CHALLENGES OF TEACHING WITH TECHNOLOGY ACROSS THE CURRICULUM:
ISSUES AND SOLUTIONS

LAWRENCE A. TOMEI, EDD
DUQUESNE UNIVERSITY, USA

Information Science Publishing

Hershey • London • Melbourne • Singapore • Beijing

Acquisition Editor:	Mehdi Khosrow-Pour
Senior Managing Editor:	Jan Travers
Managing Editor:	Amanda Appicello
Development Editor:	Michele Rossi
Copy Editor:	Lori Eby
Typesetter:	Amanda Appicello
Cover Design:	Michelle Waters
Printed at:	Integrated Book Technology

LB
1028.5
C478
2003

Published in the United States of America by
    Information Science Publishing(an imprint of Idea Group Inc.)
    701 E. Chocolate Avenue, Suite 200
    Hershey PA 17033-1240
    Tel: 717-533-8845
    Fax: 717-533-8661
    E-mail: cust@idea-group.com
    Web site: http://www.idea-group.com

and in the United Kingdom by
    Information Science Publishing (an imprint of Idea Group Inc.)
    3 Henrietta Street
    Covent Garden
    London WC2E 8LU
    Tel: 44 20 7240 0856
    Fax: 44 20 7379 3313
    Web site: http://www.eurospan.co.uk

Library of Congress Cataloging-in-Publication Data

Challenges of teaching with technology across the curriculum : issues and solutions / [edited by] Lawrence A. Tomei.
        p. cm.
Includes bibliographical references.
    ISBN 1-59140-109-7 (hardcover) — ISBN 1-59140-117-8 (ebook)
    1. Computer-assisted instruction—Handbooks, manuals, etc. 2. Curriculum planning—Handbooks, manuals, etc. 3. Educational technology—Handbooks, manuals, etc. I. Tomei, Lawrence A.
    LB1028.5 .C478 2003
    371.33'4—dc21

                                                            2002014192

British Cataloguing in Publication Data
A Cataloguing in Publication record for this book is available from the British Library.

Challenges of Teaching with Technology Across the Curriculum: Issues and Solutions

Table of Contents

Preface

Technology is embarking on a new phase in the classrooms of the future. Gone are the days when teachers were forced to rely on technologists to prepare their instructional materials. At the outset of the technology revolution, computers and software were so technically complex that only programmers dared tackle the design, development, and implementation of a   computer-assisted instruction package.

The use of microcomputers in the classroom expanded rapidly during 1980–1989. During this decade, U.S. schools acquired over two million microcomputers, and the number of schools owning computers increased to virtually 100% (Kinnaman, 1995). Even so, creating early technology-based materials demanded the use of a limited array of available design tools, such as BASIC programming language and application software such as LOGO. Preparing instructional materials remained under the purview of the technologist who understood the dialects of programming code and machine language. Fortunately, the rapid evolution of multimedia technology, both hardware and software, in the mid-1990s changed all that.

Between 1978 and 1995, prior to the advent of multimedia technology, computer processor speeds increased from 4.77 MHz (megahertz) to a phenomenal 166 MHz, a whopping factor of 40. From 1995 to 2002, multimedia-capable systems increased again from 200 MHz to speeds greater than 1 GHz (gigahertz), another factor of 5. Respectively, computer memory would advance from 16 kilobytes in the late 1970s, to megabytes in the 1990s, and now gigabytes in the new millennium. During the same periods of time, software tools and applications also exploded in capacity and capability. Spreadsheets and word processing were introduced in 1979. It would be 1987 before hypermedia was introduced, and several more years before office productivity and Web browsers could match the available speed and memory capacity of multimedia computers.

After decades of instructional technology advancements in speed, memory capacity, and software, teachers finally have at their disposal user-friendly applications that support the design and implementation of sophisticated instructional materials matching individual teaching strategies with curricular lesson objectives and student learning styles. Now, all teachers need is a comprehensive, easy-to-understand, resource to guide them through the expanding maze of Web sites and educational software. Enter *Teaching with Technology Across the Curriculum*.

This book is for educators who consider technology a viable content area in its own right and an essential tool for lifelong learning. It focuses on integrating technology into P–12 (Preschool through Grade 12) curriculum using computers, software, and the Internet to deliver academic content.

The book begins by examining how to create technology-based instruction for the classroom. The first two chapters set the stage by introducing instructional technology and how teachers create and infuse that technology into their curriculum. Readers are asked to identify their own system of beliefs about learning as they begin this book. It is important to determine which psychology of education best represents their views of teaching and learning and how that preference influences their use of technology in the classroom. The Model for Preparing Technology-Based Lessons serves to guide the reader in the design, research, development, implementation, and assessment of technology-based resources. And, a new technology classification paradigm offers a novel way of thinking about technology-based student learning.

In Chapter 2, word processing, spreadsheets, databases, graphics utilities, multimedia, and the World Wide Web are established within their historical context. Each application is explained in terms of potential use in the classroom. Standards for each content area are offered for primary, intermediate, middle, and secondary grade levels. Finally, example lesson plan ideas are suggested so that the reader may consider practical lesson goals and objectives for technology-based instructional materials.

The book focuses on infusing technology-based academic content materials into the P–12 curriculums. Chapters 3 through 10 introduce instructional technology in light of real-world classroom situations in eight key academic areas: Science, Mathematics, Social Studies, Language Arts, Fine Arts, Foreign Languages, Technology, and Special Education. Each chapter is similarly constructed, addressing critical elements in the use of technology. Specifically, each chapter deals with appropriate technologies for the classroom, including a short history of how technology has affected the area in the recent past; technology standards for teachers and students, as proposed or accepted by national and international associations particular to each area; the best in electronic media, including commercially available, shared, and free educational software at appropriate K–12 grade levels; exciting sites on the World Wide Web, offered by academic area and grade level; and integrating technology into classroom-appropriate thematic units, which will offer the reader actual thematic lessons that have successfully integrated technology.

The final chapter offers a look at how classroom teachers utilize the competencies, content ideas, and practical examples offered in the previous chapters to design, develop, and implement their own, teacher-made technology-based instructional materials. It guides the reader toward the integration of text-based, visual-based, and Web-based instructional materials into the curriculum. For those readers ready to prepare their own materials, Chapter 11 provides a step-by-step primer for creating word-processing documents, classroom presentations, and Web-based home pages. The appendices that follow the chapter offer example materials with links to an innovative Web page designed specifically for readers of *Teaching with Technology Across the Curriculum*. Teachers are encouraged to retrieve the Microsoft *Word* documents, *Power Point* presentations, and Netscape Web pages at www.duq.edu/~tomei/TAC (*Teaching Across the Curriculum*), where the online files may be downloaded for practice while reading the chapter.

Renowned educators, steeped in the methodologies for teaching the key academic areas, have prepared these chapters. The content, evaluations, rubrics, and example software packages and Internet sites have been accumulated, reviewed, and assessed over the course of several academic semesters. Technology is more than a delivery system, and *Teaching With*

Technology Across the Curriculum offers many practical uses to simulate real-world environments and replicate authentic problems. The guiding light during the preparation of this book was a hope that readers would incorporate aspects of the book as they see fit for the expressed purpose of using technology to promote student understanding and improve student learning.

Reference

Kinnaman, D. E., & Dyrli, O. E. (1995). Teaching Effectively with Technology: What Every Teacher Needs to Know About Technology. *Technology & Learning Magazine.*

Acknowledgments

The content information, evaluation classifications, proposed rubrics for software and Web sites, and model software packages and Internet sites were accumulated, reviewed, and assessed by participants in Duquesne University's Graduate Program in Instructional Technology over the course of several semesters. In our GITED 520, Teaching With Technology Across the Curriculum (from which this text derived its title), participants examine how technology is applied across specific classroom disciplines. They prepare technology-based integrated thematic units that serve as the focus for curriculum development across all grade levels. The application of appropriate technologies for teaching these subject matter areas is assessed.

The contributing authors would like to thank the students from the Summer 2001 and Fall 2001 semesters who volunteered their time and talents toward this effort. Specifically, several students went above and beyond in their review of material and quality of their recommendations. Special thanks go to Susan Carr, Susan Lewis, Erin Lynn, Barbara Bradley, Amy Rakowski, Ayano Ban, and Karen Ford.

Introduction To Technology Across The Curriculum

1

Lawrence A. Tomei, EdD

Introduction

Teaching with Technology Across the Curriculum is a book for teachers who wish to use technology as a tool to enhance the teaching–learning process. Its focus is on integrating technology into the P–12 (preschool through Grade 12) curriculum using computers, software, and Web-based instructional materials to analyze, evaluate, and apply the academic content to be delivered.

The book purports two primary themes: Creating Technology-Based Curriculum Instruction for the Classroom and Infusing Technology-Based Academic Content into the Curriculum.

Creating Technology-Based Curriculum Instruction

The first theme of the book presents an approach to creating an integrated lesson stressing the use of technology as a tool to solve real-world problems. Readers need access to the Microsoft suite of word processing, spreadsheets, presentation, and database applications along with Internet access to take full advantage of the examples and illustrations covered in the text. Specifically, the first part of the text addresses the standards and strengths of word processing, spreadsheets, databases, drawing, and the Internet and offers example lesson plan ideas for incorporating these applications into the curriculum of the school.

At the outset, readers are encouraged to think of a unit of instruction appropriate for their classroom; a lesson in which they might actually infuse the primary technologies introduced in the book. The instruction might include the integration of the following:

1. Word processing: Word processing is arguably the most popular technology for the classroom because of its relative ease of use, capacity for creativity and personalization of student work, and its many uses as a tool for promoting student understanding.

2. Spreadsheets: Electronic spreadsheets, with their use of formulas, data manipulation, and "what if" scenarios, are sufficient to promote reasoning and logic, problem solving, and analytical skills in P–12 classroom lessons.

3. Databases: Students who engage in critical thinking find that the logical sequencing, ordering, manipulating, and retrieval features of databases contribute to their development as independent thinkers.

4. Paint and draw: Drawing utilities are popular applications for today's multimedia computers. With minimal instruction, students learn how to locate their graphics on the Internet and modify those images to create new graphics, charts, icons, and visuals. Integrating these skills into a lesson is particularly appropriate when teaching concrete learners.

5.   Internet: With the meteoric rise of the Internet, it is particularly important to consider the impact of the World Wide Web in the classroom. Keep in mind that the Internet involves more than the World Wide Web; it also includes file transfer, gopher, electronic mail, listservs, newsgroups, and chat rooms.

Infusing Technology-Based Academic Content into the Curriculum

The second focus of this book introduces academic content supported by educational technology, educational software, and Internet applications. Each chapter has been developed by members of higher education faculty; leaders in the field of instructional technology who excel in its application for elementary and secondary school teaching. The text explores seven key academic areas:

- Science
- Mathematics
- Social Studies
- Language Arts
- Foreign Languages
- Fine Arts
- Special Education

Specifically, the book suggests how teachers may design instructional units that combine various technologies, selecting appropriate uses for each content area incorporated into the lesson. Consideration of national standards for technology is presented along with a proposed taxonomy for integrating technology into content area curriculum. Rubrics for evaluating educational software and an overview of some of the best content area software packages are introduced. Likewise, rubrics for assessing the educational value of Internet sites are offered along with some excellent examples of Web sites appropriate for P–12 learning.

Theories of Applied Teaching and Learning

Any text that purports to delve into aspects of technology for the classroom curriculum must first address accepted principles of teaching and learning. The primary responsibility of teachers is to ensure student learning. A teacher's selection of educational goals, instructional strategies, and classroom organization and behavior, whether focused on textbooks, audiovisual materials, or technology, must be grounded in an understanding of how teachers teach and how students learn.

Because *Teaching with Technology Across the Curriculum* is grounded in the educational psychology of teaching, it is helpful for readers to identify their system of beliefs about learning before beginning. Check the Agree or Disagree box in each of the statements in Table 1.

Table 1. Your Psychology of Teaching

		DISCOVERING YOUR PSYCHOLOGY OF TEACHING
Agree	Disagree	I Believe that...
☐	☐	1. Learners need grades, gold stars, and other incentives as motivation to learn and to accomplish school requirements.
☐	☐	2. Learners can be trusted to find their own goals and should have some options or choices in what they learn at school.
☐	☐	3. Teachers need to determine what students are thinking about while solving math problems.
☐	☐	4. Students should be graded according to uniform standards of achievement that the teacher sets for the class.
☐	☐	5. Students should set their own individual standards and should evaluate their own work.
☐	☐	6. Curriculum should be organized along subject matter lines that are carefully sequenced.
☐	☐	7. The teacher should help students monitor and control their own learning behavior.
☐	☐	8. The school experience should help students develop positive relations with their peers.

For the most part:

- Statements **1, 4, and 6** would be supported most strongly by **Behavioral** psychologists.

- Statements **3 and 7** would have been sustained by **Cognitive** psychologists.

- Statements **2, 5, and 8** would support the **Humanistic** approach to teaching.

Most teachers tend to agree with most statements in the table in an effort not to appear unresponsive to any of their students. Remember which school of psychology you initially chose. After exploring the following theories and theorists, representing the three important schools of educational psychology, you will be asked to reevaluate your initial position. Will it change or remain the same?

Behavioral Approach to Teaching with Technology

Years ago, teachers believed that the best way to learn was through repetition; a principle from the behavioral learning theories that has dominated educational thinking since the time of Ivan Pavlov. Students would spend their time practicing spelling words, copying history notes, and recalculating mathematical answers over and over again until they "learned" the information.

Contemporary behaviorists view the *environment* as key to learning; specifically, in terms of *stimuli* and *response*. They attempt to prove that behavior is controlled by the environmental contingencies of external *reward* or *reinforcement* linking the stimuli to a positive response. Teachers who accept the behavioral viewpoint of pioneers like B.F. Skinner and Alfred Bandura also accept that student behavior is a response to previous stimuli and that *all behavior is learned*. For example, classroom troublemakers "learn" to be disruptive because they seek attention (reinforcement) from their teachers and peers. Withdrawn students learn that their environment does not reinforce social interaction, so they become reserved and silent. As a result, student behavior is to be analyzed in terms of its reinforcement history.

The next logical step is to learn which behavioral processes must change to eliminate undesirable behavior by students. Teacher responsibility, according to the behaviorist, is to construct an environment in which the probability of reinforcing proper student behavior is maximized by careful organization and presentation of information in a *designed sequence*. Programmed instruction, computer-assisted instruction, and technology-reinforced mastery learning experiences are traditional methods for integrating technology into a behavioral classroom.

Behavioral teachers remain on the lookout for the best in drill and practice software, visual presentations that support continuous positive feedback, and Internet sites that offer a stimulus–response format to point and click through associated links.

Cognitive Approach to Teaching with Technology

Cognitive psychologists focus on learners as active participants in the teaching–learning process. Those who adhere to this psychology of learning believe that teachers are more effective if they know what *prior knowledge* the student possesses and how the individual processes information. Cognitive teachers use accommodation and assimilation strategies to help the learner acquire knowledge more effectively. Effective instruction for these teachers includes teaching students how to learn, remember, think, and motivate themselves.

Cognitive–developmental psychologists, such as Jean Piaget and Jerome Bruner, study the various steps in student thinking and believe they are different from adults. They stress that teachers must understand the nature of thought processes when planning instruction. And, they attribute growth to *age–stage development* and teaching to a reiterative process of *assimilation* and *accommodation*.

Cognitive–constructivist psychologists, on the other hand, view human cognition as knowledge created by the individual through various encounters with new ideas and thinking. Knowledge is a series of *building blocks* that the teacher places one on top of the other to build upon student understanding.

All constructivist principles include the concept of **schemata**, a process of organizing concepts and information into a cognitive structure that supports subsequent use and retrieval. Discovery learning, reception learning, and the information-processing model represent applications of cognitive principles in technology-based lesson design. Here, teachers search for educational software that allows students to personally explore a topic; presentations that offer the learner a scaffolding of content material from which the learner can build new knowledge; and, Internet sites that respect a learner's cognitive demand or need for encoding (gathering and representing information), storing (holding information), and retrieving (getting the information when needed).

Humanistic Approach to Teaching with Technology

Humanistic psychologists believe that how people feel about learning is as important as how they think or behave. Proponents of humanism do not describe behavior from the viewpoint of the teacher, as do behaviorists; and they do not describe behavior from the academic content presented, as do cognitivists. Instead, they describe behavior from the vantage point of the student who is performing the activity. Humanists, led by such famous authors as Abraham Maslow and Carl Rogers, embrace the idea of **self-actualization**, the growth of a person to achieve whatever degree of individual satisfaction they may be capable of achieving. The humanistic teacher creates an educational environment that fosters **self-development, cooperation, positive communications**, and **personalization** of information.

Open education and cooperative learning are the primary manifestations of humanism. Technology supports open education by diagnosing individual learning, while teachers primarily observe and ask questions. Instruction is individualized with little reliance on textbooks or workbooks. With respect to cooperative learning, technology assists in the critical area of individual accountability and the development of personal collaborative skills necessary for group work.

The humanistic teacher seeks educational software tailored to individual students; presentations that are shared in a group learning environment; and Internet sites supporting interpersonal communication rather than subject matter content alone.

Interim Summary

No teacher teaches exclusively within the domain of a single psychology. To do so would mean that every student learns in exactly the same way. However, when teaching with technology, it is important to keep a predominant psychology in mind. Decide which psychology best represents your views of teaching and learning and consider how that preference influences your predilection for using technology in the classroom. After reading this section of the chapter, did you change your psychology?

A Model for Preparing Technology-Based Instructional Materials

Teaching with Technology Across the Curriculum aids teachers in preparing instruction that combines word processing, spreadsheets, databases, and drawing into a single lesson plan, while targeting one or more content areas. Consider using the Model for Designing Technology-Based Lessons (Figure 1) to develop technology-based lessons.

A sample lesson developed by following the 8 steps of the Model and containing all the necessary elements of an effective instructional unit on Dinosaurs is found in Appendix A.

Figure 1. Model for Creating Technology-Based Cross-Curriculum Instruction

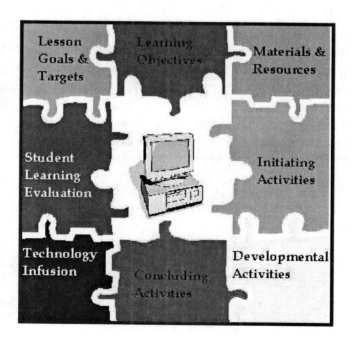

Step 1: Lesson Goals and Targets

Developing technology-based instruction begins by specifying the overall lesson goals and targets. This step precedes any search for instructional materials. It is designed to help the teacher define the purpose of the lesson <u>before</u> "surfing" Internet sites to see what content might be available. This step also helps other teachers who might be interested in using this lesson in their classroom or parents who assist their children in their studies. A technology-based lesson begins with the following information:

1. *Theme*: Select an appropriate theme reflecting the curriculum to be taught. Consider student interests and experiences, national and local issues, or community and international problems. A short overview of the lesson is also recommended.

2. *Grade-level appropriateness*: Describe the target learner(s) and any prior student knowledge required before beginning the lesson.

3. *Lesson length*: Thematic units often span more than a single class period. Often, they become the focus of learning over weeks, months, or even semesters. Describe the length of the lesson and the best methodology for presenting the content.

4. *Focus*: Develop a short focus statement summarizing the overall intent of the unit and the component topics to be explored. The focus might be expressed as the KWL model; specifically, what do students already **K**now, **W**hat do they want to learn in this lesson, and what did the student **L**earn following the lesson?

Step 2: Learning Objectives

Benjamin Bloom created what many consider the most famous classification for educators with his *Taxonomy of Educational Objectives* (Krathwohl & Bloom, 1984). In his landmark exposition, Bloom developed a theory of six progressively complex steps of cognitive development. He offered classroom teachers a rubric for developing instructional objectives at increasingly advanced levels of higher-order thinking. Knowledge, comprehension, application, analysis, synthesis, and evaluation are considered among the most practical theories of teaching and learning. But, perhaps the most appealing aspect of Bloom's taxonomy is the subsequent research that resulted in lists of action verbs representing possible intellectual activity on each level. This list for the cognitive domain is presented in Table 2.

Table 2. Taxonomy for the Cognitive Domain

Taxonomy Classification	Action Verbs that Represent Intellectual Activity on this Level
Knowledge	Arrange, define, duplicate, label, list, memorize, name, order, recognize, relate, recall, repeat, reproduce state
Comprehension	Classify, describe, discuss, explain, express, identify, indicate, locate, recognize, report, restate, review, select, translate
Application	Apply, choose, demonstrate, dramatize, employ, illustrate, interpret, operate, practice, schedule, sketch, solve, use, write
Analysis	Analyze, appraise, calculate, categorize, compare, contrast, criticize, differentiate, discriminate, distinguish, examine, experiment, question
Synthesis	Arrange, assemble, collect, compose, construct, create, design, develop, formulate, manage, organize, plan, prepare, propose, set up
Evaluation	Appraise, argue, assess, attach, choose, compare, defend, estimate, judge, predict, rate, core, select, support, value, evaluate

The taxonomy for the technology domain, like its predecessors, includes a progressive level of complexity from simple to complex, first to last, general to specific. The six interconnected levels of literacy, collaboration, decision making, instruction, integration, and societal considerations offer a new way to think about technology-based student learning. Consider the taxonomy presented in Table 3.

Table 3. Taxonomy for the Technology Domain

Taxonomy Classification	Action Verbs that Represent Intellectual Activity on this Level
Literacy Understand technology and its components	• **Understand** computer terms in oral and written communication • **Demonstrate** keyboard and mouse (click and drag) operations • **Use** basic computer software applications. • **Operate** computer input and output devices
Collaboration Share ideas, work collaboratively, form relationships using technology	• **Make use of** communications tools for individual writing and interpersonal collaborations • **Share information** electronically among students • **Communicate** interpersonally using electronic mail
Decision Making Use technology in new and concrete situations	• **Apply** electronic tools for problem solving • **Design** effective solutions to practical real-world problems • **Develop** new strategies and ideas using brainstorming software • **Prepare** an electronic spreadsheet • **Create** calendars, address books, and class schedules
Discrimination Select technology-based instructional materials appropriate for individual students	• **Appraise** educational software and determine its effectiveness with respect to individual student learning styles • **Discriminate** multimedia resources appropriate to student development, age, gender, culture, etc. • **Assess** various Internet environments for their strengths as possible student learning tools • **Employ** electronic media to construct new research and investigate lesson content
Integration Create new instructional materials using various technology-based resources	• **Design, construct**, and **implement** teacher-made Internet-based materials for learning subject content • **Design, construct**, and **implement** teacher-made text-based materials for learning subject content • **Design, construct**, and **implement** teacher-made visual-based classroom presentations for learning subject content • **Consider the uses** of technology to address the strengths and avoid the weaknesses inherent in multiple intelligences • **Focus** student learning using integrated instructional materials
Tech-ology The study of technology and its value to society	• **Defend** copyright and fair use laws for using technology • **Debate** the issues surrounding legal and ethical behavior when using technology • **Consider the consequences** of inappropriate uses of technology

Note. From *Using a taxonomy for the technology domain*, L. A. Tomei, 2001, Penn Association of Colleges and Teacher Educators.

Creating learning objectives requires the teacher to identify specific objectives for student mastery. The ABCD format and Mager's behavioral learning objectives are widely accepted models for writing lesson objectives that are specific, observable, measurable, and unambiguous.

1. ABCD Format

(A)udience. The focus of a technology-based lesson is on the learner and not the teacher. When creating a learning objective in this format, the teacher should ask, "**Who** are the students that the lesson is designed to teach?"

(B)ehavior. The behavior component of a learning objective is synonymous with student learning outcomes, and they must be measurable. Behavior consists of the following:

o   Content: Content refers to the specific subject matter to be taught. An acceptable learning objective contains a thorough description of the lesson material to be covered and answers the question, "What do I want the student to **know**?"

o   Action verb: An action verb is necessary to answer a second question, "What do I want the student to **do**?" The action verbs shown in the taxonomy above offer a more extensive list of action verbs to illustrate the concept.

(C)ondition. A properly constructed condition specifies the situation within which the expected behavior must occur. It answers the question, "What must I **give** the students to aid in their learning of this content?" For example, for fifth-grade students who must learn the capitals of all 50 states, a teacher would most likely give her students a map of the United States with a space to annotate all capital cities.

(D)egree. The degree or criterion specifies the minimum acceptable performance standard in terms of quality, quantity, or time. It must be stated if less than perfect performance is acceptable; otherwise, students should expect 100% success. This component answers the final question, "**How well** must the student learn the target material?"

2. Mager's Behavioral Objectives

Mager's model (1997) for writing learning objectives is one of the most well known. Similar to the ABCD model, Mager proposed using behavioral learning objectives that included three major components: condition, behavior, and criteria.

Conditions specify the circumstances, materials, and directions that the student is given to satisfy the expected behavior. This part of the objective usually begins with a simple declarative statement, such as "The student will be given a map of the 50 United States, a number of multiplication problems, or a paragraph from a Shakespearean play," that relates to performing the specified behavior. Like conditions in the ABCD model, Mager also answers the question, "What must I **_give_** the students to aid in their learning of this content?"

Behavior is a statement of what the learner will be able to do and includes the audience as an essential component. Behavior is the skill or knowledge to be gained (e.g., two-digit numbers, vocabulary words) and the action or skill (e.g., define, count, label, categorize, analyze, design, evaluate, add, multiply, etc.) to be mastered. It simultaneously answers the questions, "What do I want the student to **_know_**?" and "**_Who_** are the students that the lesson is designed to teach?"

Criteria measure what and how the learner will be evaluated. Like degree in the previous model, criteria describe how to judge the outcome of the behavior or performance and answer the question, "**_How well_** must the student learn the target material?" and must be compared to established standards. For example, "correctly identify 45 out of 50 states" or "correctly spell all words on our weekly vocabulary list."

Step 3: Materials and Resources

Once the specific learning outcomes have been determined, it is time to identify the necessary materials and resources to satisfy the conditions of each learning objective. Specific technology resources will be identified later in the model. For now, consider the following:

1.   _Text-based resources,_ including newspapers, pamphlets, notices, travel guides, junk mail, journals, diaries, letters,

maps, advertisements, brochures, flyers, encyclopedias, dictionaries, magazines, booklets, professional journals

2.   *Visual-based resources,* including educational software, reference works, educational games and simulations related to curriculum, and CD-ROM adaptations of literature as well as graphics presentation packages

3.   *Web-based resources,* including internal links created by the teacher and housed locally on the school's Web server and external links that provide resources found on sites throughout the Internet (Both types of Web addresses should be included in this section of the lesson plan.)

4.   *Audio/visual resources,* such as videos, films, filmstrips, movies, slide programs, overhead transparencies, records, audiotapes, books and tapes, and CDs

5.   *Community resources,* such as guest speakers, adjunct faculty, and virtual online and actual field trips

6.   *Instructional television,* including educational television and cable services, such as Channel One

7.   *Literature resources,* including fiction, nonfiction, and poetry

Step 4: Initiating Activities

Describe at least one activity that introduces the unit of instruction and sets the stage for learning the material to be covered. An initiating activity is not necessarily technology related. It may not even use technology. Rather, the initiating activity should relate directly to learning objectives of the lesson.

Step 5: Developmental Activities

Developmental activities cover a broader range of curricular areas. There should be at least one developmental activity for each of the primary objectives to be taught. However, a single objective could incorporate more than one activity. By far, this will be the more comprehensive component of the integrated unit.

Step 6: Concluding Activity

The concluding activity engages students in a meaningful summary of their discoveries and leads to new ideas, understandings, and connections. If appropriate, technologies are infused in the next step.

Step 7: Technology Infusion

In previous steps, the teacher established the goals, learning objectives, materials and resources, and activities of the lesson. Here, appropriate technologies are integrated into the lesson. A handy "Guide to Common Classroom Technologies" (shown in Table 4) offers a suite of technologies available for classroom application and provides a ready index when searching for possible instructional technologies.

Table 4. Guide to Common Classroom Technologies

1. Calculators and graphing calculators	13. List servers
2. Computer-assisted instruction	14. MIDI interfaces
3. Databases	15. Multimedia computers
4. Desktop publishing	16. Music synthesizers
5. Drill and practice instructional media	17. Newsgroups
6. Electronic mail	18. Office productivity
7. Digitized encyclopedias	19. Problem-solving instructional media
8. Games instructional media	20. Simulation instructional media
9. Groupware	21. Spreadsheet
10. Graphic presentation	22. Tutorial instructional media
11. Hypertext/hypermedia/hyperlinks	23. Video (film, videotape, laser, DVD)
12. Internet	24. World Wide Web
	25. Word processing

Step 8: Student Learning Evaluation

The final step in the development of technology-based lessons is conducting the assessment of student progress. Avoid relying on formal pencil-and-paper tests. Instead, select criteria that measure growth in learning and thinking. Use technology, if appropriate, to conduct portions of the evaluation. For example, word processing (logs and student journals), completed spreadsheets and database listings, and printouts of the best Web pages available on the Internet offer more authentic assessment of learning outcomes, while decreasing the administrative demands of individualized student evaluation.

Conclusion

This chapter introduces the two primary themes encountered in the remainder of the book. First, it presents an approach to creating an integrated inquiry lesson stressing the teacher's use of technology to solve real-world problems. Word processing, spreadsheets, databases, paint and draw, and the Internet are introduced in subsequent chapters, along with the seven key academic areas of Science, Mathematics, Social Studies, Language Arts, Foreign Languages, Fine Arts, and Special Education, and how technology is used for teaching and learning this important content material.

This chapter offers an overview of the key psychologies of behavioral, cognitive, and humanistic education and asks readers to become aware of their own primary beliefs about teaching, in general, and teaching with technology, specifically. And finally, a model for designing new instructional materials was presented.

References

Mager, R. F. (1997). *Preparing instructional objectives: A critical tool in the development of effective instruction*, Atlanta, GA: Center for Effective Performance Inc.

Tomei, L. A. (2001). *Using a taxonomy for the technology domain*, Penn Association of Colleges and Teacher Educators.

Tomei, L. A. (2002). *The technology facade.* New York: Allyn & Bacon Publishers, Inc.

Appendix A: Instructional Unit on Dinosaurs

Model Thematic Unit:
Dinosaurs of North America

Using the Model for Designing Technology-Based Lessons

Lesson Goals and Targets

I.   **Focus:** Students will explore prehistoric times to expand their knowledge of dinosaurs.

II. **Grade Level:** Primary

III. **Theme:** Dinosaurs

Millions of years ago, long before there were any people, there were dinosaurs. Dinosaurs were one of several kinds of prehistoric reptiles that lived during the Mesozoic Era, the "Age of Reptiles."

The largest dinosaurs were over 100 ft (30 m) long and up to 50 ft (15 m) tall (like Argentinosaurus, Seismosaurus, Ultrasauros, Brachiosaurus, and Supersaurus). The smallest dinosaurs, like Compsognathus, were about the size of a chicken. Most dinosaurs were in between.

It is difficult to figure out how the dinosaurs sounded, how they behaved, how they mated, what color they were, or even how to tell whether a fossil was male or female.

There were many different kinds of dinosaurs that lived at different times. Some walked on two legs (they were bipedal), and some walked on four (they were quadrupedal). Some could do both. Some were speedy, and some were slow and lumbering. Some were armor-plated; some had horns, crests, spikes, or frills. Some had thick, bumpy skin, and some even had primitive feathers.

The dinosaurs dominated the Earth for over 165 million years during the Mesozoic Era, but they mysteriously went extinct 65 million years ago. Paleontologists study their fossil remains to learn about the amazing prehistoric world of dinosaurs.

Although dinosaurs' fossils have been known since at least 1818, the term "dinosaur" (deinos means terrifying; sauros means lizard) was coined by the English anatomist Sir Richard Owen in 1842.

Learning Objectives

Objective I: Using a personal computer and Web address list, students will navigate the Internet locating two specific Dinosaur Web sites, and locate, download, and print at least two images of their favorite dinosaurs.

Objective II: After locating a given Web site, a student will review the information and answer the questions in the Workbook: *"What is the difference between an omnivore and a carnivore? When did the dinosaurs live? And, what were the most common dinosaurs in North America?"*

Objective III: Given a Web address, students will click on a dinosaur's name to go to a simple black-and-white printout, and color, cut out, and mount their favorite dinosaur. Students will share a 3 to 5 min presentation on their favorite dinosaur and discuss why the dinosaur is their favorite and why this lesson was important to them.

Materials and Resources

I. Text-Based Resources

1. Science adventures: *Dinosaurs*, by Kayne Quinn and Jan Hutchings
2. Plastic dinosaur figures
3. Clay for making dinosaur models
4. Dinosaur model sets (available in most toy stores): dinosaur models that come in eggs with posters and books: Tyrannosaurus Rex, Brachiosaurus, Leptoceratops, Stegasaurus. and Triceratops
5. Collection of books relating to dinosaurs (See "Related Literature" at the end of this section.)

II. Visual-Based Resources

Check out the following videotapes from the school library:

- *If the Dinosaurs Come Back*, by Bernard Most
- *Danny and the Dinosaur*, by Syd Hoff
- *The Secret Dinosaur*, by Marilyn Hirst
- *Dinosaurs*, by Kathleen Daly

III. Web-Based Resources

Web Site	URL
Paper Dinosaurs, 1824–1969	http://www.lhl.lib.mo.us/pubserv/hos/dino/welcome.htm
American Museum of Natural History	http://www.amnh.org
National Geographic Dinosaur Eggs	http://www.nationalgeographic.com/dinoeggs/
Dinosaur Exhibit from Honolulu Community College	http://www.hcc.hawaii.edu/hccinfo/dinos/dinos.1.html
The Field Museum, Chicago, IL, Dinosaur Exhibit	http://www.fmnh.org/exhibits/web_exhibits.htm
University of California Museum of Paleontology, Berkeley, CA	http://www.ucmp.berkeley.edu/index.html
Visit a Dig — The Dinosaur Society	http://www.webscope.com/webscope/dino/digs.html
Guide to Dinosaur Sites in Western Colorado and Eastern Utah	http://www.rmwest.com/dinosaur/guide.htm
Dinosaur Illustrations Online	http://web.syr.edu/~dbgoldma/pictures.html

IV. Other Resources

Field Trip to the Carnegie Science Center's Dinosaur Exhibit and Omnivision

Initiating Activities

Purchase three to four medium-sized watermelons and paint them white. Hide them in a "dinosaur nest" somewhere on the playground before the start of the lesson. Tell the students they must find the dinosaur's nest to begin the dinosaur unit. Once they find the "eggs," cut them open and share them with the group. After returning to the classroom, have the students draw pictures of imaginary creatures that may have laid those "eggs."

Developmental Activities

It is not necessary, or suggested, that all of the activities be included. They are intended to be used as a guide to illustrate the scope of activities that can be developed. Selection should be based on student needs, interests, and objectives.

1. Provide students with large paper bags. Have them create a paper-bag puppet to represent their favorite dinosaur. Next, have students create skits with the puppet (e.g., a fight between a meat eater and a plant eater).

2. Tell students to use the names of dinosaurs to create new names for foods (e.g., fabrosaurus french fries, megalosaurus milkshakes, stegosaurus spaghetti). Then, have them write a menu for lunch using these "new foods." Allow time for students to share menus. Plan a dinosaur lunch for the entire class. Have students sign up to bring some of the "new foods" from home.

3. Scientists have proposed several reasons for the dinosaurs' disappearance (the Earth became too cold, there was not enough food, etc.). Have students research these reasons and then divide them into groups, each group supporting one of the reasons. Provide time for them to discuss and defend their positions.

4. Using a variety of sources, list some dinosaurs and their lengths on the chalkboard. To help students understand how long the different dinosaurs were, measure their exact lengths with a ball of yarn (in which you have previously tied knots every 5 ft). Count by fives as the yarn is unrolled. Use a meter stick to convert these lengths to meters.

5. Have students become paleontologists (scientists who specialize in finding and studying ancient fossil remains) by bringing clean chicken or turkey bones to school. Place each bone in wet, packed sand to make an imprint. Remove the bone, and pour plaster of Paris into the imprint (or mold). Let it harden, and then remove it from the sand. Have students label and display their fossils.

6. Have students pretend they want to move Tyrannosaurus Rex, the largest of the meat-eating dinosaurs, which weighed approximately 8 tons and was over 20 ft high, from a zoo in New York City to a zoo in Paris, France. Provide time for a brainstorming session on how this could be done.

7. Give each student a large piece of butcher paper and have them draw their favorite dinosaur and color or paint it. Place a second sheet of paper under the first sheet, and staple them together loosely, leaving a small opening for stuffing. Stuff the dinosaur with crumpled newspaper, and add legs, horns, tails, and so on. Label and display these stuffed dinosaurs.

8. Ask students to create riddles about dinosaurs (e.g., What is the best way to get a piece of paper out from under a dinosaur? Wait until it moves, etc.). Compile these riddles into a class booklet, "Dinosaur Riddles."

9. Have students take on the role of a particular dinosaur. If possible, mime the dinosaur, in addition to giving out one clue at a time: I weigh _____. I am _____ tall. I eat _____ . Allow four clues. If students have not guessed the dinosaur after four guesses, have the dinosaur-student provide the answer.

10. Plan a field trip to a museum of natural history to see dinosaur skeletons. If this is not possible, then plan a virtual trip via the Internet. (See Materials and Resources.)

11. Provide students with plastic dinosaur figures, clay, dinosaur model sets, and so on. As a class, create a display or diorama that depicts a prehistoric time when dinosaurs roamed the world. Use real greenery or plastic or silk. A mirror makes a great lake. Do not forget the volcano in the background!

Concluding Activities

There is at least one dinosaur name for each letter of the alphabet. Assign one letter to each student or group of students, and tell them to find a dinosaur whose name begins with that letter. Have them draw the dinosaur and write a one-page summary describing it. The summary should include the pronunciation of the dinosaur's name, its size, where it lived, what it ate, and so on. Finally, compile these reports into an "ABC of Dinosaurs."

Technology Infusion

The following Web sites have been selected for this course. Examine each of the sites in order. If you have any trouble locating a site, please ask for assistance.

> Jason's Dinosaur Site
>
> Dinosaur Classroom Activities
>
> Dinosaur Information Sheets and Printouts
>
> Honolulu Community College Dinosaur Exhibit

Student Learning Evaluation

You will receive a grade for this lesson based on the following criteria:

Assessment	Possible Points	Percent of Points
Attendance and participation	100 points	10%
Web site navigation	500 points	50%
Workbook	100 points	10%
Presentation	300 points	30%
Total possible	**1000 points**	**100%**

Teacher: Miss Tammy Brown

Email Address: brown@schoolwise.edu

Fifth-Grade Science Teacher

Schoolwise Elementary School

Major Applications Of Instructional Technology

Claudia A. Balach, MSEd, NBCT

Introduction

In the words of Malcolm X, "education is our passport to the future, for tomorrow belongs to the people who prepare for it today." One such passport for educators grappling with the preparation of their students is the use of technology applications as tools for learning. Not only will children need these tools to successfully navigate their years of formal schooling, but they will also need these tools to successfully navigate their lives in the 21st century. To effectively use these tools, educators and their students must become comfortable via an ongoing daily integration of the major instructional technology applications in the classroom.

The goal of this chapter is to provide a road map for effectively integrating technology in the classroom. It is not intended to provide detailed instruction in specific applications but rather to offer a preliminary view of each application as an instructional tool. The chapter first defines the six major software tools used in classrooms today:

- Word processing
- Spreadsheets
- Databases
- Paint and draw
- Multimedia/hypermedia software
- The World Wide Web

Following an introduction, the major benefits of each application and the commonly accepted content and technology standards for using these tools in the classroom will be explained. Next, some 20 lesson plan ideas, along with associated learning objectives, are offered for consideration. Lesson plan ideas are divided into Primary (pre-K through Grade 2), Intermediate (Grades 3 through 5), Middle (Grades 6 through 8), and Secondary (Grades 9 through 12), following the International Society for Technology in Education (ISTE) National Educational Technology Standards for Students (ISTE, 2000). Within each of the four grade levels are sample lessons that integrate the standards and applications into a curriculum following principles of best practice.

The question "Why do we use technology in the classroom" closely parallels the questions asked when any new technology first arrived on the educational scene. "Why bring pencils to the classroom?" "Why give textbooks to the students?" "Why use blackboards for teaching?" Each technology must be considered in light of its use as a tool for increasing student understanding. Ultimately, the choice depends upon the resources available in the school, their availability to the teacher, and the skills of a teacher to select resources that most effectively enhance student learning.

Technology should only be chosen if and when it enhances student learning. It should not be used because the school has recently spent thousands upgrading its computer lab, or because it has just invested in a technology in-service program for its teacher, or because the school wishes to impress its parents. Instructional technologies are tools, and like other tools, "they can be used well or badly, they can be used appropriately or inappropriately (or not at all), they can save money or cost too much, and in the hands of a skilled craftsman, beautiful, long-lasting results become possible" (Peck, 2001).

Table 1. Best Practices: New Standards for Teaching and Learning in America's Schools

Student-centered. The best starting point for schooling is young people's real interests; all across the curriculum, investigating students' own questions should always take precedence over studying arbitrarily and distantly selected "content."

Experiential. Active, hands-on, concrete experience is the most powerful and natural form of learning. Students should be immersed in the most direct possible experience of the content of every subject.

Holistic. Children learn best when they encounter whole ideas, events, and materials in purposeful contexts, not by studying subparts isolated from actual use.

Authentic. Real, rich, complex ideas and materials are at the heart of the curriculum. Lessons or textbooks that water-down, control, or oversimplify content ultimately "disempower" students.

Expressive. To fully engage ideas, construct meaning, and remember information, students must regularly employ the whole range of communicative media: speech, writing, drawing, poetry, dance, drama, music, movement, and visual arts.

Reflective. Balancing the immersion in experience and expression must be opportunities for learners to reflect, debrief, and reflect on their experiences.

Social. Learning is always socially constructed and often "interactional"; teachers need to create classroom interactions that "scaffold" learning.

Collaborative. Cooperative learning activities tap the social power of learning better than competitive and individualistic approaches.

Democratic. The classroom is a model community; students learn what they live as citizens of the school.

Cognitive. The most powerful learning comes when children develop true understanding of concepts through higher-order thinking associated with various fields of inquiry and through self-monitoring of their thinking.

Developmental. Children grow through a series of definable but not rigid stages, and schooling should fit its activities to the developmental level of students.

Constructivist. Children do not just receive content; in a very real sense, they re-create and reinvent every cognitive system they encounter, including language, literacy, and mathematics.

Challenging. Students learn best when faced with genuine challenges, choices, and responsibility in their own learning.

Source: Zemelman, Daniels, and Hyde, 1998

Best practice, which stems from the work of Zemelman, Daniels, and Hyde (1998), easily applies to the use of technology applications in the classroom. Some widely accepted best practices include teaching that is student-centered, experiential, holistic, authentic, expressive, reflective, social, collaborative, democratic, cognitive, developmental, constructivist, and challenging. Throughout this chapter, the use of the major instructional technology applications is referenced to these practices. For a more detailed explanation of each of these terms, refer to Table 1.

Another pertinent pedagogical framework relevant to technology as a tool in the classroom is Bloom's taxonomy. Discussed in the previous chapter, Bloom's taxonomy addresses different levels of cognitive learning. When using technology as a tool in the classroom, educators must teach with cognitive variety, addressing the higher-order thinking levels of analysis, synthesis, and evaluation. Applied to instructional technology, Table 2 demonstrates the broad categories of educational software and the best learning supported by each.

Table 2. Software Types and the Kinds of Learning They Support

Software Type and Example	Skills Used or Involved	Related Bloom's Levels
Drill and skill practice; example: typing	Practice facts; usually, games are involved	Knowledge level
Tutorial/Web page tutorial; example: Reader Rabbit	Information is gained through presentation and practice on a computer	Knowledge and comprehension levels
Role play and simulation; example: Sim City	Student plays a prescribed role	Application and analysis levels
Reference and Web search; example: Microsoft Encarta	Information available in text formats	Comprehension through evaluation levels
Productivity and creativity; example: Microsoft Publisher	Allows student to create materials in whatever manner suits the project at hand	Synthesis and evaluation levels
Presentation; example: Hyperstudio and Microsoft Power Point	Student uses multimedia format to present	Analysis, synthesis, and evaluation levels
Authorware and Web page; example: Microsoft Front Page	Student uses multimedia format to present information in an interactive format	Synthesis and evaluation levels

Finally, this chapter and the remainder of the book consider the use of technology in education and distinguish between using technology as a teacher-centered instructional delivery device and technology as a tool for student-centered learning. While there is no single right or wrong answer to this issue, in following with the best practice research-based premises of Zemelman, Daniels, and Hyde (1998), this chapter focuses on the latter perspective. The teacher must structure the learning experience so that the student is the technological carpenter; so that the student is the one using the tool to discover learning, process and retrieve information, and communicate.

Word Processing

A Definition and Brief History

Word processing uses the computer to create, edit, and print documents (Webopedia, 2001). Its precursor was the typewriter. In 1979, Seymour Rubenstein created *WordStar*, a word processor for the CP/M (Computer Program/Management) operating system of Digital Research Corporation. In 1980, Alan Ashton and Bruce Bastian created *Word Perfect*. Unchallenged for many years, development of WYSIWYG (What You See Is What You Get) word processing was to receive its primary impetus in 1981, when IBM rolled out its version of the personal desktop computer. Over the next 4 years, many word-processing programs, including *MacWrite* (Apple), *Microsoft Word* (Microsoft Corporation), and *AppleWorks* (Apple), appeared. Users were able to perform on-screen tasks such as changing fonts and font size as well as cutting, pasting, and deleting text.

Classroom Benefits

Word processing is the most commonly used computer application in the office, classroom, and home (Pfaffenberger, 2000). Its use transcends content and pedagogy and, from an educational perspective, more effectively enhances a learner's self-perception as a "real writer." Word processing produces a more professional image, brings student writing in line with accepted standards for communication and publishing, and enables students to reflect on the thinking that goes on behind the writing rather than the syntax of spelling and grammar (to some extent). This makes it easier for learners to share their work with others, encourages and facilitates collaborative writing, provides learners with more control over the pace and direction of their own learning, encourages experimentation and risk taking, helps learners adopt an appropriate self-critical distance from their writing, and encourages experimentation and risk taking (Keith & Glover, 1987).

While, presently, the use of word processing is ubiquitous in the classroom, educators must keep foremost in their minds that the benefits of word processors in the classroom for pedagogical goals remain inconclusive. Current research implies that students who use word processing write more, revise more, and develop a better attitude toward the writing process. There are also studies that are unable to draw conclusive results correlating quantity with the quality of student writing (Geisert & Futrell, 2000). As with any tool, the delivery and structure of the learning experience, as well as the attention paid to the student's needs, comprise the significant factors in the effectiveness of the tool.

Standards for Classroom Application

The list of popular word-processing applications includes *Microsoft Word*, *Microsoft Works*, *ClarisWorks*, and *Word Perfect*.   Software selection, however, has been rendered practically obsolete by the dominance of *Microsoft Word*. Even so, standards for using word processing in the classroom are only now becoming widely accepted. From a public school district, word-processing technology standards are offered for consideration here and applied to the lesson plans that follow (Andover Public School District, 2001).

Primary Grades (Pre-Kindergarten through Grade 2)

Word-Processing Skills	Skill Level
Create a document	Practice
Type in story with added graphic	Practice
Save, edit, retrieve, print	Introduction
Highlight/select text	Introduction
Recognize alphanumeric keys	Application
Recognize return	Application
Recognize all keys	Practice

Intermediate Grades (Grade 3 through Grade 5)

Word-Processing Skills	Skill Level
Create a document	Application
Type in story with added graphic	Mastery
Save, edit, retrieve, print	Mastery
Highlight/select text	Application
Use shortcuts	Practice
Cut, copy, paste	Mastery
Select all	Mastery
Spell check and thesaurus	Mastery
Font, style, size	Mastery
Document formatting	Practice
Apply indent	Practice
Shrink and enlarge	Practice
Insert page numbers	Introduction
Use find and then change	Introduction
Apply columns	Introduction
Recognize alphanumeric keys	Application
Recognize return	Application
Recognize all keys	Practice

Middle Grades (Grade 6 through Grade 8)

Word-Processing Skills	Skill Level
Create a document	Application
Type in story with added graphic	Application
Save, edit, retrieve, print	Application
Highlight/select text	Application
Use shortcuts	Practice
Cut, copy, paste	Application
Select all	Application
Spell check and thesaurus	Application
Font, style, size	Application
Document formatting	Application
Apply indent	Application
Shrink and enlarge	Application
Insert page numbers	Application
Use find and then change	Application
Apply columns	Application
Advanced document format	Mastery
Set page and column breaks	Mastery
Use tab stops and leaders	Mastery
Headers and footers	Mastery
Format paragraphs	Practice
Use style sheets	Practice
Create lists and outlines	Practice
Create and format sections	Introduction
Mail merge	Introduction
Recognize alphanumeric keys	Application
Recognize return	Application
Recognize all keys	Application

Secondary Grades (Grade 9 through Grade 12)

Word-Processing Skills	Skill Level
Create a document	Application
Type in story with added graphic	Application
Save, edit, retrieve, print	Application
Highlight/select text	Application
Use shortcuts	Practice
Cut, copy, paste	Application
Select all	Application
Spell check and thesaurus	Application
Font, style, size	Application
Document formatting	Application
Apply indent	Application
Shrink and enlarge	Application
Insert page numbers	Application
Use find and then change	Application
Apply columns	Application
Advanced document format	Application
Set page and column breaks	Application
Use tab stops and leaders	Application
Use headers and footers	Application
Format paragraphs	Mastery
Use style sheets	Mastery
Create lists and outlines	Mastery
Create and format sections	Practice
Mail merge	Practice
Recognize alphanumeric keys	Application
Recognize return	Application
Recognize all keys	Application

Lesson Plan Ideas for Integrating Word-Processing Applications

Word processing is already required in today's educational environment. Applications range from computerized test taking (e.g., driving permits and job applications) to completing loan applications or searching for a book at the local library. As students progress through their education, they enter subsequent grades bringing with them skills considered previous learning. Still, a comfort level does not yet exist for what children should know about word-processing skills as they enter particular grades. Perhaps the following example lesson objectives can help.

Lesson Idea #1

Category: Primary Grades

Title: Christmas Celebrations (Grade 2), by Brenda Olmstead

Adapted from: www.clis.com/staffdev/TRLP/secondgr.htm

Lesson Goals/Objectives: The students will note likeness and differences in holiday celebrations (Christmas) in the United States and Germany. The students will write a paragraph using "power writing" (main idea and supporting details). The student will use the computer to enter their paragraph, save, retrieve, and print for display.

Comments: This lesson employs the best practice principles of student-centered, authentic, expressive, and experiential. Students will know basic computer skills, comprehend a sense of their story, apply word processing to create a document, analyze and synthesize for likenesses and differences, and evaluate favorite parts of stories.

Lesson Idea #2

Category: Intermediate Grades

Title: Get in the Green (Grade 3), by North Carolina Department of Public Instruction

Adapted from: www.dpi.state.nc.us/Curriculum/ computer.skills/lssnplns/wordproc/wpg3-2.htm

Lesson Goals/Objectives: Use a word-processing program to load, enter, save, and print text.

Comments: In terms of best practice, this lesson is student-centered, experiential, reflective, democratic, and constructivist. The teacher could augment the lesson so that it addresses higher-order thinking skills by asking students to relate their learning to habitats/environments around the world, by asking students to relate what they discover from their investigations, or by asking the students to compare the amount of resources needed to grow versus the amount of energy derived.

Lesson Idea #3

Category: Middle Grades

Title: Opinion Articles (Grades 6 through 8), by Lisa Nash

Adapted from: www.education-world.com/a_tsl/archives/01-1/lesson0016.shtml

Lesson Goals/Objectives: Students research opinion pages and create documents in newspaper-style column format. They will research information on assigned topics, formulate opinions about current topics, combine the research and opinion into word-processing documents, type the research and opinion into word-processing documents, format the text into columns, use spell checking, insert a header that includes the name of the article, and insert a graphic into the body of the text.

Comments: Some team teachers may want to collaborate on this lesson. Students could receive grades for English, history, computers, etc. This lesson takes word-processing skills up a notch to include a greater amount of formatting. In terms of best practice, the lesson is student-centered, cognitive, reflective, and expressive. The assessment takes the lesson and extends it to make it more constructivist, more collaborative, and more holistic. Regarding Bloom's taxonomy, the lesson innately addresses the higher-order levels involving opinion and attitudes.

Lesson Idea #4

Category: <u>Secondary Grades</u>

Title: <u>Class Directory</u> (Grades 9 through 12), by Marge Arnold

Adapted from: www.lcet.doe.state.la.us/conn2/sections/lessons/preview.asp?ID=136

Lesson Goals/Objectives: The purpose of this unit is to enhance students' writing, speaking, and listening skills. Students will produce a class directory of newsletters about themselves. Each newsletter will include a biography written by a class member after an interviewing activity, an autobiographical essay written by the student, and writings by other students in the class and by the teacher. Microsoft Word or WordPerfect will be used for basic word processing. Students will import their documents into Microsoft Publisher or other desktop publishing software to create their newsletter. Photographs taken with a digital camera, photographs brought from home to be scanned, and clip art will be added to the published documents. The completed class directory will be placed in the high school library for future generations of students to read. Students will also produce a presentation using *PowerPoint*, *KidPix*, or other software.

Comments: This particular lesson incorporates many principles of best practice — it is student-centered, experiential, holistic, authentic, expressive, reflective, social, collaborative, cognitive, constructivist, and, depending upon standards set, challenging. This lesson also addresses all level of Bloom's taxonomy, and it incorporates all learning preferences.

Spreadsheets

A Definition and Brief History

A spreadsheet organizes information into columns and rows and manipulates numeric information using arithmetic functions. The term "spreadsheet" came from the word for an accountant's ledger; a book used to track large amounts of quantitative information (Norton & Sprague, 2001). According to Power (2001), "the spreadsheet literally spreads or shows all of the costs, income, taxes, etc., on a single sheet of paper for a manager to make decisions." In 1979, Dan Bricklin, a Harvard student, and Robert Frankston, an MIT student, created the first spreadsheet, *VisiCalc*, to run on the Apple II computer. Initially, spreadsheets had limited abilities; however, when *Lotus 1-2-3* was introduced in 1982, expanding features lifted it to the forefront of spreadsheet programs. *Microsoft Office's* spreadsheet application is *Excel*, while *ClarisWorks* and *AppleWorks* have their spreadsheet applications integrated within their respective software suites.

Classroom Benefits

There are many benefits to spreadsheet programs in the classroom. They are faster than manual analysis and calculator-based analysis. They offer greater flexibility as users change entries and immediately view the results. Additionally, spreadsheets allow for graphical displays, copy-and-paste editing, and formula revisions as necessary. Pedagogically, spreadsheets help students move from the concrete to the abstract as their attention switches from symbol manipulation to sense making; that is, they have the opportunity to reflect, discuss, analyze, and evaluate procedures performed on numbers and quantities (Battista & Van Auken Borrow, 1998). Historically, teachers have used spreadsheets as a management tool for grading, attendance charts, surveys, and checklists. However, spreadsheets are also used for "timelines, game boards, and graphs or to solve problems, keep track of classroom experiments, explore mathematical relationships, and delve into social studies or science investigations" (Sharp, 2002).

Standards for Classroom Application

Microsoft's *Excel* dominates spreadsheet use, however, spreadsheet features of *ClarisWorks* make it a popular second in schools. *Lotus 1-2-3* and *Quattro Pro*, while still popular in the business sector, are used little, if at all, in the classroom. In terms of user friendliness, the spreadsheet employs the same GUI (graphical user interface) as word-processing programs, and its range of features requires more cognitive development to master. Use of spreadsheets does not begin in earnest until the intermediate grades (Andover Public School District, 2001).

Primary Grades (Pre-Kindergarten through Grade 2)

Spreadsheet Skills	Mastery Level
Not applicable	N/A

Intermediate Grades (Grade 3 through Grade 5)

Spreadsheet Skills	Mastery Level
Adjust row and column height	Practice
Enter text	Practice
Add a graphic	Practice
Work with formulas	Practice
Highlight cells	Practice
Format numbers	Introduction
Use page view	Introduction
Print a document	Introduction
Use display	Introduction
Sort	Introduction
Create pie chart	Introduction
Create bar chart	Introduction
Create whole table	Introduction
Clear, delete, insert	Introduction
Insert worksheets into a word-processing document	Introduction

Middle Grades (Grade 6 through Grade 8)

Spreadsheet Skills	Mastery Level
Adjust row and column height	Application
Enter text	Application
Add a graphic	Application
Work with formulas	Application
Highlight cells	Application
Format numbers	Application
Use page view	Application
Print a document	Application
Use display	Application
Sort	Application
Create pie chart	Application
Create bar chart	Application
Create whole table	Application
Clear, delete, insert	Mastery
Insert worksheets into a word-processing document	Mastery
Use headers and footers	Mastery
Format dates and times	Mastery
Set displays and borders	Mastery
Shading	Mastery
Divide window	Practice
Lock and unlock cells	Practice

Secondary Grades (Grade 9 through Grade 12)

Spreadsheet Skills	Mastery Level
Adjust row and column height	Application
Enter text	Application
Add a graphic	Application
Work with formulas	Application
Highlight cells	Application
Format numbers	Application
Use page view	Application
Print a document	Application
Use display	Application
Sort	Application
Create pie chart	Application
Create bar chart	Application
Create whole table	Application
Clear, delete, insert	Application
Insert worksheets into a word-processing document	Application
Use headers and footers	Application
Format dates and times	Application
Set displays and borders	Application
Shading	Application
Divide window	Mastery
Lock and unlock cells	Mastery

Lesson Plan Ideas for Integrating Spreadsheet Applications

The use of spreadsheets is not as widespread a skill as word processing. However, as time progresses, much of the world's financial record keeping will be conducted using spreadsheets. So, it is important that children become literate with their use. Alternatively, teachers will not use spreadsheets if they are not familiar with them. In-service staff development should help teachers become familiar with the use of spreadsheet applications. The following lesson objectives may provide a learning opportunity for teachers as well as their students.

Lesson Idea #5

Category: Intermediate Grades

Title: Santa's Elf Spreadsheet (Grade 4), by Patricia K. Asher

Adapted from: –HYPERLINK "http://www.askeric.org/Virtual/Lessons/Mathematics/AppliedMath/APM0007.html" — www.askeric.org/Virtual/Lessons/Mathematics/AppliedMath/APM0007.html

Lesson Goals/Objectives: Students will learn how to estimate prices of items; use catalogs and advertisements to research costs of items; and use problem-solving strategies and a spreadsheet template to determine what can be bought within a budget.

Comments: This lesson is an authentic learning experience for students. It also is student-centered, expressive, cognitive, and developmental. It focuses on analysis and synthesis of data (which is inherent to spreadsheet use) and addresses all learning styles.

Lesson Idea #6

Category: Middle Grades

Title: SOS: Save Our Shrimp Industry (Grade 8), by Patricia K. Asher

Adapted from: –HYPERLINK "http://www.dpi.state.nc.us/Curriculum/computer.skills/lssnplns/SSlesson.G8.3.2.1b.html"

—www.dpi.state.nc.us/Curriculum/computer.skills/
lssnplns/SSlesson.G8.3.2.1b.html

Lesson Goals/Objectives: Given a prepared spreadsheet on the income from shrimping in North Carolina, test "What if?" scenarios by entering possible amounts of pollutants dumped into the water and by observing the resulting effects on shrimp harvests. Enter and edit data into a prepared spreadsheet to test "What if?" statements.

Comments: This lesson incorporates all of the best practices. It is student-centered, experiential, holistic, authentic, expressive, reflective, social, collaborative, democratic, cognitive, developmental, constructivist, and challenging. In this instance, technology enables the student to focus on higher-order analysis rather than on lower-order calculations. It is another lesson that can be adapted to a variety of grade levels above and below Grade 8. It develops higher-order thinking skills in the students, and it uses a variety of learning styles.

Lesson Idea #7

Category: Secondary Grades

Title: Aviation Collision (Grades 9 through 12)

Adapted from: www.nasaexplores.com/lessons/01-063/9-12_1-t.html

Lesson Goals/Objectives: Use a real-life situation to create computer spreadsheets and graphs and to enter formulas to organize large amounts of data.

Comments: The lesson is a highly authentic learning experience for the students. Through creative assessment, it can be made holistic, reflective, and challenging. Such a lesson can readily be differentiated based upon student's individual needs. Lessons such as this integrate all levels of Bloom's taxonomy and learning styles.

Note: A more comprehensive lesson plan, including several exercises and a student assessment, is provided in Appendix A.

Databases

A Definition and Brief History

A database organizes information structured as fields, records, and files. Precursors to electronic databases include index cards and lists. In 1960, General Electric's Charles Bachman developed the Integrated Data Storage, one of the first database management systems to store and organize data logically. According to Manetti (2001), "The first commercial release (issued in 1979) was Vulcan Database Program, created by Wayne Ratliff who sold the rights to Ashton-Tate, that renamed it into dBase II. Modern databases execute operations and instructions, and code (like a normal program) that at the beginning were not proper database characteristics but that are now essential."

There are three kinds of databases. First, text-based databases include alphanumeric information only. Second, hypermedia databases involve information related through hyperlinks. Third, multimedia databases include information from two or more media linked to a single product and may be linear or nonlinear. Commercial software used in educational settings, *AppleWorks*, *Microsoft Works*, and *Access*, typically include text-based databases.

Classroom Benefits

There are numerous instructional benefits to using databases in the classroom. Much of the strength of databases lies in their ability to search and sort information quickly. In years past, when students created index cards for research papers, much time was spent sorting and organizing. With database software, a mouse click re-sorts and retrieves the desired information. Organizing content information is logical even for elementary-level students. Importantly, the use of databases in the classroom helps develop student thinking skills, including analyzing, comparing and contrasting, generalizing, classifying, inferring, and interpolating. According to Norton and Sprague (2001), structure in a database lesson is crucial. The introduction to the lesson should stress the problem to be solved, not the computer. Clear expectations are vital. Teachers should model key problem-solving elements and guide student practice. Daily summary sessions of where each group has been, its achievements, and next steps are very useful. There should be final, public sharing of results.

Standards for Classroom Application

Most database programs are integrated into office productivity software suites such as *Microsoft Office* and *AppleWorks*. Purchase decisions are typically removed from the classroom teacher and held in central office administration. However, should the classroom teacher be included in acquisition decisions (highly recommended), ease of use and availability of technical support are important selection criteria.

As with spreadsheets, the use of databases is not found in younger grades; they do not typically begin until the intermediate grades. The Andover Public School District standards for integrating databases into the curriculum follow (Andover Public School District, 2001).

Primary Grades (Pre-Kindergarten through Grade 2)

Database Skills	Mastery Level
Not applicable	N/A

Intermediate Grades (Grade 3 through Grade 5)

Database Skills	Mastery Level
Enter data in a field	Practice
Create new record	Practice
Alter layout	Practice
Move through records	Practice
Define field	Introduction
Add and delete fields	Introduction
Sort records	Introduction
Match records	Introduction
Hide selected and unselected	Introduction
Show all records	Introduction
Create and rename layouts	Introduction
Edit layout: header and body	Introduction
Edit layout: move fields	Introduction
Edit layout: resize fields	Introduction
Edit layout: text styles	Introduction

Middle Grades (Grade 6 through Grade 8)

Database Skills	Mastery Level
Enter data in a field	Application
Create new record	Application
Alter layout	Application
Move through records	Application
Define field	Mastery
Add and delete fields	Mastery
Sort records	Mastery
Match records	Mastery
Hide selected and unselected	Mastery
Show all records	Mastery
Create and rename layouts	Mastery
Edit layout: header and body	Mastery
Edit layout: move fields	Mastery
Edit layout: resize fields	Mastery
Edit layout: text styles	Mastery
Find records	Mastery
Store sorts and searches	Mastery
Create reports	Mastery
Edit layout: number format	Practice
Calculations: create database	Practice
Calculations: enter data	Practice
Calculations: change formats	Practice
Calculations: grand summary	Practice
Calculations: subsummary	Practice
Data: lists and ranges	Introduction
Data: set auto entries	Introduction
Data: use new tools	Introduction

Secondary Grades (Grade 9 through Grade 12)

Database Skills	Mastery Level
Enter data in a field	Application
Create new record	Application
Alter layout	Application
Move through records	Application
Define field	Application
Add and delete fields	Application
Sort records	Application
Match records	Application
Hide selected and unselected	Application
Show all records	Application
Create and rename layouts	Application
Edit layout: header and body	Application
Edit layout: move fields	Application
Edit layout: resize fields	Mastery
Edit layout: text styles	Mastery
Find records	Mastery
Store sorts and searches	Mastery
Create reports	Mastery
Edit layout: number format	Mastery
Calculations: create database	Mastery
Calculations: enter data	Mastery
Calculations: change formats	Mastery
Calculations: grand summary	Mastery
Calculations: subsummary	Mastery
Data: lists and ranges	Practice
Data: set auto entries	Practice
Data: use new tools	Practice

Lesson Plan Ideas for Integrating Database Applications

Lesson Idea #8

Category: Intermediate Grades

Title: America's Richest People Lesson Plan (Grades 4 and 5), by Ted MacDonald and Mary Beth Castonguay

Adapted from: www.mcps.k12.md.us/departments/isa/elit/el/mathtrav/real_life_bignumbers.html

Lesson Goals/Objectives: Students will use newly acquired numeration skills to understand and analyze a real-life database. Students will be introduced to the Forbes 400 Richest People in America Web site. Students will use this data to complete the student activities worksheet, examining real-life "big" numbers and writing them in standard form. Students will use the data to compare/contrast and manipulate (sum and mean) "big" numbers. They will use the database to gather, organize, and analyze information. They will have the opportunity to use expository reading skills to learn about various successful people by reading brief biographical summaries. They will provide a citation to document their source of information.

Comments: This lesson plan is student-centered, authentic, expressive, cognitive, and constructivist. It can be adapted to address other areas of best practice. It is a fine example of how students use information from a database rather than just enter information into a database. It focuses on higher-level thinking skills and addresses a variety of student learning styles.

Lesson Idea #9

Category: Middle Grades

Title: Europe (Grade 6)

Adapted from: www.dpi.state.nc.us/Curriculum/computer.skills/lssnplns/database/grad6311.htm

Lesson Goals/Objectives: Use a database to sort records. Given a prepared database of European countries, sort the countries in ascending order by elevation, and identify the five countries with the highest elevations.

Comments: This lesson plan incorporates many best practice teaching techniques. It is student-centered, experiential, collaborative, social, reflective, developmental, and constructivist. The students use all levels of Bloom's taxonomy from knowledge, comprehension, applying, analysis, synthesis, and evaluation.

Lesson Idea #10

Category: Secondary Grades

Title: Casualties in War (Grade 11)

Adapted from: www.teach-nology.com/tutorials/databases/example/

Lesson Goals/Objectives: Students will be able to debate the reliability and validity of data found in an online database.

Comments: Due to their innate ability to organize information and to enable students to visually see connections, database applications should be integrated into the regular activities of the classroom. Use of a database to organize information can free the learner to focus on applying, analyzing, synthesizing, and evaluating the information.

Graphics/Paint and Draw Utilities

A Definition and Brief History

Images play a significant role in the world around us. In computer applications, images refer to the Web-based graphics and clip art that are created using paint and draw software. A variety of programs are available, ranging in functionality from design, presentation, and productivity to painting and drawing.

Classroom Benefits

All too frequently in the classroom, verbal and mathematical intelligences take precedence over visual representation. The multitude of available computer graphics tools for teachers and students is beginning to balance this equation. The most successful learning theorists include visual and artistic tools in their bag of teaching tricks.

Standards for Classroom Application

There is abundant graphics software for computers in the classroom, including *ClarisWorks, Microsoft Works* and *Word, KidPix, Corel Draw,* and *Adobe Photoshop.* Most classroom computers host more than one of these graphic programs; sometimes, a choice of two or three programs is loaded onto a school computer. Choice of graphics software often depends upon age appropriateness, ease of use, cost, support, reliability, and purpose. Andover standards for graphics/paint and draw utilities begin with the primary grades and include the following (Andover Public School District, 2001).

Primary Grades (Pre-Kindergarten through Grade 2)

Graphics Skills	Mastery Level
Basic tools	Introduction
Create a new drawing	Introduction
Draw shapes	Introduction

Intermediate Grades (Grade 3 through Grade 5)

Graphics Skills	Mastery Level
Basic tools	Mastery
Create a new drawing	Practice
Draw shapes	Practice
Add and delete objects	Practice
Select objects	Practice
Resize objects	Practice
Change line appearance	Practice
Change fill and line pattern	Practice
Gradient fill	Practice
Copy, paste, and duplicate object	Practice
Turn autogrid off and on	Practice
Rotate and reflect	Introduction
Align objects	Introduction
Text box: insert text	Introduction
Group and ungroup	Introduction
Show and hide ruler	Introduction

Middle Grades (Grade 6 through Grade 8)

Graphics Skills	Mastery Level
Basic tools	Application
Create a new drawing	Application
Draw shapes	Application
Add and delete objects	Application
Select objects	Application
Resize objects	Application
Change line appearance	Application
Change fill and line pattern	Application
Gradient fill	Application
Copy, paste, and duplicate object	Application
Turn autogrid off and on	Application
Rotate and reflect	Application
Align objects	Application
Text box: insert text	Application
Group and ungroup	Application
Show and hide ruler	Application
Link text box	Mastery
Add painting box	Mastery
Use painting tools	Mastery
Select area of painting	Mastery
View master page	Mastery
Edit master page	Mastery
Create body pages	Mastery

Secondary Grades (Grade 9 through Grade 12)

Graphics Skills	Mastery Level
Basic tools	Application
Create a new drawing	Application
Draw shapes	Application
Add and delete objects	Application
Select objects	Application
Resize objects	Application
Change line appearance	Application
Change fill and line pattern	Application
Gradient fill	Application
Copy, paste, and duplicate object	Application
Turn autogrid off and on	Application
Rotate and reflect	Application
Align objects	Application
Text box: insert text	Application
Group and ungroup	Application
Show and hide ruler	Application
Link text box	Application
Add painting box	Application
Use painting tools	Application
Select area of painting	Application
View master page	Application
Edit master page	Application
Create body pages	Application

Lesson Plan Ideas for Integrating Graphics and Paint and Draw Utilities

Educators must keep in mind that image and paint and draw programs are useful well beyond the confines of the art classroom. Images and paint and draw programs allow for student ownership of their learning. Students can express themselves through a variety of means, with the potential for creativity being boundless. Visual representations of concepts and ideas require metacognitive thinking and deep cognitive understanding. When assessing using such tools, the educator must be cautious to allow time for the student to think without feeling hurried. Images and paint and draw can be used in pretesting as well as in posttesting, and their use can show the teacher a truer depth and breadth of the student's understanding.

Lesson Idea #11

Category: Primary Grades

Title: Habitats (Grade 1)

Adapted from: www.k12.hi.us/~dtisdell/training/haines.html by Maria Haines

Lesson Goals/Objectives: This is a small group activity, but it can also be adapted to use with the whole class. In order to do this activity with the whole class, it would be best to do the draw portion of the lesson in the computer lab. Through this activity, students will learn new vocabulary words, make connections between habitats discussed in science and the story character's habitat, find rhyming words throughout the story, write about their inventive animals and the animal's living environment, experiment with the draw/paint program in *KidPix*, make up a story with text, respond to literature in a variety of ways, and use a computer to assist in the completion of a task.

Comments: As written, the lesson addresses the lower levels of Bloom's taxonomy, however, it could easily be extended to apply what is learned to endangered species to incorporate an evaluative component. In terms of learning styles, this lesson uses visual, aural, read–write, and kinesthetic components.

Lesson Idea #12

Category: Intermediate Grades

Title: Cue Set (Grade 4)

Adapted from: www.macomb.k12.mi.us/eastdet/Plans/EL-langCharlotte.htm by David A. Jackowicz

Lesson Goals/Objectives: Students describe their experiences catching bugs, either earlier in life or at the present time. Students describe the different types of spiders with which they are familiar, and then explain what they know about each type.

Comments: This lesson follows the best practices of being student-centered, holistic, expressive, collaborative, cognitive, and developmental. The students work at all levels of Bloom's taxonomy, including evaluative, when they explain how technology enhances the written text material.

Lesson Idea #13

Category: Middle Grades

Title: Trees of Our Region (Grade 8)

Adapted from: www.wvaworldschool.org/html/lesson/lplans/science/oconnell/trees2.htm by Marty Burke, Carol O'Connell, and Lana Turner

Lesson Goals/Objectives: Acquaint students with the trees native to West Virginia and the skills necessary for tree identification. Create an online tree identification key. Develop techniques in digital imagery and Web page building.

Comments: The best practices include its being student-centered, experiential, holistic, authentic, expressive, reflective, cognitive, developmental, and challenging. Each of Bloom's levels is addressed through this lesson, as are all of the learning styles.

Lesson Idea #14

Category: <u>Secondary Grades</u>

Title: <u>Railroad Safety</u> (Grade 9)

Adapted from: www.oli.org/for_teachers/oli_cdrom/lessons/
9_12_ms_lp.html

Lesson Goals/Objectives: Students will be able to communicate clearly and convincingly a specific position on rail safety. Students will use details, illustrations, statistics, comparisons, and analogies to defend their positions. Identify, evaluate, and synthesize information in order to support a thesis. Present information in a logical, well-organized format. Cite sources of information using a standard method of documentation. Communicate ideas to an intended audience. Work collaboratively and cooperatively to develop a cohesive campaign.

Comments: This inclusive lesson addresses all of the best practices in a strikingly authentic manner. It uses a mix of all of the Bloom's levels, and it approaches the student's learning from all learning styles. Also note that this lesson can be altered for students at lower grade levels, as it can be adapted for students for enrichment purposes.

Hypermedia and Multimedia Software

A Definition and Brief History

Multimedia and hypermedia are two frequently misunderstood technology terms. Multimedia is "the field concerned with the computer-controlled integration of text, graphics, drawings, still and moving images, animation, audio, and any other media where every type of information can be represented, stored, transmitted and processed digitally" (Marshall, 2001). It is important to note that this definition does not address how that information is organized. Multimedia is not a new concept. It encompasses slides, cassette players, and even overhead projectors.

Hypermedia is defined as "using the computer to input, manipulate, and output graphics, sound, text, and video as part of a hypertext system. The different forms of information are linked together so that the user can move from one to another" (Sharp, 2002). In hypertext, all bits of information are connected to all other bits of information through a network of links. Multimedia includes linearly organized data, while hypermedia is nonlinear.

Vannevar Bush created hypertext in 1945; around 20 years later, Ted Nelson took this idea, named it, and developed *Xanadu*, a software framework that allows users to connect electronic documents (Keep, McLaughlin, & Parmer, 2000). In 1987, Bill Atkinson (also the author of MacPaint) at Apple Computer created *HyperCard* for the Macintosh computer, followed by Roger Wagner's *HyperStudio* for the Apple IIGS. Contemporary software allows users to create multimedia linear presentations and includes *PowerPoint, AppleWorks*, and *KidPix*. The World Wide Web is an example of hypermedia in action.

Classroom Benefits

According to Dede (1994), hypermedia "offers new methods for structured discovery, addresses varied learning styles, is motivating and empowers students, and allows educators to present information as a web of interconnections rather than a stream of facts." A meta-analysis (Najjar, 1996) has shown that "learning was higher when the information was presented via computer-based multimedia systems than traditional classroom lectures. Another very significant finding was that learning appeared to take less time when multimedia instruction was used." Using these instructional tools places the student in the driver's seat in control of the learning process and of transforming the lesson into an engaging, active form of learning. Other research has shown that the development of critical thinking skills in language and reading is enhanced by the use of hypermedia tools. Thus, hypermedia sets the stage for a constructivist-learning situation. It enables the classroom to readily become a student-centered, cognitive, developmental, and challenging environment.

Standards for Classroom Application

There is an array of multimedia and hypermedia application from which educators may choose. Most school districts install *Microsoft Office* or *AppleWorks*, offering *Power Point* or the *Presentation* module, respectively. These two applications, in combination with *HyperStudio* and *KidPix*, depend more on the computer platform in the school than on any other single factor. Windows-based systems typically host *Power Point*; Macintosh-based systems provide *Power Point* or *HyperStudio* and *KidPix*. Standards, however, breech the gap, providing a common set of skills and competencies for all learners, as provided again by the Andover Public School District.

Primary Grades (Pre-Kindergarten through Grade 2)

Multimedia Skills	Mastery Level
Slide show sequence: linear	Introduction

Intermediate Grades (Grade 3 through Grade 5)

Multimedia Skills	Mastery Level
Slide show sequence	Mastery
Create new multimedia	Practice
Choose a background	Practice
Use ready-made border	Practice
Create your own border	Practice
Add text	Practice
Add graphics	Practice
Edit graphics	Practice
Use the tool palette	Practice
Save the card	Practice
Add buttons	Practice
Sound	Practice
Link	Practice
Transition	Practice
Use ready-made cards	Practice
Create a new card	Practice
Edit button actions	Practice
Record a sound	Practice
Use the storyboard	Practice
Use button icons	Practice
Test functions	Practice
Create magic button	Introduction
Scale artwork	Introduction
New button actions	Introduction
Animation	Introduction
Quick-time movies	Introduction
Create hyperlogo button	Introduction
Import audio	Introduction
Import movies	Introduction
Use fat bits	Introduction
Import graphics	Introduction
Link to the Internet	Introduction

Middle Grades (Grade 6 through Grade 8)

Multimedia Skills	Mastery Level
Slide show sequence	Application
Create new multimedia	Application
Choose a background	Application
Use ready-made border	Application
Create your own border	Application
Add text	Application
Add graphics	Application
Edit graphics	Application
Use the tool palette	Application
Save the card	Application
Add buttons	Application
Sound	Application
Link	Application
Transition	Application
Create a new card	Application
Use ready-made cards	Application
Edit button actions	Application
Record a sound	Application
Use the storyboard	Application
Use button icons	Application
Test functions	Application
Create magic button	Application
Scale artwork	Application
New button actions	Application
Animation	Application
Quick-time movies	Mastery
Create hyperlogo button	Application
Import audio	Mastery
Import movies	Mastery
Use fat bits	Mastery
Import graphics	Mastery
Link to the Internet	Mastery

Secondary Grades (Grade 9 through Grade 12)

Multimedia Skills	Mastery Level
Slide show sequence	Application
Create new multimedia	Application
Choose a background	Application
Use ready-made border	Application
Create your own border	Application
Add text	Application
Add graphics	Application
Edit graphics	Application
Use the tool palette	Application
Save the card	Application
Add buttons	Application
Sound	Application
Link	Application
Transition	Application
Create a new card	Application
Use ready-made cards	Application
Edit button actions	Application
Record a sound	Application
Use the storyboard	Application
Use button icons	Application
Test functions	Application
Create magic button	Application
Scale artwork	Application
New button actions	Application
Animation	Application
Quick-time movies	Application
Create hyperlogo button	Application
Import audio	Application
Import movies	Application
Use fat bits	Application
Import graphics	Application
Link to the Internet	Application

Lesson Plan Ideas for Integrating Hypermedia/Multimedia Applications

Hypermedia and multimedia in the classroom, despite the fact that both have been around for some time, are still considered in their infancy. Together, they are natural authentic assessment vehicles, demanding critical thinking, comprehension, and understanding of relationships between concepts and content. Few schools are able to afford multimedia hardware and software. Fortunately, the lesson ideas that follow provide examples of applications well within any school budget. Still, teachers must ensure that students do not become overly engrossed with the novelty of the multimedia and hypermedia at the expense of true content understanding.

Lesson Idea #15

Category: Primary Grades

Title: Leyendas and Children's Literature (Grade 2)

Adapted from: ladb.unm.edu/retanet/plans/search/ retrieve.php3?ID%5B0%5D=423 submitted by Diane Forsyth

Lesson Goals/Objectives: Second-grade students develop a connection with a kindergarten or first-grade counterpart by reading children's literature to them. At the same time, they explore the cultural writings, legends, and folk tales from the Southwest and Latin America. Students complete two projects using two different cultural writings, legends, or folk tales. One project is completed on the computer and the second in some other format. At least one of the projects must be completed in a form that can be given to the kindergarten student to keep.

Comments: This lesson is student-centered, holistic, authentic, expressive, reflective, collaborative, cognitive, developmental, constructivist, and challenging. These instructional dimensions are trademarks of lessons that incorporate hypermedia in the classroom. All of the students' learning styles are addressed, and the students learn at all levels of Bloom's taxonomy.

Lesson Idea #16

Category: Intermediate Grades

Title: Architecture (Grades 4 and 5)

Adapted from: communitydisc.wst.esu3.k12.ne.us/CGI/TAF/ by Betty Desaire

Lesson Goals/Objectives: Students will learn how things fit together by studying tessellations and the work of M.C. Escher. They will then learn the terminology of architecture, become aware of the historical significance of architecture in different parts of the world, and problem solve in creating their own pieces of architecture out of cardboard boxes. They will access the Internet for research purposes, and learn how to save images from the Internet to a disk. They will also use the video camera to save snapshots of local architecture to a disk. Finally, they will create a *HyperStudio* stack depicting images and text.

Comments: This unit incorporates all of the best practices in a meaningful manner. The student's thinking is addressed at all levels of Bloom's taxonomy, and all learning styles are addressed.

Lesson Idea #17

Category: Middle Grades

Title: Human Rights/Civil Rights (Grades 7 and 8)

Adapted from: communitydisc.wst.esu3.k12.ne.us/CGI/TAF/ by Ruby Morrisett

Lesson Goals/Objectives: What rights should be common to all people, regardless of time or place? The purpose of this unit is for students to connect their learning of the novel *Roll of Thunder, Hear My Cry* to historical and contemporary study of the issue of human rights/civil rights by creating a multimedia presentation.

Comments: This interdisciplinary unit addresses all best practices, learning styles, and levels of Bloom's taxonomy.

Lesson Idea #18

Category: <u>Secondary Grades</u>

Title: Civil War Presentations (Grades 10)

Adapted from: www.sendit.nodak.edu/uswftn/net_lessons/ lesson_plans/civilwar.html by Jerry Strahm

Lesson Goals/Objectives: Students will be able to use the Internet to locate four events related to the Civil War, make a list of related Web sites, arrange events of the Civil War in chronological order, save graphics related to the four events of the Civil War to a folder on the computer, combine graphics and information with headings from these resources found on the Internet into the presentation program Microsoft *Power Point*, and post the presentation on the school's home page.

Comments: In terms of best practice and Bloom's taxonomy, the classroom teacher is able to readily adapt the above lesson idea. In this type of lesson, it is important that the teacher maintain the focus of the lesson on the research and learning rather than on the presentation capabilities of *PowerPoint*.

The World Wide Web

A Brief Definition and History

The Internet is "a worldwide system of computer networks; a network of networks in which users at any one computer can, if they have permission, get information from any other computer (and sometimes talk directly to users at other computers)" (TechTarget, 2001). In 1969, the Advanced Research Projects Agency of the Department of Defense created the Internet to support command and control communication in case of a nuclear attack. In 1986, the Internet expanded beyond its original objectives as universities became more involved in the potential of instantly sharing files and data. In its original state, the Internet was a challenge for novices to navigate; however, by 1989, Tim Berners-Lee developed the beginnings of the World Wide Web. According to Kroop (2001), "1995 is the year the World Wide Web is indisputably established as the most important service on the Internet. The social, political and cultural impact of the Internet gradually becomes undeniable." The impact of the World Wide Web is now so widespread that it is quite difficult to envision life without it.

Classroom Benefits

The Internet and the World Wide Web together tear down the traditional walls of the classroom and connect it electronically to the rest of the world. The time required to retrieve information is reduced to seconds; distances are virtually eliminated. Unlike trips to the library that were inconvenient and time-consuming, research via the World Wide Web is conducted online at the office, school, or home. The definition of "current" information changed to include events that happened only seconds ago. Updating history and science textbooks has been rendered nearly obsolete. The opportunity to teach critical, analytic thinking skills to students has become real-time, as students learn to discern quality Web sites and pages from those with less reputable content. The ease with which differentiation in the classroom takes place is given a new meaning, as teachers have students research a variety of different perspectives on the same topic or on the same perspective on a variety of topics. The World Wide Web lessens the passivity of learners, while the spectra of learning styles (visual, auditory, artistic, musical, and kinesthetic) have been increased geometrically.

In addition to the standard use of the World Wide Web as a source of information, technology for learning synchronously (chats) and asynchronously (discussion boards) has expanded. Email is now the communications media of choice for nearly all students, teachers, and experts in the field.

Standards for Classroom Application

The most commonly used Web browsers are Netscape Communicator and Internet Explorer. Less frequently used by educators, commercial Internet service providers such as America Online and CompuServe are also available. The choice of browser software is less important than meeting certain minimum levels of competency demonstrated by the following standards combined from efforts by the Liverpool Central School District, Curriculum and Standards Site, New York (URL: www.liverpool.k12.ny.us/standards/lstandards/mst/k-12computerskills.html) and Fayette County Public Schools, Lexington, Kentucky (URL: www.fayette.k12.ky.us/instructtech/standards/).

	Primary Grades P–2	Intermediate Grades 3–5	Middle Grades 6–8	Secondary Grades 9–12
Communications (email skills)				
• Send and receive electronic communications	NA	Introduction	Practice	Practice
• Use appropriate electronic etiquette	Introduction	Practice	Practice	Practice
• Transfer files over email	NA	NA	Introduction	Practice
Communications (Internet, intranet)				
• Access and post to a bulletin board	NA	NA	Introduction	Practice
• Subscribe and unsubscribe to a list serve	NA	NA	Introduction	Practice
• Participate in digital–audio conferencing	NA	NA	NA	Introduction
• Participate in digital–video conferencing	NA	NA	NA	Introduction

Research–Information Access				
• Use electronic library resources to gather data	Introduction	Practice	Practice	Practice
• Use electronic bibliographies as a research tool	NA	Introduction	Practice	Practice
• Use key words to search the Internet	NA	NA	Introduction	Practice
• Use Boolean logic with various search engines and tools	NA	NA	NA	Introduction
• Bookmark authoritative research sites	NA	NA	Introduction	Practice
• Use advanced search techniques	NA	NA	Introduction	Practice
• Save information from telecommunication services and other online sources	NA	NA	Introduction	Practice
Impact of the World Wide Web				
• Demonstrate understanding that what you do on a network affects other users	Introduction	Practice	Practice	Practice
• Use various Web browsers to navigate the World Wide Web	Introduction	Practice	Master	Application
• Use advanced features of Web browsers	NA	Introduction	Master	Application
Other World Wide Web features				
• Locate and use video and audio information	NA	NA	Introduction	Practice
• Open, reply, reply all, forward, and attach messages	NA	Introduction	Master	Application
• Set up and effectively use an address book	NA	Introduction	Master	Application
• Publish information on the Internet	NA	NA	NA	Introduction

Lesson Plan Ideas for Integrating World Wide Web Applications

Lesson Idea #19

Category: <u>Primary Grades</u>

Title: <u>Food Chains</u> (Grade 3)

Adapted from: www.tamu-commerce.edu/coe/shed/espinoza/ s/ellis-b-lp2.html by Bruce Ellis

Lesson Goals/Objectives: Create a model of food chains to create a food web.

Comments: This lesson uses the World Wide Web to search for information. It enables students to take ownership of the information they choose and uses the best practices of being student-centered, expressive, collaborative, cognitive, developmental, and constructivist. Differentiation through use of a variety of extensions could make the lesson challenging for each student at an appropriate level. The lesson addresses the lower levels of Bloom's taxonomy.

Lesson Idea #20

Category: <u>Intermediate Grades</u>

Title: <u>Global Food Trek</u> (Grade 5)

Adapted from: www.plainfield.k12.in.us/hschool/webq/ webq105/ by Rose Clawson

Lesson Goals/Objectives: Exploring the customs and the cuisine from other cultures and comparing personal diets to the food guide pyramid.

Comments: The lesson addresses all best practices, attends to all learning styles, and implements the higher levels of Bloom's taxonomy.

Note: A more comprehensive lesson plan, including several exercises and a student assessment, is provided in Appendix B.

Lesson Idea #21

Category: Middle Grades

Title: The Life of Edgar Allan Poe (Grades 7 or 8)

Adapted from: home.aol.com/odysseybms/poe.htm by Ms. Debbie Dowdy

Lesson Goals/Objectives: Students will learn about the life of Edgar Allan Poe and about the history of our country and the world during the early- to mid-1800s. They will use a variety of research methods and modes, including computer technology, to collect information. Students will also keep a log of any conflicting information that they may find. Students will then organize and synthesize the information to plan a creative oral presentation.

Comments: This higher-level thinking lesson incorporates all of the best practices as well as all levels of Bloom's taxonomy. Structure for the presentations to the class can help to ensure a standard above which the students must reach.

Note: A more comprehensive lesson plan, including several exercises and a student assessment, is provided in Appendix C.

Lesson Idea #21

Category: Secondary Grades

Title: Chemical Element Internet Research (Grade 12)

Adapted from: www.nisd.net/holmesww/technology/integration/tips/elements/ElementResearch.htm by Alice Fiedler

Lesson Goals/Objectives: Chemistry students use online sources to investigate the element of their choice and relate their findings to what they have learned in class.

Comments: In this lesson, high school chemistry students use the student-centered, expressive, cognitive, developmental, and constructivist best practices. The lesson uses all levels of Bloom's taxonomy and addresses all learning styles. In order to add a metacognitive dimension to the lesson, the teacher could instruct various groups to present their information in ways that attend to varying learning styles. In addition, the teacher could have students identify the different Bloom's levels within their own products.

References

Andover Public School District (2001, December 21). *Technology*. Retrieved December 31, 2001 from the World Wide Web: www.andoverpublicschools.com/District/Tech/technolo.htm.

Battista, M. T., & Van Auken Borrow, C. (1998). Using spreadsheets to promote algebraic thinking. *Teaching Children Mathematics* (pp. 470–478).

Dede, C. (1994). *Making the most of multimedia. Multimedia and learning: A school leader's guide.* Alexandria, VA: National School Board Association.

Geisert, P. G., & Futrell, M. K. (2000). *Teachers, computers, and curriculum: Microcomputers in the classroom.* Boston: Allyn & Bacon.

Horn, J. (2001). *Middle School Net.* Retrieved October 20, 2001 from the World Wide Web: www.dpi.state.nc.us/Curriculum/computer.skills/lssnplns/database/grad6311.htm.

Keep, C., McLaughlin, T., & Parmar, R. (2000). *Ted Nelson and Xanadu.* Retrieved November 1, 2001 from the World Wide Web: www.iath.virginia.edu/elab/hfl0155.html.

Keith, G. R., & Glover, M. (1987). *Primary language learning with microcomputers.* Wolfeboro, NH: Croom Helm.

Kroop, T. (2001, 2000). *w3history.* Retrieved November 3, 2001 from the World Wide Web: www.w3history.org/.

Liverpool Central School District, *Curriculum and standards site in New York State.* Retrieved December, 2001 from the World Wide Web: www.liverpool.k12.ny.us/standards/lstandards/mst/k-12computerskills.html.

Manetti, S. (2001, April 4, 2000). *Database History*. Retrieved October 15, 2001 from the World Wide Web: www.nostalgia.itgo.com/Software/Tipo/enDatabase.html.

Marshall, D. (2001, October 4, 2001). *What is Multimedia?* Retrieved November 1, 2001 from the World Wide Web: www.cs.cf.ac.uk/Dave/Multimedia/node10.html.

Najjar, L. J. (1996). Multimedia information and learning. *Journal of Educational Multimedia and Hypermedia, 5*, 129–150.

National Educational Technology Standards for Students: Connecting Curriculum and Technology. (2000). International Society for Technology in Education.

Norton, P., & Sprague, D. (2001). *Technology for Teaching*. Needham Heights: Allyn and Bacon.

Oddo, L., Wang, L., Ucer, S., LaTorre, A., & Lin, K. (1997). *History of Computer Graphics*. Retrieved October 24, 2001 from the World Wide Web: www.imagesunlimited.com/History.html.

Overview of Technology and Education Reform. Retrieved October 6, 2001 from the World Wide Web: www.ed.gov/pubs/EdReformStudies/EdTech/overview.html.

Peck, K. (2001, August 28, 2001). *Messages from the Frontier*. Paper presented at the Quaker Valley School District In-service Program, Sewickley, Pennsylvania.

Pfaffenberger, B. (2000). *Webster's new world dictionary of computer terms* (8th ed.). New York: IDG Worldwide.

Power, D. J. (2001, August 19). *A Brief History of Spreadsheets*. Retrieved October 6, 2001 from the World Wide Web: dssresources.com/history/sshistory.html.

Sharp, V. (2002). *Computer Education for Teachers: Integrating Technology into Classroom Teaching* (Fourth ed.). New York: McGraw-Hill Higher Education.

A Short History of Databases. (2001). Retrieved October 6, 2001 from the World Wide Web: www.databaseanswers.com/history.htm.

Swan, K., & Meskill, C. (1996). Using hypermedia in response-based literature classrooms: A critical review of commercial applications. *Journal of Research on Computing in Education, 29*(2), 167–195.

TechTarget. (2001). *Internet — A whatis definition*. Retrieved November 3, 2001 from the World Wide Web: whatis.techtarget.com/definition/0,289893,sid9_gci212370,00.html.

Worcester, T. (1997). *Tammy's Technology Tips for Teachers*. Retrieved October 18, 2001 from the World Wide Web: www.essdack.org/tips/index.html.

Word processing - Webopedia.com. (2001). Retrieved October 4, 2001 from the World Wide Web: www.pcwebopedia.com/TERM/w/word_processing.html.

Zemelman, S., Daniels, H., & Hyde, A. (1998). *Best practice: New standards for teaching and learning in America's schools*. Portsmouth, NH: Heinemann.

Appendix A

Aviation Collision (Grades 9 through 12)
Spreadsheet Exercises

Exercise #1: Opening an *Excel* Spreadsheet

To open *Excel* from Windows, double click on the icon labeled Microsoft *Excel* or click on the Start button in the lower left-hand corner of the screen, go to the folder labeled program, then click on the Microsoft *Excel* program.

When *Excel* is first opened, across the top of the screen is the File → Edit → View menu bar. On the next line is the tool bar with icons for commonly used tools.

Below the menu bar is the actual worksheet composed of cells. Each cell is designated with a letter and a number. The letters indicate which column the cell is in, and the numbers indicate which row the cell is in.

	A	B
1	This is cell A1.	This is cell B1.
2	This is cell A2.	This is cell B1.

Moving from cell to cell can be done in two ways. Use the arrow keys to move, or use the mouse to click inside the cell to be used. Usually, there are several worksheets within a workbook. Near the bottom of the window there are several tables labeled "Sheet 1," "Sheet 2," etc. Clicking on a tab provides access to the worksheet.

Exercise #2: Entering Data into a Spreadsheet

On Sheet 1, click inside the appropriate cells, and enter the following data in the assigned cells:

A1	Altitude
B1	Count
C1	% of Total
D1	Cost
A2	0
A3	50
A4	100

After cell A4, increase the value by 100 for each cell in the A column. In cell A13, the number 1000 should be entered. Finish entering the altitude values as follows:

A14	1500
A15	2000
A16	3000
A17	4000
A18	5000
A19	>5000

Under the other headers, enter the following values:

Count	Percent of Total (%)	Cost in U.S. Dollars ($)
5893	29.94	107,134,807
2150	10.92	4,024,544
1407	7.15	12,856,207
1426	7.25	3,258,258
1078	5.48	2,260,010
485	2.46	557,162
1052	5.35	3,383,946
288	1.46	1,514,222
254	1.29	1,024,802
327	1.66	959,055
115	0.58	91,143
1314	6.68	2,462,739
1336	6.79	7,036,778
1363	6.93	1,498,842
817	4.15	3,140,545
172	0.87	228,375
103	0.52	164,081
100	0.51	968,497

To ensure that the percent of total is equal or close to 100, add the values. Click on cell C20, then find the Autosum icon in the tool bar, and click. Using the Autosum icon enters the formula "=sum()" to add a range of cells. If the cell is too small for the formula, click on cell C. This highlights all the cells under header C. Go to the format tab, and under column click, on autoformat. Use the Autosum icon to total the cost column. Next, graph the altitude and count.

The Graph Wizard icon gives access to all graph types available. Highlight columns A and B, and then click on the Graph Wizard icon. Choose the line graph. Follow the directions. Do not forget to label the x and y axes.

Exercise #3: Using *Excel* Functions

On Worksheet 2, begin a new spreadsheet, and enter the following data:

Common Name	Cost	Count	Average Cost
American white pelican	256,917,876	6	
Canada goose	82,288,968	66	
Turkey vulture	35,948,493	419	
Griffon vulture	26,833,390	6	
Red-tailed hawk	12,733,987	340	
Common starling	12,670,813	239	
Black vulture	8,893,695	139	
Snow goose	6,652,888	31	
Herring gull	4,717,464	88	

To calculate the average cost, enter cell D2 = B2/C2. Copy this formula, and enter it in the remaining cells in column D. Next, using the Tool icon "fx," find the average for the total cost (Column B). Click in cell B11, then click the Function Wizard icon that displays all the functions available.

Choose the "average" function. The computer averages cells B2 through B10. Using a calculator, check the answer given by the computer. On the same spreadsheet, alter the number format. Select column B by clicking on the "B" button at the top of the column. Click on Format → Cells → Number. Under the Category tab, highlight currency, and select two decimal places. Select the Symbol "$". Click OK.

Highlight the first two columns, and use the chart wizard to graph the data into a pie chart. In the chart wizard, in step 3 of 4, type an appropriate title.

Exercise #4: Summative Assessment

Refer to the 9–12 NASA Explores article, "Proceed to Plan B." With this information and after completing the previous exercises, respond to the following activities:

1. Discuss how the Intelligent Flight Control could be a major benefit for pilots.

2. Print all work in hard copy, and save all files to a floppy disk to be submitted as a single project to the instructor.

3. Compare your results to the following example, and explain any differences in how the student spreadsheets look.

Common Name	Cost	Count	Average Cost
American white pelican	256,917,876	6	42,819,646
Canada goose	82,288,968	66	1,246,802.545
Turkey vulture	35,948,493	419	85,795.92601
Griffon vulture	26,833,390	6	4,472,231.667
Red-tailed hawk	12,733,987	340	37,452.90294
Common starling	12,670,813	239	53,015.95397
Black vulture	8,893,695	139	63,983.41727
Snow goose	6,652,888	31	214,609.2903
Herring gull	4,717,464	88	53,607.54545
Average cost		49,739,730.44	

4. Compare your results to the following example, and explain any differences in how the graph looks.

Figure 1. Example Graph from the Intelligent Flight Control Spreadsheet

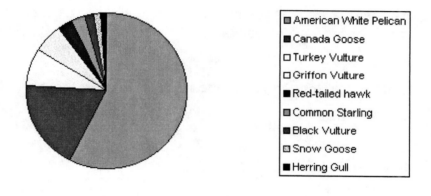

Cost Of Collisions Caused By Different Types of Birds

- American White Pelican
- Canada Goose
- Turkey Vulture
- Griffon Vulture
- Red-tailed hawk
- Common Starling
- Black Vulture
- Snow Goose
- Herring Gull

Appendix B
Global Food Trek (Grade 5) World Wide Web Exercises

Exercise #1

Print and read the Food Guide Pyramid located at www.eatright.org/erm/erm032698.html.

Exercise #2

Print and read the Food Guide Pyramid located at www.kidshealth.org/kid/stay_healthy/food/pyramid.html.

Exercise #3: How Do You Compare?

Complete a personal assessment of your own diet.

Name: _____

How Do You Compare?

Food Guide Pyramid Recommendations	Your Daily Servings
Bread, Cereal, Rice, and Pasta Group — 6 to 11 servings daily	_____
Milk, Yogurt, and Cheese Group — 2 to 3 servings daily	_____
Meat, Poultry, Fish, Beans, Eggs, and Nuts Group — 2 to 3 servings daily	_____
Vegetable Group — 3 to 5 servings daily	_____
Fruit Group — 2 to 4 servings daily	_____
Fats, Oils, and Sweets — "use sparingly"	_____

Exercise #4: Children in Other Countries

Complete the worksheet as a group project.

Children in Other Countries

After completing your research, do you think children in other countries consume <u>more</u> or <u>less</u> than the servings recommended by the Food Guide Pyramid?

Food Guide Pyramid	Mexico	Japan	China	Russia	France
Bread, cereal, rice, and pasta	_____	_____	_____	_____	_____
Milk, yogurt, and cheese	_____	_____	_____	_____	_____
Meat, poultry, fish, beans, eggs, and nuts	_____	_____	_____	_____	_____
Vegetables	_____	_____	_____	_____	_____
Fruits	_____	_____	_____	_____	_____
Fats, oils, and sweets	_____	_____	_____	_____	_____

Exercise #5: What Did You Learn?

Write three sentences stating what you learned from your mini-nutrition lesson. Then, share with your group, and add several of these statements to the school Web page.

1. _____

_____

_____

2. _____

_____

_____

3. _____

_____

_____

Exercise #6: Enrichment Activities

Continue your Global Food Trek using the following Web resources, and complete the Web site worksheets.

Visit These Sites	Check Here After Viewing
http://www.ameritech.net/users/macler/intrntlfoods.html	
http://www.ars.usda.gov/is/kids/nutrition/nutritionintro.htm	
http://www.eatethnic.com	
http://www.educ.uvic.ca/faculty/mroth/438/CHINA/chinese_new_year.html	
http://explora.presidencia.gob.mx/index_kids.html	
http://www.familyfoodzone.com/	
http://www.foodwine.com/destinations	
http://www.kidsfood.org	
http://mexico.udg.mx/cocina/ingles/	
http://www.russianfoods.com/	
http://www.wcsu.ctstateu.edu/socialsci/area.html	
http://www.yahooligans.com/Around_the_World/Food_and_Eating/	

Web Site Worksheets

Name: _____

Complete a Web site worksheet for each site visited, and offer two new facts that you learned about global food issues at that site.

1. Web Site Title: _____
Fact: _____
_____

Fact: _____
_____

2. Web Site Title: _____
Fact: _____
_____

Fact: _____
_____

3. Web Site Title: _____
Fact: _____
_____

Fact: _____
_____

Exercise #7: Global Food Trek Rubric

Global Food Trek Rubric Student Name:_____			
	Fair 5	Good 10	Excellent 15
Individual grade			
Group grade			
Oral presentation			
Web site			
Project objective			
Total points			
Final grade: _____			
Teacher comments:			

Appendix C
The Life of Edgar Allan Poe (Grade 7 or 8) World Wide Web Exercises

Exercise #1: Explore these historical and other great Web sites about Edgar Allen Poe's life and contributions to literature.

Biography Sites

  Qrisse's Edgar Allan Poe Pages www.poedecoder.com/Qrisse/

  The Edgar Allan Poe Museum www.poemuseum.org/

  The Poe Museum - A Brief Poe Bio www.poemuseum.org/bio.htm

  Edgar Allan Poe's House of Usher www.comnet.ca/~forrest/

  Edgar Allan Poe Biographical Information — National Historical Site — Park Brochure www.nps.gov/edal/brochure.htm

  Payge's Poe Page www.geocities.com/EnchantedForest/Dell/3627/

  Edgar Allan Poe — An In-depth Look at empirezine.com/spotlight/poe/poe1.htm

Sites Especially Helpful for the Historical Events Group

  A Poe Chronology www.nadn.navy.mil/EnglishDept/poeperplex/chronhis.htm

  TrackStar: The Pratuck Experience! Growth of a Nation scrtec.org/track/tracks/s06515.html

Sites About the Last Years of Poe's Life

  TrackStar: The Mysterious Death of E. A. Poe scrtec.org/track/tracks/s06147.html

  How did Poe Survive for Forty Years? www.nadn.navy.mil/EnglishDept/poeperplex/survivp.htm

  Who Is Buried in Edgar Poe's Grave? www.nadn.navy.mil/EnglishDept/poeperplex/gravep.htm

Other Great Poe Places to Visit

The Poe Decoder www.poedecoder.com/

Martha Womack's Home Page — Precisely Poe www.poedecoder.com/PreciselyPoe/

The Complete Works of Edgar Allan Poe www.mindspring.com/~thorazine/Poe/

Passions in Poetry — Classical Poems by Edgar Allan Poe netpoets.com/classic/049000.htm

Appendix D

Chemical Element Internet Research (Grade 12) World Wide Web Exercises

Exercise #1: Investigate the following characteristics of your selected element, and complete the table that follows.

www.shef.ac.uk/chemistry/web-elements/

chemicalelements.com

qlink.queensu.ca/~7gg2/elements.html

www.chemicool.com/

pearl1.lanl.gov/periodic/

www.ucc.ie/ucc/depts/chem/dolchem/html/elem/periodic.html

www.klbproductions.com/yogi/periodic/

Element selected: _____	Complete the following information
Origin of the element's name and symbol, its name in other languages	
Discovery date/circumstances	
Atomic number, atomic mass	
Isotopes: mass numbers of the most common, most stable, and least stable isotopes	
Metal/nonmetal/metalloid classification	
Group and period	
Electron configuration and valence electron configuration	
Physical properties	
State and appearance at room conditions	
Melting and boiling points	
Chemical properties	
Likely ionic charge	
Common chemical reactions	
Uses/applications	
Other pertinent information	

Exercise #2: Student Presentation Rubric

Criteria	Points Awarded 0–5 (Poor → Outstanding)
Information appropriate for the chosen element	0 1 2 3 4 5
Information accurate	0 1 2 3 4 5
Documentation of Internet sources adequate	0 1 2 3 4 5
Analysis of the information, judging what is most significant and filtering out superfluous data	0 1 2 3 4 5
End product attractive and interesting	0 1 2 3 4 5

TECHNOLOGY IN THE SCIENCE CLASSROOM

3

BARBARA M. MANNER, PHD

Introduction

> Technology, when properly used as an integral part of the curriculum and the instructional approach, can be a very effective tool for improving and enhancing instruction and learning experiences in the content area involving all students in complex, authentic tasks. (Kimmel, Deek, & Frazer, 2001)

In the information age, classroom emphasis is changing from teaching to student learning, as the role of the teacher transforms from instructor to facilitator. As the saying goes, the teacher is no longer "the sage on the stage" but is rather the "guide by the side."

The use of technology in teaching science has advanced more rapidly than perhaps any of the other disciplines. Both teacher and student use a variety of technologies well beyond the simple applications of word processing and multimedia. Motion sensors, computers, and air tracks are used for velocity and acceleration studies in the physics laboratory. Specialized microscopes and computer programs enhance observations of cells and genetic material in biology. Instrumentation, such as resistivity meters, is taken into the field for indirect geophysical measurements to identify subsurface rock units and locate sources of petroleum and water.

Historical Evolution of Science-Based Technologies

In the early 1960s, science technologies consisted primarily of filmstrips and movies with all their associated limitations and problems. As newer technologies were developed, experts warned that science teachers would become obsolete, and computers would replace instructors. Of course, that simply has not happened. More and more, as the previous quote proposes, technology is accepted as a tool to enhance instruction not to replace it. Even now, as distance education becomes more popular in the science classroom, many teachers and students believe that technology eliminates or severely limits the teacher–student and student–student interaction so integral to learning.

As science instruction moved into the 1990s, technology changed from filmstrips and movies to overheads, videos, World Wide Web, and computer simulations. With the introduction of the digital camera, students found themselves in the role of scientist, developing a keener set of science process skills. For example, active, inquiry-based oceanography exercises use the National Oceanic and Atmospheric Administration (NOAA) Internet site to investigate basic differences in salinity and temperature in various parts of the ocean during different seasons. This data is used at a more sophisticated level, with temperature and salinity variations and basic surface water circulation statistics to determine interactions between the ocean and the atmosphere and to trace the flow of energy and matter between these two systems (Martin & Howell, 2001). Recent research has also shown that differences in salinity are now seen as an important measurement of global climate and global warming (CCPO & NOAA, 1998).

Not only have science experiments and real-world simulations changed dramatically as a result of evolving technologies, but also, teachers and students now avail themselves of technologies hardly imagined a few years ago. In a typical science lab, teachers and students use digital cameras to capture their experiments and review their procedures in real time (Hargis & Stehr, 2001). Web sites offer safe, current, close-up views of Mt. St. Helens and other active and inert natural disasters (www.fs.fed.us/gpnf/mshnvm/volcanocam/). Classrooms connect across the world to share information for projects such as stream evaluation or clean up and tracking migration patterns of butterflies. Students explore worlds they would otherwise never see, and as a result, they appreciate science more. Web sites from NASA show up-to-date weather on other planets (www.deepspace.ucsb.edu/ia/nineplanets/nineplanets.html). Another site allows students and teachers to look at different cells without the expense of sophisticated microscopes on site (www.cellsalive.com/). More advanced technologies, such as panorama and object movies, allow the user to interact with images in a nonlinear fashion. Objects are panned 360° and rotated to be viewed from different perspectives (Rodriguez, 2001).

The Australian Alice Springs School of the Air (www.assoa.nt.edu.au/) illustrates an interesting example of the use of technology to teach science as well as other subjects. The school started in 1951 as a means of providing a community aspect to the education of the bush children lacking social contact. Communication was primarily by means of two-way radios, and lessons were delivered over the air. Today, Alice School provides educational service to 130 children covering 1.3 million square kilometers of the Australian Outback. Students access the World Wide Web, adding a new dimension to the possibilities of what can be taught and how the students at a distance access information.

Standards for Technology in Science

With the advent of National Science Education Standards (National Research Council, 1996) and adoption of state-level science standards, teachers require a much higher level of technology understanding. Relevant parts of the National Science Education Standards require the following:

- Teachers must possess skills necessary to guide inquiries based on students' questions.
- Teachers must be able to interpret data using appropriate technologies.
- Inquiry provides opportunities for teachers to use technology beyond the scope of immediate inquiries.
- Teachers use a variety of technology tools.

"Academic Standards for Science and Technology" (Pennsylvania Department of Education, 2002) include the following general standards related to these topics. Knowledge of content, process, and skills in technology involves learning processes that include these components:

- Methods of designing and developing solutions
- Standards for selecting and using appropriate materials, tools, and processes
- Experimental and design specifications for testing and evaluating solutions
- Criteria for judging the performance and impact of the solutions
- Evaluation of the impact of modifying a system to improve performance

Educational Software for the Science Classroom

Introduction

Using technology in the science classroom benefits teachers and students. Generally, teachers who use technology are more motivated, knowledge-able in scientific inquiry, and positive about teaching than those who do not. The use of technology enables students to collaborate on meaningful research projects with their classmates and students throughout the world. By working on research projects, students learn to use scientific tools and technologies appropriately (Colley, 2001).

Evaluation Classifications

Technology is adaptive and multisensory; its proper use accommodates these individual differences and maximizes student learning efficiency.

Levels of Difficulty and Multiple Intelligences

Students and their vastly different learning styles and multiple intelligences have major implications for instruction (Manner, 2001). Students become responsible for their own learning and, as a result, are more highly motivated with increased retention abilities. An example of software that includes various levels of difficulty and multisensory components is David Macaulay's "Pinball Science," distributed by Dorling Kindersley. This program helps students answer multilevel questions about various physics aspects of the pinball machine and build their own machine, piece by piece, with all the action and sounds of real pinball (Rodriguez, 2001).

Reinforcement of Principles and Concepts

Effective technology reinforces complex science concepts. It helps students having difficulty understanding concepts by providing opportunities for remediation. Technology enriches students who wish to explore a particular science principle in more detail but cannot due to limited class time that prevents additional instruction. For example, Edmark's "Thinkin' Science Series — ZAP!" allows students to apply the principles of science to create and test experiments with lasers, sound waves, and circuits.

Integration of Science with Other Content Areas

Finally, technology eases the integration of science with other subject areas. Social studies and science integration is possible with software incorporating various content areas. An example is "The Digital Field Trip to the Rainforest," distributed by TASA Graphic Arts, Inc. Students learn about the location of rainforests around the world (geography), the implications of loss of rainforests (social studies), and the types and adaptations of animals and plants in the rainforest (science). Multimedia technology provides a learning environment that fosters creativity and discovery through computer visualization, simulation, and modeling (Kimmel, Deek, & Frazer, 2001). "Digital Frog 2" software, as well, engages students in dissection with animations and interactions allowing students to see how the frog's body works—from blood pumping through the heart to joints moved by the user (Digital Frog International).

Rubric for Evaluating Science Software

Once a teacher has decided to use software to enhance instruction, the challenge is in choosing the appropriate software. A teacher should choose carefully so that student understanding and retention is maximized and a deep knowledge base is developed, leading to inquiry-based learning experiences. Learning should be sequential, progressing from basic to more complex. Not only should content be a goal of incorporating software, but process skills such as observation, prediction and hypothesizing, classifying, and drawing conclusions should also be developed.

A rubric for evaluating science software is included in Table 1. Ideally, a teacher would select software with ratings of 30 in all categories; however, the purpose of the lesson and student learning outcomes are the primary criteria upon which to choose software. For example, emphasizing content places more weight on that element of the rubric. On the other hand, an emphasis on skill acquisition shifts the final selection, making content less important. In general, teachers should avoid software that scores less than half of the available points, because they are based on meeting technology-based standards.

Table 1. Rubric for Evaluation of Software for the Science Classroom

Criteria	Little or No Evidence of Achievement 0	Meets Minimum Expectations 10	Nearly Achieved Expectations 20	Achieves Expectations 30
Content				
Instructional content is accurate and up-to-date				
Content and implementation are free from race, ethnic, or gender stereotyping				
Information is presented logically and clearly				
Reading level is appropriate				
Accommodates a wide range of abilities				
Content of the software fits the purpose of the instruction				
Teaching				
Increases understanding and skills				
It is appropriate for use by a variety of learners				
Facilitates higher-level thinking				
Technology-Related Support				
Graphics and sound enhance the program and stimulate interest				
Gives positive feedback				
Provides for review of content and skills				
Includes teacher support materials				
Is user friendly				
Layout of screen has a consistent format				
Student performance can be stored and easily retrieved				

Examples of Best Educational Software

Elementary School Science Software

Fifteen graduate preservice and inservice elementary teachers evaluated the software, "Sammy's Science House" (1994 version) by EdMark as part of a technology lesson in a Teaching Elementary School Science class. The software is labeled for ages three to six but was found to be appropriate for use with older children. A summary of their ratings and some anecdotal comments are provided in Table 2. Numbers reflect students awarding each level ($n = 15$). Not all criteria were evaluated (N/E = Not Evaluated).

Table 2. Evaluation of Elementary Level Software for the Science Classroom

Criteria	Little or No Evidence of Achievement 0	Meets Minimum Expectations 10	Nearly Achieved Expectations 20	Achieves Expectations 30
Content				
Instructional content is accurate and up-to-date	0	0	1	14
Content and implementation are free from race, ethnic, or gender stereotyping	1	0	1	13
Information is presented logically and clearly	0	0	4	11
Reading level is appropriate	1	0	2	12
Accommodates a wide range of abilities	N/E	N/E	N/E	N/E
Content of the software fits the purpose of the instruction	N/E	N/E	N/E	N/E
Teaching				
Increases understanding and skills	0	0	0	15
Is appropriate for use by a variety of learners	0	0	4	11
Facilitates higher-level thinking	0	1	5	9
Technology-Related Support				
Graphics and sound enhance the program and stimulate interest	0	0	0	15
Gives positive feedback	1	0	0	14
Provides for review of content and skills	0	0	3	12
Includes teacher support materials	0	13	1	1
Is user friendly	0	0	3	12
Layout of screen has a consistent format	N/E	N/E	N/E	N/E
Student performance can be stored and easily retrieved	N/E	N/E	N/E	N/E

Anecdotal comments for Sammy's Science House:

> "...Can be used with children older than 6 — up to the third grade."

> "...Provides opportunities to increase difficulty levels."

> "...Stimulates interest and attention."

> "...Can also be used for special needs children."

> "...Deals with a variety of appropriate content but not to any depth."

> "...Allows for development of classification skills."

> "...Helps students to comprehend in a self-paced environment."

Secondary School Science Software

Twelve graduate and undergraduate preservice and inservice secondary science teachers evaluated "The Theory of Plate Tectonics" (version 1.3, produced by TASA Graphic Arts, Inc.) as part of a technology lesson in a Teaching Secondary School Science class. The following is a summary of their ratings and some anecdotal comments. Numbers in the rubric reflect the number of students giving the software that rating level ($n = 12$). Again, not all criteria were evaluated (N/E = Not Evaluated).

Anecdotal comments for The Theory of Plate Tectonics:

> "...Has both college and high school levels, and a Spanish version."

> "...Stimulates interest and attention."

> "...Test questions for both levels are included."

> "...Can be used by both the teacher or by students in a self-paced environment."

Table 3. Evaluation of Secondary Level Software for the Science Classroom

Criteria	Little or No Evidence of Achievement 0	Meets Minimum Expectations 10	Nearly Achieved Expectations 20	Achieves Expectations 30
Content				
Instructional content is accurate and up-to-date	0	0	0	12
Content and implementation are free from race, ethnic, or gender stereotyping	N/E	N/E	N/E	N/E
Information is presented logically and clearly	0	0	0	12
Reading level is appropriate	0	0	0	12
Accommodates a wide range of abilities	N/E	N/E	N/E	N/E
Content of the software fits the purpose of the instruction	N/E	N/E	N/E	N/E
Teaching				
Increases understanding and skills	0	0	0	12
It is appropriate for use by a variety of learners	0	0	2	10
Facilitates higher-level thinking	0	0	3	9
Technology-Related Support				
Graphics and sound enhance the program and stimulate interest	0	0	0	12
Gives positive feedback	0	0	0	12
Provides for review of content and skills	0	0	0	12
Includes teacher support materials	0	5	7	0
Is user friendly	0	0	0	12
Layout of screen has a consistent format	N/E	N/E	N/E	N/E
Student performance can be stored and easily retrieved	N/E	N/E	N/E	N/E

Internet Use in the Science Classroom

Introduction

The number of science sites has continued to grow exponentially until it seems as though there are more Web pages than could ever be used. On the positive side, however, there are many truly exceptional sites applicable to the science classroom.

Evaluation Classifications

For teachers who wish to integrate the Internet into a science lesson, there are basically three different degrees to consider. First and simplest is to use data taken directly from an Internet site relative to a particular topic. For example, for lessons on earthquakes, students use the Internet to track the occurrence of quakes and add global locations to a classroom map. Second, a more involved use of the Internet occurs when developing activities that correlate with specific Web sites, enhancing direct instruction in the classroom with activities that remediate and enrich the topic. Students are encouraged to develop online research skills and personalize their individual learning strategies. Third, at the highest degree, the study of a particular topic becomes almost exclusively Web based. Students develop their own questions and, with facilitation by the teacher, access preselected Web sites, using their developing online research skills to meet the lesson objectives (Kelly, 2001).

A teacher must follow additional guidelines to make the incorporation of the Internet educationally sound. First, determine the lesson goals and student learning outcomes before considering the Internet. (Note: This is the same sound principle that applies to all lessons.) Second, choose the curricular area to be reinforced by use of the Internet (the only defensible use of the Web). Focusing on lesson objectives encourages all subsequent decisions from that perspective (Kelly, 2001). Third, divide the curriculum into manageable portions and set schedules. Allow time for using computers or the computer lab. Technology almost inevitably takes more time to implement than scheduled by the teacher. Fourth, decide on the learning activities for each part of the curriculum. Determine which learning activities the Internet best supports. Such activities are obtained directly from reputable Web sites or are teacher-made from information harvested from various sites.

Searching for Appropriate Science Sites

Many Web sites have lesson plans (Figure 1, Site 1) for all areas and grade levels of science. In addition, there are good databases, such as that of the National Oceanic and Atmospheric Administration (NOAA) (Figure 1, Site 2), which contains actual weather and climate data suitable for students. These resources also promote inquiry exercises that mimic real-world job responsibilities and encourage thinking processes used by everyday scientists. Students learn to think like scientists rather than simply learn course content. There are also sites that offer Web-based science lessons (Figure 1, Site 3) that incorporate Web-based competencies into the lesson, simultaneously expanding the technology skills of students.

At elementary and secondary levels, Web sites support the integration of science with other curricular areas. For teachers wishing to integrate science, colonial history, and a unit about presidents, there is the combined project conducted by the National Park Service-George Washington Birthplace National Monument and Richmond County Public Schools (Figure 1, Site 4). Optical Research Associates of California created an excellent site for teachers who want to reinforce learning objectives on the nature of light, written especially for children (Figure 1, Site 5). At the

Figure 1. Appropriate Science Curriculum Internet Sites

Site Sponsor	URL
Schoolhouse, the Encarta Lesson Collection	encarta.msn.com/schoolhouse/lessons/
National Oceanic and Atmospheric Administration (NOAA)	www.noaa.gov/
Connecting Students	connectingstudents.com/
George Washington Birthplace National Monument	www.nps.gov/gewa/edweb.htm
Optical Research Associates of California	www.opticalres.com/kidoptx.html
The Great Kapok Tree	www.sdcoe.k12.ca.us/SCORE/kapok/kapoktg.htm
Stellaluna	projects.edtech.sandi.net/chavez/batquest/batquest.html
Get Outside!	sfgate.com/cgi-bin/article.cgi?file=/getoutside/archive/1996/06/01/whytide.DTL
University of Wisconsin	ssec.wisc.edu/data/sst/latest_sst.gif

elementary level, children's literature books or science-based books are reinforced by information from Web sites. For example, if children are learning about the rainforest, *The Great Kapok Tree*, by Lynn Cherry (Figure 1, Site 6) provides excellent basic instruction and plenty of enrichment information and activities related to the topic. Finally, a Web site related to bats and the book *Stellaluna* (Figure 1, Site 7) encourages students to learn even more about bats, play bat games, design bat art, and then make a bat expert.

In some cases, use of a Web site has the sole purpose of illustrating an event or concept, fostering understanding in ways simply not possible without technology. For example, the relationship between the moon, earth, sun, and the tides is difficult to convey in the static environments of overhead transparencies or drawings on the blackboard. The use of an animated Web site demonstrates the gravitational action of the sun and moon on the Earth's oceans and brings this dynamic process to life for the student in the classroom (Figure 1, Site 8). Topics of climates, ocean characteristics, or El Niño/La Niña rely on maps and animated simulations provided by the Web site (Figure 1, Site 9) to illustrate the latest sea surface temperatures. Using this site periodically allows students to track changes in these temperatures and relate anomalies in climates.

Rubrics for Evaluating Science Web Sites

Choosing a science curriculum Web site that matches learning objectives with student developmental and reading levels is essential. A teacher never wants to go online just to fill in the "use of technology" block of a lesson plan. The only key to successful integration is the *meaningful* use of Internet resources. Table 4 provides a rubric to evaluate possible science-specific Web sites.

Table 4. Rubric for Evaluation of Web Sites for the Classroom

Criteria	Little or No Evidence of Achievement 0	Meets Minimum Expectations 10	Nearly Achieved Expectations 20	Achieves Expectations 30
Content				
Content is appropriate for the planned lesson				
Content is appropriate for the ability level of the students				
Sponsor or author of the site is reputable and responsible				
Information is accurate, up-to-date, and reliable				
Information is presented logically and clearly				
Information is at a developmentally appropriate grade and reading level and is comprehensive				
Teaching				
Increases understanding and skills				
Content promotes inquiry learning, and critical thinking skills are needed to analyze and synthesize information				
Content encourages students to think and reflect				
Appropriate references and copyright statements are included				
There is a real task to do				
Technology-Related Support				
There is consistent appearance within the Web site				
There is linking within and outside of the Web site; capable of moving around the Web site easily				
Visually appealing design and style of the site enhance information delivery				
Web site designed to be viewed by a variety of graphics browsers (Netscape Navigator and Microsoft Internet Explorer at a minimum)				
Waiting for Web pages to load large graphics not distracting to students				
Site usually accessible (not difficult to connect during peak class hours)				

Examples of Best Web Sites for Teaching Science

A listing of the more popular Web sites for the Science classroom is provided at Appendix A to this chapter. The sites are classified as General, Primarily for Students, Primarily for Teachers, For Adults and Children, and Research Issues. For purposes of example, two science sites were assessed using the proposed rubric. Somewhat differently than the reviews of educational software, the Web sites were evaluated and scores averaged before being assigned specific assessment points.

Elementary School Science Web Sites

Fifteen graduate preservice and inservice elementary teachers evaluated selected Web sites. The following is a summary of the student ratings and some anecdotal comments for the United States Environmental Protection Agency Web site (www.epa.gov/kids/). The site contains links to games, pictures, and activities related to issues involving water, air, garbage and recycling, plants and animals, and the environment in general. Recall that the scores given for each criterion represent an average of all scores received from the evaluating teachers.

Anecdotal comments for the United States Environmental Protection Agency Web site:

> "...Some aspects of the site are more appropriate for secondary students."

> "...Good site though 'wordy'."

> "...Coloring and other activities geared towards lower elementary grades, most of the reading is more appropriate for grades 5–7."

> "...Covers a broad level."

> "...Some material suitable for 5 year old and others much too difficult."

Table 5. Evaluation of Elementary Web Sites for the Classroom

Criteria	Little or No Evidence of Achievement 0	Meets Minimum Expectations 10	Nearly Achieved Expectations 20	Achieves Expectations 30
Content				
Content is appropriate for the planned lesson				X
Content is appropriate for the ability level of the students			X	
Sponsor or author of the site is reputable and responsible				X
Information is accurate, up-to-date, and reliable				X
Information is presented logically and clearly				X
Information is at a developmentally appropriate grade and reading level and is comprehensive			X	
Teaching				
Increases understanding and skills				X
Content promotes inquiry learning, and critical thinking skills are needed to analyze and synthesize information			X	
Content encourages students to think and reflect			X	
Appropriate references and copyright statements are included		X		
There is a real task to do				X
Technology-Related Support				
There is a consistent appearance within the Web site				X
There is linking within and outside of the Web site; capable of moving around the Web site easily		X		
Visually appealing design and style of the site enhance information delivery				X
Web site is designed to be viewed by a variety of graphics browsers (Netscape Navigator and Microsoft Internet Explorer at a minimum)				X
Waiting for Web pages to load large graphics not distracting to students			X	
Site usually accessible (not difficult to connect during peak class hours)			X	

Secondary School Science Web Sites

Twelve graduate and undergraduate preservice and inservice secondary science teachers evaluated GeoCities "Rain Forests of Indonesia" (www.geocities.com/RainForest/3678/gerbang.html) as part of a technology lesson in a Teaching Secondary School Science class. The following is a summary of their ratings and some anecdotal comments. Remember, scores given for each criterion represent an average of all scores received from the evaluating teachers.

Anecdotal comments for the GeoCities "Rain Forests of Indonesia" Web site:

> "...Is not user-friendly."
>
> "...Is told as a simulation; I like that. (paraphrased)"
>
> "...Could be overwhelming if not focused for a student."
>
> "...Is an information site only, teacher would have to make adaptations."
>
> "...Is not reliable because it is a home page."
>
> "...Has not been updated for over 5 years!"

Table 6. Evaluation of Secondary Level Web Site for the Science Classroom

Criteria	Little or No Evidence of Achievement 0	Meets Minimum Expectations 10	Nearly Achieved Expectations 20	Achieves Expectations 30
Content				
Content is appropriate for the planned lesson			X	
Content is appropriate for the ability level of the students			X	
Sponsor or author of the site is reputable and responsible	N/E	N/E	N/E	N/E
Information is accurate, up-to-date, and reliable	X			
Information is presented logically and clearly			X	
Information is at a developmentally appropriate grade and reading level and is comprehensive		X		
Teaching				
Increases understanding and skills			X	
Promotes inquiry learning, and critical thinking skills are needed to analyze and synthesize information				
Content encourages students to think and reflect		X		
Appropriate references and copyright statements are included		X		
There is a real task to do	X			
Technology-Related Support				
There is a consistent appearance within the Web site				X
There are links within and outside of the Web site; capable of moving around the Web site easily		X		
Visually appealing design and style of the site enhance information delivery			X	
Web site is designed to be viewed by a variety of graphics browsers (Netscape Navigator and Microsoft Internet Explorer at a minimum)			X	
Waiting for Web pages to load large graphics is not distracting to students			X	
Site is usually accessible (not difficult to connect during peak class hours)			X	

Other Technology Considerations in the Science Curriculum

Introduction

Occasionally, classroom teachers may have a curriculum topic for which there is no suitable educational software or Web site available. Or, the software and Web sites that are available do not sufficiently illustrate a particular concept. Rather than disregarding technology altogether, there is an option: develop teacher-made instructional materials using Microsoft *Word* and *Power Point*, Netscape *Composer*, or even more advanced packages such as Macromedia's *Authorware*, *Dreamweaver*, or *Fireworks*. A few personal examples demonstrate the potential of teacher-made materials.

Mineral Bonding

One of the challenges of teaching mineral formations and the effects on rocks, erosion, weathering, mass movements, and earthquake damage is to show and explain how elements bond to form minerals. Transparencies are not effective, and students who do not deal well with abstract ideas find lectures unproductive. A *Power Point* presentation illustrates all of the above concepts through a series of slides that simulate animation. Students see the "movement" of electrons and the bonding of atoms of different elements to form particular examples of minerals. Digital photos of actual mineral samples as well as scanned illustrations from books were incorporated into the presentation. A review section was added at the end of the presentation that addressed all of the science concepts and theories required by the course.

Ocean Currents

To meet objectives for an Earth Science class, the instructor harvested various resources from the Internet to develop a short *Power Point* presentation on the topic of ocean currents. The topic was introduced by a segment of Thor Heyerdahl's book, *Kon Tiki*, that described floating on ocean currents. A map of the Gulf Stream developed by Benjamin Franklin from reports by sailors and supplemented by a modern-day satellite imagery map traced the ocean currents. Both were remarkably similar, even though

Franklin's map was obviously many years older. Animation or movies of the prevailing winds, cold and warm ocean currents, the Coriolis Effect, and upwellings allowed students to better visualize and understand these phenomena. An Internet site related a news story about the loss of a shipment of Nike athletic shoes; a journey of floating shoes that visually tracked current movements in the North Pacific. Last, a section of review questions allowed students to focus on what they had learned, while assisting students who needed remediation and presenting the information individually to those who had not been in class.

Earthquakes

The challenges of this project, which went way beyond the previous two, involved an effective way of presenting a variety of information relating to earthquakes in a single program. The topics addressed were initiation, travel, and effect of the various seismic waves; deformation of land; wave tracking by seismographic stations; and determination of the epicenter of an earthquake. To illustrate each of these concepts, an original animation of seismic waves and the resulting land deformation were rendered using *Authorware*. Superimposed over actual seismograph readings showing travel time and receiving of seismic waves was a video of the Loma Prieta earthquake during the 1989 World Series game. A step-by-step illustration of the triangulation system using the Alaska earthquake of 1964 illustrating the determination of the epicenter was also added to the animation. Finally, unlike the previous two projects, this stand-alone presentation included instructor voice-overs describing each segment of the video. Students use this presentation without the lecture to receive basic information, revisit material for remedial learning, and enhance their understanding of the many concepts presented in the lesson.

Conclusions

Anytime technology is incorporated into the classroom, there are challenges. Choosing the right software, locating the best Web sites, and
preparing instructional materials are just some of these considerations.
Regardless, each of these challenges boils down to a single critical element
— time.

The rubrics offered in this chapter will help evaluate potential software and
possible Web sites. But, with the abundance of software on the market and
the infinite number of Web sites, it will be difficult to narrow the field. Talk
to other teachers about particular software packages they have used. Seek
reviews from professional journals and organizational newsletters. For
example, the National Science Teachers Association (NSTA) journals include
Science and Children, *Science Scope*, and *Science Teacher*, and their
newspaper, *NSTA Reports*. Each publication reviews at least one or two
science-oriented software packages. Also, Web sites, such as www.uwm.edu/
~kahl/CoVis/Software, offer reviews of middle school and secondary school
science software.

Most educators are willing to try new technologies, especially when they
see that they can advance student learning. Success, however, also depends
on accessibility to equipment, opportunities for technical training, and
reliable technical assistance. Without support, busy teachers may not
expend the effort necessary to incorporate technology into their science
classes. Finally, when introducing technology to the classroom teacher,
begin with simple technologies first; foster a sense of success. Progress to
the more complex technologies only after support, reliability, and individual teacher confidence have been established.

References

Center for Coastal Physical Oceanography and National Data Buoy
    Center (NOAA). (1998). Salinity measurements in the coastal
    ocean. Workshop at Old Dominion University, September
    1998.

Colley, K. (2001). Technology-based learning. *The Science Teacher*,
    68, 6, 49–52.

Hargis, J. & Stehr, J. (2001). Chemistry on Camera. *The Science Teacher, 68,* 4, 24–27.

Kelly, D. (2001). Creating Web Units. *Instructor,* November/December, 56–59.

Kimmel, H., Deek, F., & Frazer, L. Technology and hands-on strategies for teaching science and mathematics. Retrieved from the World Wide Web: www.rit.edu/~easi/easisem/handson.html.

Manner, B. M. (2001). Learning styles and multiple intelligences in students. *Journal of College Science Teaching, XXX,* 6, 390–393.

Martin, E. E. & Howell, P. D. (2001). Active inquiry, web-based oceanography exercises. *Journal of Geoscience Education, 49,* 2, 158–165.

National Research Council. (1996). *National Science Education Standards,* National Academy Press, Washington, D.C.

Pennsylvania Department of Education. (2002). Academic Standards for Science and Technology. 22 Pa. Code, chap. 4, Appendix B.

Rodriguez, A. (2001). The virtual reality skeleton project. *T.H.E. Journal, 29,* 1, 64–71.

Appendix A
Web Sites for Teaching Science

URL	Description
www.firstscience.com	Sections include articles, poems, quizzes, games, fact file, links, and science cams
www.sciencepage.org	Links page — includes links to lesson plans, content areas, organizations, and more
www.cln.org/subjects/science.htm./	Community Learning Network — curricular and instructional resources and theme pages
Primarily for Students	
web.mit.edu/invent/	Inventors of present and past
kids.earth.nasa.gov	Information on air, natural hazards, land, water, and careers; educational games
yahooligans.com	Pathways through this for good science information for elementary age children
www.chem4kids.com/	Chemistry at the elementary level
www.omsi.edu/online/whatzit/home.html	Answers to science questions
www.epa.gov/kids/	EPA's kid page
kidscience.about.com/kidsteens/kidscience	Links to science sites for children
www.yucky.kids.discovery.com/	Worms and other "yucky" stuff
www.kaytee.com/discovery/	Information about birds; endangered and extinct species
Primarily for Teachers	
nsta.org	National Science Teachers Association
nagt.org	National Association of Geoscience Teachers
acs.org	American Chemical Society
aapt.org	American Physics Teachers
nabt.org	American Association of Biology Teachers
sohowww.nascom.nasa.gov/	Solar and Heliospheric Observatory — lesson plans, materials, programs (TV- and Internet-related), Ask Questions, links, and glossary (for Middle School and higher)
instruct1.cit.cornell.edu/courses/taresources/	Resources for Scientists Teaching Science (for Secondary, College)
www.tetra-fish.com	Aquarium lesson plans
www.teacherpathfinder.org	Educational links, including science
www.exploratorium.edu	Online Exploratorium
www.MonarchWatch.org/	Monarch butterfly: anatomy, migration, etc.
kidscience.miningco.com/	General science-related articles, experiments, etc.
littleshop.physics.colostate.edu	Little Shop of Physics
www.colorado.edu/physics/2000/	Physics site with good information
www.fi.edu/tfi/units/life/	General biology site with links
www.sciencedaily.com	Current science information
encarta.msn.com/schoolhouse/lessons/	Lessons with Web links
score.kings.k12.ca.us	Internet-infused lessons
geology.er.usgs.gov/eastern/environment/environ.html	Free materials; questions about the environment

www-sci.lib.uci.edu/SEP/SEP.html	Links to Web resources for classroom use
www.csun.edu/~vceed009/science.html	Science lessons galore
faldo.atmos.uiuc.edu/WEATHER/weather.html	Lessons on weather for Grades 2 through 4
www.physics.umn.edu/groups/demo/	Physics teaching strategies
www.physlink.com	Physics resources
For Teachers and Children	
www.astr.ua.edu/4000WS/4000WS.html	Women in science
home.olemiss.edu~dnschill/science_careers/	Science careers
www.nceet.snre.umich.edu/EndSpp/Endangered.html	Endangered species Web site
school.discovery.com/teachers/	Discovery Channel Web site
nesen.unl.edu/teacher/lesacttoc.html	Activities for parents to do with child, also has other Web links
www.aces.uiuc.edu/uplink/gpe/	Learning about plants through mystery games
www.lessonplanspage.com/popcode.html	Lesson plans plus magazine suggestions for teachers, students, and parents; academic tips; and links
Research Issues	
www.nap.edu/issues	Issues in science and technology — online journal
www.popsci.com	Popular Science articles
www.narst.org	National Association for Research in Science Teaching
Add Your Own URLs	**Personal Science Web Sites**

Technology In The Mathematics Classroom

4

Robin J. Ittigson, EdD and John G. Zewe, MSEd

Introduction

According to the National Council of Teachers of Mathematics, technology is essential in teaching and learning mathematics. It influences how mathematics should be taught and enhances what students learn. Calculators and computers present visual images of mathematical ideas for students. They help students organize information, support investigations, and develop decision-making, reflection, reasoning, and problem-solving skills.

Technology enhances the teaching of mathematics by presenting concepts in exciting new ways. Children learn the concept of place value by reading their textbook, then translating the words and numbers to a calculator or math software. They use technology to gain basic skills or to practice instant recall of facts and figures. For higher-level thinking, calculators and computers enable students to explore patterns and relations of very large numbers and offer explanations about why certain sequences occur. To promote problem-solving abilities, technology presents complex scenarios of how numbers are used in real life; scenarios that mathematics students have sought for years. Enabling students to perform routine computations quickly and efficiently, technology allows students to focus on the language, meaning, and applications of their answers. Students gain ownership with abstract mathematics and are enriched by the range, quality, and realism of the investigations presented.

Technology in mathematics classes enhances teaching for understanding. Students can examine more examples using technology than was ever possible by hand. The power of the graphics calculator addresses the visual learner, while manipulatives connect the symbols and pictorial representations for the more tactile student. Geometry software allows students to experiment with properties of shapes and draw conclusions about relationships when measurements are adjusted. Computational capacity extends the range of problems presented to students and provides choices to teachers when presenting abstract mathematical concepts.

The boundaries of mathematical landscape are suddenly transformed. With technology, teachers connect student skills to basic development of mathematical understanding, enabling elementary students to organize and analyze large sets of numbers. Middle school students in grades 5 through 8 study linear relationships, experimenting with variables and large amounts of data represented by scatter plots. High school students use simulations to visualize complex computer algebra systems. Random generators enhance probability experiments that approach realistic situations. Sample sizes become huge, and students suggest more realistic predictions about real-life situations using technology-based tools such as spreadsheets.

With the use of technology, adaptations are now possible for differentiated classrooms, allowing individual instructional needs to be met. Programs individualize specific content area, and their personalized reports give feedback to teachers who modify their presentations accordingly. Students who are visual, pictorial, and tactile are stimulated by learning in modes that better afford them the greatest success.

Historical Evolution of Technology in the Mathematics Classroom

With the range of essential technological devices available today, mathematics education takes on a whole new perspective. Students are exploring very large numbers at a relatively young age. Using technology, students encounter real-world simulations not limited to paper and pencil computations, pointless numbers, or meaningless emphasis on getting the "right" answer. Using technology correctly requires time; familiarizing students with media may be comfortable initially. The results are quite gratifying, seeing how much additional motivation students have to explore mathematical concepts. With more students achieving greater success and satisfaction, teachers are realizing how integral technology has become in their classroom.

Primary grade students who are beginning to count use the automatic constant feature on four-function calculators to show numbers increasing in given intervals. At the intermediate level, students make use of all four operations (addition, subtraction, multiplication, and division) to understand why the order is important when deriving a certain answer. They explore the meaning of the remainder when looking at decimal notation and the importance of zero when exploring problems related to place value and money. Upper elementary and middle school calculators have fraction keys to add and subtract as well as simplify fractions. The goal in instruction becomes comparing sizes and relationships among fractions rather than spending numerous lessons finding least common denominators.

Graphing calculators in middle schools provide instruction in data entry, charts, construction of coordinates for graphs, and exploration of ideas of variable numbers. Instructional time is spent gaining insights into relationships between equations, integers, and graphs. On the middle and high school levels, statistical functions allow students to identify landmarks of realistic data (mode, mean, range, standard deviation) stored and altered as the need arises. Histograms, box and whisker graphs, and stem and leaf charts allow students to look at trends and predict the future. Scatter plots of ordered pairs encourage students to experiment with linear equations and best-fit lines. In addition, calculators are now programmable; students can write their own programs to find answers to quadratic formulas and to formulate strategies for playing an opponent in a chess tournament.

Numerous other technologies exist for all grade levels. All it takes is a little research to find them and enjoy. Problem solving, strategic thinking, logical reasoning, and number sense develop with technologies used to supplement content material. Keep in mind that consistency is the key. In order to get the highest learning outcomes possible, technologies should be integrated into the curriculum on a regular basis.

The debate over whether or not to use technology in the classroom has been around since the introduction of the calculator, perhaps before then. The first debate concerns the use of the calculator in the class; a second debate involves when to use the calculator. Some researchers insist that calculators not be used until the later grades. Others are adamant that calculator use should be established as soon as possible. This debate will undoubtedly continue.

Knowing when and how, not if, to use the calculator should be debated. The calculator, like all other forms of technology, is not appropriate for all instruction. Rather, technology should be viewed as another effective tool in the suite of teaching strategies, and school administrators must provide their staff with effective and appropriate training on the use of any new technology.

Standards for Technology in Mathematics

The NCTM (National Council of Teachers of Mathematics) has taken a strong stand on the use of technology in the classroom. The NCTM recommends that all students use technology to concentrate on the problem-solving process rather than on the calculations associated with problems; gain access to mathematics beyond students' level of computational skills; explore, develop, and reinforce concepts including estimation, computation, approximation, and properties; experiment with mathematical ideas and discover patterns; and work with real data in problem-solving situations. The NCTM further recommends that publishers, authors, and test writers integrate the use of the calculator into their mathematics materials at all grade levels. (The above information was taken from a brochure prepared by Charleen M. DeRidder, Knox County Schools, and Joseph R. Caravella, NCTM.)

In 1996, the NCTM established its *Principles and Standards for School Mathematics*, a resource guide for mathematics education of students in pre-kindergarten through Grade 12. Its recommendations are grounded in the belief that all students should learn important mathematical concepts and processes with understanding. *Principles and Standards* has been revised several times since its earliest publication. The current version makes an argument for the importance of technologies and describes ways for integrating these goals. Table 1 provides the standards for instructional programs and offers selected Web-based examples of technologies integrated into a mathematics curriculum. [Note: Suggested technologies taken from Table 1 ("Guide to Common Classroom Technologies," Chapter 1) have been added for additional understanding of the various technologies pertinent to a mathematics classroom.]

As stated in the NCTM *Professional Standards for Teaching Mathematics: Executive Summary*, "Today's students will be citizens of the twenty-first century, a century that promises to be dramatically different from the one we have known. The effects of technological innovation will continue to permeate every aspect of life...computational skills alone do not suffice...by the turn of the century, the need to understand mathematics in order to succeed in all walks of life will be without precedent."

Table 1. Standards for School Mathematics

Instructional Programs from Pre-Kindergarten Through Grade 12 Should Enable all Students to:	Examples of Suggested Technology Applications (http://standards.nctm.org/document/eexamples/index.htm)	Specific Technologies
Number and Operations • Understand numbers, ways of representing numbers, relationships among numbers, and number systems • Understand meanings of operations and how they relate to one another, compute fluently and make reasonable estimates	4.5 Learning about Number Relationships and Properties of Numbers Using Calculators and Hundred Boards. Virtual 100 boards and calculators furnish a visual way of highlighting and displaying various patterns and relationships among numbers.	• Calculators • Hundred boards • Computers
Algebra • Understand patterns, relations, and functions; represent and analyze mathematical situations and structures using algebraic symbols • Use mathematical models to represent and understand quantitative relationships • Analyze change in various contexts	5.2 Understanding Distance, Speed, and Time Relationships Using Simulation Software. Software simulation of two runners along a track. Students control the speeds and starting points of the runners and examine a graph of the time-versus-distance relationship.	• Simulation software • Graphic presentation
Geometry • Analyze characteristics and properties of two- and three-dimensional geometric shapes and develop mathematical arguments about geometric relationships • Specify locations and describe spatial relationships using coordinate geometry and other representational systems • Apply transformations, and use symmetry to analyze mathematical situations • Use visualization, spatial reasoning, and geometric modeling to solve problems	4.3 Learning Geometry and Measurement Concepts by Creating Paths and Navigating Mazes. The three-part example presents a rich computer environment in which students can use their knowledge of number, measurement, and geometry to solve interesting problems. 4.4 Developing Geometry Understandings and Spatial Skills through Puzzle-like Problems with Tangrams. Describing figures and visualizing what they look like when they are transformed through rotations or flips or are put together or taken apart in different ways are important aspects of geometry in the lower grades. This two-part example demonstrates the potential for high-quality experiences provided by computer "shape" environments for students. 5.3 Exploring Properties of Rectangles and Parallelograms Using Dynamic Software. Geometry software provides an environment in which students can explore geometric relationships and make and test conjectures.	• Computers • Spreadsheets • Problem-solving instructional media • Games instructional media • Graphic presentation

Note. From *Principles and Standards for School Mathematics*, National Council of Teachers of Mathematics (NCTM), 2000, Reston, VA, http://www.nctm.org.

Table 1. Standards for School Mathematics (continued)

Measurement • Understand measurable attributes of objects and the units, systems, and processes of measurement • Apply appropriate techniques, tools, and formulas to determine measurements	7.4 Understanding the Least Squares Regression Line with a Visual Model. This example allows students to explore three methods for measuring how well a linear model fits a set of data points.	• Spreadsheet • Graphing calculators
Data Analysis • Formulate questions that can be addressed with data, and collect, organize, and display relevant data to answer them • Select and use appropriate statistical methods to analyze data • Develop and evaluate inferences and predictions based on data • Understand and apply basic concepts of probability	6.6 Comparing Properties of the Mean and the Median through the use of Technology. Experimenting with this software helps students compare the utility of the mean and the median as measures of center for different data sets.	• Simulation instructional media • Video
Problem Solving • Build new mathematical knowledge through problem solving • Solve problems that arise in mathematics and in other contexts • Apply and adapt a variety of appropriate strategies to solve problems • Monitor and reflect on the process of mathematical problem solving	7.5 Exploring Linear Functions: Representational Relationships. Technology allows the linking of multiple representations of mathematical situations and the exploration of the relationships that emerge.	• Drill and practice instructional media
Reasoning • Recognize reasoning and proof as fundamental aspects of mathematics • Make and investigate mathematical conjectures • Develop and evaluate mathematical arguments and proofs • Select and use various types of reasoning and methods of proof		
Communications • Organize and consolidate their mathematical thinking through communication • Communicate their mathematical thinking coherently and clearly to peers, teachers, and others • Analyze and evaluate the mathematical thinking and strategies of others • Use the language of mathematics to express mathematical ideas precisely	5.1 Communicating about Mathematics Using Games. Video clips illustrate communication about mathematics among teachers and their students. Games show students how to use communications as a tool to deepen their understanding of mathematics.	• Electronic mail • World Wide Web • List servers
Connections • Recognize and use connections among mathematical ideas • Understand how mathematical ideas interconnect and build on one another to produce a coherent whole • Recognize and apply mathematics in contexts outside of mathematics	7.1 Learning about Properties of Vectors and Vector Sums Using Dynamic Software. Students manipulate a velocity vector to control the movement of an object in a game-like setting.	• Games instructional media
Representation • Create and use representations to organize, record, and communicate mathematical ideas • Select, apply, and translate among mathematical representations to solve problems • Use representations to model and interpret physical, social, and mathematical phenomena	5.5 Collecting, Representing, and Interpreting Data Using Spreadsheets and Graphing Software. Spreadsheets and graphing software are tools for organizing, representing, and comparing data.	• Spreadsheets • Graphing software • Simulation instructional media

Note. From *Principles and Standards for School Mathematics,* National Council of Teachers of Mathematics (NCTM), 2000, Reston, VA, http://www.nctm.org.

Educational Software for the Mathematics Classroom

Introduction

Technology empowers learners with tools to enhance their learning styles and make concepts understandable and interesting. There are a plethora of products involving educational software formats such as mathematical manipulatives; data collection and graphing tools, including spreadsheets; and problem-solving, simulation, games, and drill and practice instructional programs. The classroom teacher remains the critical factor in making important decisions regarding on-task time and desired learning outcomes.

Evaluation Classifications

Manipulatives provide materials for learning basic mathematics concepts and problem-solving skills. These materials include geoboards, pattern blocks, counters, base-10 blocks, and Unifix cubes. The learner abandons the tactile experience of a real model for images on a screen, linked to symbolic representations (numbers and equations) so that mental relationships, comparisons, and contrasts are developed. The ability to adjust size and shape of the computer model, thus adapting the model to a specific problem, is accomplished with relative ease. The teacher continues to weigh the advantages of computer screen manipulations with real-world, tactile reinforcements.

Data collection and graphing software enables students to gather, organize, and analyze data by graphic representations. Students analyze the problem and find correct scales, maximum and minimum numbers, and other statistical parameters. As students construct their own graphs, teachers exchange the time saved using technology with the increased thinking and learning time, as students increase their understanding of the importance in choosing the correct manner and size of the graph, the proper scale, and the appropriate titles and labels for accurate presentations.

Spreadsheets analyze and present data in graphic form. Students manipulate numbers in rows and columns and input simple formulas, derive averages, and compute ranges and averages. Students change the cells and parameters of data and analyze the "what if" aspects of how such changes affect their lists. They analyze data and investigate patterns in numbers and view the graphical shapes of the data using bar, line, and circle diagrams.

Instructional programs include mathematics software that enables students to explore shapes and shape properties. It can help students create new shapes and then manipulate and measure them by dragging points or lines with a computer mouse. Software options construct lines with varying properties and maintain these properties while superimposing new shapes. Students experiment with constructions, compare and contrast relationships, and make hypotheses about endless variations or original constructions by dragging different shapes and making rotations, flips, turns, and slides. Most software programs produce measurements, instantly revising the attributes, geometric constructions, and functions as the relationships between them change.

Instructional software consists of drill and practice, problem solving, and simulations that build conceptual understanding. Most software enables the classroom teacher to individualize the type of instruction, presentation, method of feedback, and correction given to the student as well as the time allotted for each task and method of assessment. They motivate student learning with inviting graphics, enhanced sounds, real-life problems, and game situations, where students earn points while moving toward lesson goals.

Rubric for Evaluating Mathematics Software

Evaluating mathematical software involves consideration of technology specification, content desirability, management concerns, and correct mathematics applications. Computer operating systems, memory, and hard disk requirements; availability of hard-copy and online documentation or phone assistance; and licensing, upgrade, and installation costs must be considered.

The software content must be examined with particular attention to appropriate grade and age levels; accuracy of the content information; and suitability for remediation, direct instruction, guided practice, independent practice, or enrichment. Clear directions, teacher support materials (worksheets, teacher's manual, user's manual, lesson plans, projects, links), and visual appeal of the screen images are also important.

The better mathematics software packages usually offer computerized lesson management, individual student tracking, and statistical cohort analysis. Also included are pretests and posttests, hard-copy progress reports, adjustable levels of difficulty, and a review of prior knowledge and prerequisite student skills.

Last, teachers should evaluate the potential use of mathematics software to ensure it compliments and enhances the curriculum and standards set by the district and state. The best software promotes interdisciplinary activities, addresses different learning styles, adjusts learning experiences, and actively engages its students.

A rubric for evaluating mathematics software is included in Table 2. Ideally, a teacher would select software with the highest overall ratings in all categories. Student learning outcomes are the primary criteria upon which to choose software.

Table 2. Rubric for Evaluation of Mathematics Software for the Classroom (30 = Outstanding; 20 = Satisfactory; 10 = Acceptable; 0 = Extremely poor; N/A = Not applicable)

Criteria	30	20	10	0	N/A
Technology Specifications (Maximum Points: 90)					
Appropriateness of software for platform, storage capacity, memory					
Availability of hard-copy and online documentation					
Costs of licensing, upgrade, and installation					
Content (Maximum Points: 180)					
Appropriateness of grade and age levels					
Accuracy of the content information					
Suitability for remediation, direct instruction, guided practice, independent practice, or enrichment					
Clarity of directions					
Availability of teacher support materials (worksheets, teacher's manual, user's manual, lesson plans, projects, links)					
Visual appeal of the screen images					
Lesson Management (Maximum Points: 210)					
Provision of computerized lesson management					
Provision of individual student tracking					
Provision of statistical cohort analysis					
Provision of pre- and posttests					
Provision of hard-copy progress reports					
Provision of adjustable levels of difficulty					
Review of prior knowledge and prerequisite student skills					
Correct Mathematics Applications (Maximum Points: 360)					
Increase in understanding and skills					
Appropriate for use by a variety of learners					
Facilitation of higher-level thinking					
Assurance that instructional content is accurate and up to date					
Assurance that content and implementation are free from race, ethnic, or gender stereotyping					
Presentation of information, logically and clearly					
Appropriateness of reading level					
Accommodation of a wide range of abilities					
Assurance that content of the software fits the purpose of instruction					
Promotion of interdisciplinary activities					
Assurance that is addresses different learning styles					
Hope that it actively engages math students					
TOTAL POINTS (Maximum Points: 840)					

Examples of Best Educational Software

There are many uses for software technology in the mathematics classroom environment. Demonstrations sent to a network of computers allow students to participate in lessons involving personal investigations, group explorations, or even multimedia classroom presentations. Many software vendors offer free downloads readily available on the Internet and allow free 30-day previewing periods with certain restrictions to test the capabilities of this software package. A listing of the best programs for mathematics instruction is found in Table 3.

Table 3. Examples of Mathematics Educational Software

Title	Classification	Evaluation Score	Cost	Comments
Geometer's Sketchpad	Manipulatives	T = 90 C = 170 M = 160 A = 340 Total = 560	$30	Dynamic construction and exploration tool that enables students to explore and understand mathematics in ways that are simply not possible with traditional tools — or with other mathematics software programs
The Graph Club	Manipulatives	T = 90 C = 140 M = 200 A = 310 Total = 740	Free 90-day demo $80 License	Helps students make graphs and easily compare the different kinds of graphs and how they relate to each other
Mathville VIP	Instructional programs	T = 70 C = 170 M = 100 A = 250 Total = 690	$30	Presents the virtual town of "mathville" and allows middle school and high school students to practice everyday math skills in real-life activities
JumpStart Math for Kindergartners	Manipulatives and instructional programs	T = 80 C = 180 M = 100 A = 340 Total = 700	Unknown	Outstanding math program for preschoolers includes activities, songs, and links to learn basic math facts
Math Arena	Instructional programs	T = 90 C = 180 M = 100 A = 340 Total = 710	$100	Interactive math challenges: practice a vast array of critical math skills and begin to think about numbers and shapes in new ways

Note. T = Technology; C = Content; M = Management; and A = Application.

Table 3. Examples of Mathematics Educational Software (continued)

Math Munchers Deluxe	Manipulatives	T = 60 C = 140 M = 100 A = 260 Total = 560	$15	A simulated TV game show of math problems, numbers, simple equations, or shapes, each of which represents a right or wrong answer to a simple question
Oregon Trail	Manipulatives	T = 90 C = 170 M = 210 A = 350 Total = 820	$15	Real-life decision-making and problem-solving skills used while serving as the leader of a wagon party
Shape Makers	Data collection and graphics	T = 70 C = 100 M = 120 A = 240 Total = 530	$15	Squares and triangles are reassembled to create larger squares, larger triangles, parallelograms, and trapezoids
The Cruncher	Instructional programs	T = 90 C = 180 M = 100 A = 360 Total = 730	$14	Fast and easy way to find the answers to real-life math questions
The Factory Deluxe	Data collection and graphics	T = 80 C = 150 M = 180 A = 300 Total = 810	$20	Create professional-quality mathematics worksheets to provide students with the skills development, practice, and review they need as part of a complete program to develop mathematical literacy

Note. T = Technology; C = Content; M = Management; and A = Application.

Internet Use in the Mathematics Classroom

Introduction

Many educators today use Web sites to infuse technology into their mathematical curriculum. Many excellent Web sites exist for students to access and satisfy mathematical educational outcomes established by standards, government, and teachers. Lesson objectives are matched with features from a site, and sites are typically categorized as to their focus on primary, intermediate, and middle grades at the elementary level, and secondary grades at the high school level.

Evaluation Classifications

Time spent on the Internet enhances student understanding of the primary content areas within mathematics, including numbers and operations, algebra, measurement, reasoning, geometry, data analysis and probability, and applied and advanced mathematics. Numbers and operations involve the competencies of computation, counting, fractions, money, numbers, and word problems. Algebra requires mastery of equations, graphing, functions, and word problems. Measurement is divided into the concepts of perimeter, area, volume, etc. Reasoning includes proof, problem solving, and patterns. Geometry skills consist of figures, theorems, ratios, proportions, scale, and transformations. Data analysis and probability require an understanding of data collection, graphing, probability, and real data. Finally, applied and advanced mathematics relates to consumer math, modeling, real-world applications, calculus, discrete numbers, and trigonometry.

Rubric for Evaluating Mathematics Web Sites

Table 4 provides a rubric for evaluating the strengths and weaknesses of a mathematics Web site for the K–12 classroom and ensuring that the Web site under consideration meets the learning outcomes targeted for mathematics lessons.

Table 4. Rubric for Evaluating Mathematics Web Sites

Title of the Web Site _____

Internet Address of Web Site __http://_____

Grade Level(s)_____

Mathematics Skills Addressed/Skill Level	Low	Average	Advanced
Numbers and operations • Computation • Counting • Fractions • Money • Numbers • Word problems			
Algebra • Equations • Graphing • Functions • Word problems			
Measurement • Perimeter • Area • Volume			
Reasoning • Proof • Problem solving • Patterns			
Geometry • Figures • Theorems • Ratios • Proportions • Scale • Transformations			
Data analysis and probability • Data collection • Graphing • Probability • Real data			
Applied and advanced mathematics • Consumer math • Modeling • Real-world applications • Calculus • Discrete numbers • Trigonometry			

Table 4. Rubric for Evaluating Mathematics Web Sites (continued)

Site Analysis	20	15	10	5	0
General Design Considerations (Maximum Points: 100)					
For navigation, links are clearly labeled, enabling users to move readily from page to page.					
Site offers interactivity to the mathematics student. Student engages with the site.					
Site uses appropriate page format. Pages are not inordinately long.					
Students easily find information.					
Site is aesthetically appealing. There is good use of graphics and color.					
Holistic Design and Mathematics Presentation (Maximum Points: 150)	50	—	25	—	0
Site shows complete understanding of the mathematics concepts presented, thoroughly addresses all points relevant to the solution, shows logical reasoning and valid conclusions, communicates effectively and clearly through text and diagrams, and offers correct computations and explanations. Rate the following separately:					
Mathematical Knowledge Appropriate mathematical terminology and notation are used. Algorithms are completely and correctly executed.					
Strategic Knowledge Important elements of the problem are identified, and the relationship between them is understood. Reflects an appropriate and systematic strategy for solving the problem. Gives clear evidence of a solution process, and solution process is complete and systematic.					
Problem-Solving Skills Site helped student understand the problem. Special factors that influenced the approach were identified before starting the problem. The reasons for the correct decisions made throughout the problem were clearly explained.					
Content (Maximum Points: 100)	20	15	10	5	0
Additional resource links are included.					
Site will likely be revisited due to rich content.					
The content information was accurate.					
Cultural sensitivity was displayed.					
Web site compares in content to similar Web sites.					
Technical Elements (Maximum Points: 80)	20	15	10	5	0
All links work.					
Graphics download quickly.					
Alternative text page is offered when heavy graphics or frames are used.					
Meaningful information loads within 30 seconds.					
Credibility (Maximum Points: 80)	20	15	10	5	0
Contact person is stated, and email address is included.					
Page identifies date of last revision, and links are current.					
Resource links used to develop content are included.					
Host school or institution is identified.					
TOTAL POINTS AVAILABLE (510 MAXIMUM POINTS)					

Examples of Best Web Sites for Teaching Mathematics

The best mathematics Web sites are those individually targeted to students, teachers, and parents. Perhaps unlike any other category of Web site, mathematics sites must focus on exacting content and specific learners to be most effective. Adjacent subject areas may be included on the site to infuse related content material and to emphasize the importance of mathematics in the real world. Parental assistance may be necessary, sometimes even desirable. However, no mathematics Web sites have been found to provide instruction, direct, remedial, or enhanced, equally as well to a range of students, much less teachers and parents.

Younger children may need help with directions or with navigation through the screens. There should be no advertisements on the site. The pages must be clean and appealing, with supplemental links for teachers and parents containing additional information for remediation and enhancement. Some excellent Web sites for mathematics students and teachers are included in Table 5.

Table 5. Web Sites for Teaching Mathematics*

Title	Focus/Description	Evaluation Score	Math Skills Addressed	URL Address
Bigchalk Integrated Classroom	Student focus Targeting instructional resources to standards; educator-reviewed Web sites, lesson plans, periodicals, and multimedia resources — aligned to the subjects and textbooks and correlated to state and national benchmarks	D = 200 C = 100 T = 70 Cr = 80 Total = 450	All	http://bigchalk.com/
Webmath	Student focus Discovery Channel mathematics site; separate sites for students, teachers, and parents	D = 250 C = 90 T = 80 Cr = 80 Total = 500	All	http://school.discovery.com/homeworkhelp/webmath/
MegaMath	Student focus The MegaMath project is intended to bring unusual and important mathematical ideas to elementary school classrooms so that young people and their teachers can think about them together	D = 220 C = 90 T = 50 Cr = 80 Total = 440	All	http://www.c3.lanl.gov/mega-math/
House of Math Word Problems	Student focus The goal of this math Web site is to help elementary and middle school children improve their math problem-solving and critical-thinking skills	D = 240 C = 100 T = 80 Cr = 80 Total = 500	Algebra reasoning	http://www.mathstories.com/ Membership fee required
Math Goodies	Student focus Educational Web site featuring interactive math lessons, homework help, worksheets, puzzles, forums, and more	D = 200 C = 90 T = 80 Cr = 80 Total = 450	All	http://www.mathgoodies.com/
National Council of Teachers of Mathematics	Teacher focus Site accesses information about conferences, job opportunities, breaking news, and other items of interest to all teachers of mathematics	N/A	N/A	www.nctm.org
Eisenhower National Clearinghouse for Mathematics	Teacher focus Accesses information about successful programs that can be adopted by local schools and school districts; ENC services can help teachers find the latest information about mathematics and science education	N/A	N/A	www.enc.org
Canadian Mathematical Society	Teacher focus Presents lesson plans and worksheets for a variety of content areas; offers topics related to data and classroom management	N/A	N/A	www.camel.math.ca/home.html
Swarthmore's Math Forum	Teacher focus Focuses on mathematics education; newsgroups, projects, an archive, and a search feature lead teachers to many resources; "Ask Dr. Math" is a part of this site	D = 240 C = 100 T = 80 Cr = 80 Total = 500	N/A	http://mathforum.org/
National Science Foundation	Teacher focus Provides information teachers and schools can use in the selection and implementation of a standards-based mathematics curriculum	N/A	N/A	www.edc.org/mcc/index.htm
Classic Fallacies	Teacher focus Site sets up false mathematical "proofs" and explains their flaws	D = 200 C = 80 T = 30 Cr = 80 Total = 390	N/A	www.math.toronto.edu/mathnet/falseProofs/fallacies.html

Note. D = Design ; C = Content ; T = Technical ; Cr = Credibility ; N/A = Not Applicable.

Conclusions

Teachers of mathematics should utilize technology to present basic concepts and develop lifelong mathematics skills; simulate real-world situations that promote logical reasoning and theoretical connections; and encourage predictions and problem-solving strategies rather than computation only. In addition, technology should offer multimedia (visual, auditory, and sensory) stimulation. The main strength of technology, however, is modeling real-life situations with actual or cumbersome data that cannot be handled during the daily restrictions of available classroom instruction time.

Mathematics teachers should not view technology as the panacea for learning. Effective use of technologies depends on instructors closely monitoring learning outcomes and revising instruction better suited to the demands of their students. Computers and calculators will never replace the competent teacher who must decide when, if, and how technology is to be used in the classroom. In addition, assessment tools must be designed so that students demonstrate mastery of state and local standards. Technology must be used carefully. It must not become a replacement for basic understanding and intuitions, but rather, it should be used responsibly. Enhancing student learning must always be the goal.

References

Hambree & Dessart. (1999, May/June). Research on Calculators in Mathematics. *Mathematics Education Dialogues*. Reston, VA: NCTM.

Jackiw, N. (1995). *The Geometer's Sketchpad*. Berkeley, CA: Key Curriculum Press, Software.

Kerrigan, J. (2002). Powerful Software to Balance and Enhance the Elementary School Mathematics Program. *Teaching Children Mathematics, 8*, 3, 364–370.

National Council of Teachers of Mathematics (NCTM). (2000). *Principles and Standards for School Mathematics*. Reston, VA: NCTM, http://www.nctm.org.

Olive, J. (2002). Bridging the Gap, *Teaching Children Mathematics*, *8*, 3, 356–361.

Scherno, D. (2001, August 3). Children Improving in Math, *Pittsburgh Post-Gazette*, Pittsburgh, PA.

Sconiers, S. (1986). *Calculator Mathematics*. University of Chicago, USMP, Chicago, IL.

Smith, B. (1999, May/June). A Meta-Analysis of Outcomes from the Use of Calculators in Mathematics Education. *Mathematics Education Dialogues*. Reston, VA: NCTM.

Stenmark, T. & Cossey. (1986). *Family Math*. Berkeley, CA: University of California.

Endnote

*Acknowledgements: With the help of Erin Lynn, Susan Lewis, and Amy Rakowski.

Technology In The Social Studies Classroom

V. Robert Agostino, EdD

Introduction

Claude Shannon died in my hometown, Medford, Massachusetts, in February, 2001. Age 84, he apparently had Alzheimer's disease. It is a great irony that the man most responsible for digital memory and information transmission ended his life not being able to remember. I am not sure why Claude Shannon was in my hometown at the end of his life; perhaps his long connection to the Massachusetts Institute of Technology (MIT) made him buy a house there, or maybe it was the Alzheimer's care facility. When he died, his obituary was carried by a number of national newspapers and several Web sites.

These obituaries all mentioned the same facts. Shannon was a genius, receiving dual bachelor degrees in 1936 in electrical engineering and mathematics from the University of Michigan. He also received a master's degree in electrical engineering and a PhD in mathematics in 1940 from MIT. His master's degree thesis, "A Symbolic Analysis of Relay and Switching Circuits," is regarded as the most important thesis ever written about the topic of information. Combined with his 1948 paper, "A Mathematical Theory of Communication," Shannon revolutionized the way engineers thought about hardware, and how technologists today are reconceptualizing learning theory, software design, and electronic communications. It is that evolution of technological thought that has impacted social studies so directly.

Historical Evolution of Social Studies-Based Technologies

Claude Shannon's Vision

Oddly enough, Shannon became famous by completely ignoring the content of telephone and electronic messages. His work does not concern the message being sent. Shannon did not care if the communication system contained words, pictures, sound files, smoke signals, music, art, hieroglyphics, or the secrets of the universe. What he examined was the amount of error that an electronic system such as the telephone relay systems could tolerate. Obviously, if the message arriving at the receiver was significantly different from the one originally sent, there was no effective communication. Shannon defined the term "entropy" to mean the amount of uncertainty in an information channel. He discovered that Boolean algebra and binary digits could describe the capacity of a channel. The amount of information that could be sent through a channel and the ways to reduce "noise" became the foundations of modern communications.

Digitization of the world is abundantly evident. Compact data disks, digital video disks, and digital music come straight from Shannon's insight that 1s and 0s are all that are needed to transmit any kind and amount of information. Sending digital packets of data over the Web and the Internet is the direct result of his insights. It is the content of those packets that interests teachers and students. Our pedagogical interest in the contents of the electronic media lead us to the second seminal figure in this discussion of information and its impact on the social fabric of a culture.

Marshall McCluhan's Contributions

Marshall McCluhan (1911–1980) is perhaps a more familiar name than Claude Shannon. McCluhan's contributions centered on the concept that basic elements of any general communications system include the following:

- A source of information that is a transmitting device which transforms the information or "message" into a form suitable for transmission by a particular means.
- The means or channel over which the message is transmitted.
- A receiving device that decodes the message back into some approximation of its original form.
- The destination or intended recipient of the message.
- A source of noise (i.e., interference or distortion) that changes the message in unpredictable ways during transmission.

While Shannon envisioned a digital future, McCluhan predicted that the "transmitting device" could ultimately change the meaning or perception of the message; that is, the form of the medium impacts how the recipient perceives the information. In his over-quoted phrase, "the medium is the message," McCluhan argued that the shift in the physical form that "packaged" the information made a difference in the receiver's or perceiver's understanding of the information.

Hot and Cold Media

One of McCluhan's most useful insights for teachers is his distinction between "hot" and "cold" media. His concepts of hot and cold media are often applied to information presented, formed, or packaged. A medium is hot if it engages the mind and imagination of the user, demanding a reaction and participation, both intellectual and emotional. Cold media does not engage the user; rather, it sends information irrespective of receiver involvement. Hot media is capable of actually changing meaning because of user feedback. Cold media has no such feedback loops. Television and books serve as excellent examples to illustrate the difference.

By the mid-1950s in the United States, more homes had television sets than indoor plumbing. Early educational technologists saw television as the ultimate delivery system combining motion pictures, sound, animation, and voice-over commentary, all supplemented by professionally prepared teacher guides. In the last 10 years, the Channel One enterprise has combined in-classroom TV with captive audience advertising. Other than Sesame Street, most people would be hard-pressed to name any significant educational TV show. McCluhan provided a key psychological and media insight about why educational television has not worked, and why it probably will never work.

A television broadcast transmits signals irrespective of its viewers. A signal occupies physical space without regard to viewer awareness. There is no feedback to indicate that anyone is watching. Turning on a television set causes no action or reaction, so McCluhan argued that television is a cold medium. A two-way communication system is absent. The lack of interactivity, of participation possibilities, doomed television as an educational medium. History and social studies classes are regarded by most students as incredibly boring, not because of an inherent lack of interesting information, but because the teaching methodologies, the media of presentation, are so often monologic, memory level, linear, sequential communication from teacher to students.

The basal textbook is the dominant medium or sole source of information in over 85% of American history and social studies courses and classes. It is interesting to speculate whether books are hot, cold, or a mixed media.

Secondary social studies texts are cold media; an anecdotal argument easily verifies this fact. Ask any social studies students if they ever voluntarily read their history text. My prediction is that the more students asked, the more laughter will be heard. Textbooks are cold in the same way television is cold — they do not invite feedback, participation, or student reaction.

The medium contains the information and influences how that information is perceived. In the 1956 classic, *Taxonomy of Educational Objectives*,

Benjamin Bloom defines a subcategory of comprehension (his second level of the taxonomy) called "translation," which he defines as putting communication into your own words or into other forms (Bloom, 1956). He further suggests that these forms of communications (which he also termed forms of "experience") occur in learning as enactive, iconic, and symbolic. "Enactive" is direct and experiential; "iconic" is pictorial or graphically representational; and "symbolic" is primarily language, although mathematical and other symbol systems are included. Developmentally, children learn in the enactive mode to age 5 and in the iconic mode from ages 5 through 8. Although language acquisition obviously starts at birth, the cognitive ability to use language symbolically (i.e., with abstractions, metaphor, simile, and figurative elements) matures in the preteen years (Biggs & Shermis, 1992).

Applied Technologies

This idea of learning in multiple forms is illustrated by examining the evolution of technologies in the social studies classroom from the contributions of Shannon and McCluhan to information theory. Shannon is the intellectual source of the globe-changing insight that all information can be represented and transmitted using binary digits and bits. McCluhan is the guru of the media theory school that argues that the physical form of a communication influences the receiver's perception and understanding of the message—the medium is the message. Hot and cold media enhance or minimize the classroom teacher's chances for enthusiastic participation. These characteristics of technologies dovetail with the psychological insights of Bloom and others about the levels of cognitive functioning needed to produce mastery levels of learning.

Research identifies state-of-the-art technology used in today's social studies classroom. Using the definitions and descriptions above, a few of the most promising technologies are presented in Table 1. Note how the technologies associated with social studies have matured from cold to hot media.

Table 1. Evolving Technologies in the Social Studies Classroom

Technology	Description	Application	Hot or Cold
Electronic communication	Individual and group email for all aspects of classroom interaction including, but not limited to, student–teacher communication, student–student interaction, course updates, etc.	Students learn email is an efficient way to contact a very busy instructor who manages to check email messages several times daily	Hot
Electronic classroom presentations	Graphics presentation used judiciously for class presentation of research and text material	Laptop and an LCD panel to introduce the course and loaded on the hard drive of the education department computer lab for perusal when students are preparing social studies assignments or reviewing classroom content	Cold when used by the didactic teacher Hot when used interactively by the student
Computer software	Most popular of the technologies, includes drill and practice, tutorial, simulation, and utility packages	Students use software to increase, teacher–student usability, user interaction, content development, instructional value, record-keeping ease, assessment capabilities, and modifications for a range of intellectual abilities	Hot
Multimedia	Multimedia is best when focused on a particular social studies content area, while addressing one or more of the standards	Multimedia should stimulate the user to think critically, respond reflectively, or react creatively; it often includes use of a map or globe, user interaction, thoughtful use of sound, text, graphics, animation, and clear navigational guidelines	Hot
Internet	Rapidly overtaking computer software as the technology of choice, the Internet offers a blend of all the previous forms of hot and cold media	Important to understanding geography, history, economics, political science, sociology and psychology, or current events; students analyze attributes of Web sites and their potential for higher-level thinking	Hot

Standards for Technology in Social Studies

The importance of social studies standards ensures that educators, parents, and the local citizenry will know what students are taught, how they will be taught, and how student achievement will be evaluated. The national curriculum standards in social studies define what students should be learning in social studies programs in the early grades, middle grades, and high school grades; the standards specify what students should know and when they should know it. The 10 themes that form the framework of the social studies standards (summarized from the NCSS standards) include study of the following:

- Culture, which prepares students to deal with geography, history, sociology, anthropology, and multicultural issues
- Time, Continuity, and Change, which helps students understand their historical roots and locate themselves in time
- People, Places, and Environment, which affords students a personal view and geographic perspective of the world beyond their personal environment
- Individual Development and Identity, which is shaped by culture, social groups, and assorted institutional influences
- Individuals, Groups, and Institutions, where students learn how institutions are formed, what controls and influences them, how they influence individuals and culture, and how they are maintained or changed
- Power, Authority, and Governance, which provides the developmental history of power, authority, and governance in the United States and other parts of the world
- Production, Distribution, and Consumption, which discusses the most effective allocation of the factors of production, including land, labor, capital, and management
- Science, Technology, and Society, and how they are managed to benefit the greatest number of people
- Global Connections, including the increasing importance of global connections and the frequent tensions that arise between national interests and global priorities

- Civic Ideas and Practices, critical to full participation in society and the primary purpose of social studies

A summary of the key themes of the NCSS (2001) standards is depicted in Table 2. [Note: Suggested technologies are taken from Table 4 ("Guide to Common Classroom Technologies," Chapter 1).]

Table 2. Key Standards and Their Technology Implications

Strand	Specific Standards	Suggested Technologies
Culture	Social studies programs should include experiences that provide for the study of culture and cultural diversity.	World Wide Web, video
Time, Continuity, and Change	Social studies programs should include experiences that provide for the study of the ways human beings view themselves in and over time.	Graphic presentation, tutorial instruction
People, Places, and Environments	Social studies programs should include experiences that provide for the study of people, places, and environments.	Electronic mail, list servers, World Wide Web
Individual Development and Identity	Social studies programs should include experiences that provide for the study of individual development and identity.	Electronic mail
Individuals, Groups, and Institutions	Social studies programs should include experiences that provide for the study of interactions among individuals, groups, and institutions.	Electronic mail, list servers, newsgroups, videoconferencing
Power, Authority, and Governance	Social studies programs should include experiences that provide for the study of how people create and change structures of power, authority, and governance.	Digitized encyclopedias
Production, Distribution, and Consumption	Social studies programs should include experiences that provide for the study of how people organize for the production, distribution, and consumption of goods and services.	Computer assisted instruction, games instruction, simulation instruction
Science, Technology, and Society	Social studies programs should include experiences that provide for the study of relationships among science, technology, and society.	All technologies
Global Connections	Social studies programs should include experiences that provide for the study of global connections and interdependence.	Electronic mail, list servers, newsgroups, videoconferencing
Civic Ideals and Practices	Social studies programs should include experiences that provide for the study of the ideals, principles, and practices of citizenship in a democratic republic.	Electronic mail, list servers, newsgroups, videoconferencing

Note. From *Social Education*, The Official Journal of the National Council for the Social Studies, Yearly Issues on Computer Resources for Social Education, 1997–2001.

Educational Software for the Social Studies Classroom

Introduction

Finding appropriate software to meet the needs of social studies teachers and their students is not an easy task. While the use of software in social studies is fairly recent, instructional technology and, more specifically, computer software, has quickly come to affect the teaching of social studies and the relationship between each of its major fields of study.

Evaluation Classifications

There are three important criteria for evaluating social studies software. The criteria include the following:

- **Objectivity, bias, and accuracy:** The information must be verifiably accurate. The interplay between print sources and Web sites can create students with appropriate skepticism about both.
- **Efficiency:** Time is the learner's ultimate resource. The preorganization of the learner's needs and goals will reduce redundant information and reduce search time.
- **Age appropriateness:** This criterion involves controversial materials, readability, comprehension, navigation, and the balance between text and iconic information.

In addition, each student mentally constructs the content of social studies facts, concepts, and generalizations. Content is constructed by using social studies learning process skills that enable us to gather, organize, process, and communicate data. Therefore, it is necessary for teachers to consider why they should be concerned with using technology in their classrooms. Technology can be used to promote visual and tactile or kinesthetic learning in cooperative groups that are focused on higher levels of Bloom's taxonomy. Software, in particular, helps young people learn those higher-level thinking skills that have always been a part of the social studies curriculum.

Drill and Practice

Social studies software has always been dominated by drill and practice packages. The goal of social studies software is to transmit information and determine student understanding by questioning. Well-designed drill and practice software provides the content of economics, politics, psychology and philosophy, as well as geography and history.

Simulation

Simulation is an effective strategy for helping students learn about possible courses of action and their potential consequences (Barr, 1977). Computer simulations serve as tools for developing thinking skills in the social studies and, after drill and practice, represent the second most popular type of social studies software. Simulations vary the learning experience available to students and provide a deeper understanding of another time or situation. Research suggests that nearly 40% of social studies software is now simulation. Interest in social simulation has been growing rapidly world-wide, as a result of increasingly powerful hardware and software, and rising interest in the application of ideas such as complexity, evolution, and adaptation in the social sciences (Gilbert & Troitzsch, 1999).

Tutorials

In tutorials, computers provide the information and ask the questions. They analyze student responses and alter the path of the instruction to provide deeper student understanding and thinking. Tutorial software teaches gathering skills, allowing the student to explore the content and, in the process, acquire rich sources of new information (Lengel, 1987).

Utilities

Utilities are software tools that organize and present social studies data to illustrate concepts, define trends, test hypotheses, and draw conclusions. Included are databases, paint and draw software, and instructional assessment packages. Also included are office productivity packages, including word processing and spreadsheets, both widely used in the social studies classroom.

In 1990, Northrup and Rooze gathered responses to the question of what types of computer software social studies teachers use in the classroom. Their results are summarized in Table 3.

Table 3. Software Found in Social Studies Classrooms

Type of Software	Number of Users	Percent of Users	Number Responding as Primary Software	Percent Responding as Primary Software
Drill and Practice	80	43.0	34	18.3
Simulation	112	60.2	44	23.7
Tutorials	57	30.6	10	5.4
Utilities	206	53.2	98	29.0

Note. From Northrup & Rooze, 1990.

Rubric for Evaluating Social Studies Software

Well-designed software, regardless of the content area, is concerned with general, instructional, and technical quality. Perhaps more than any other subject matter area, social studies content must be accurate, reliable, and current. Significant importance is placed on the validity of the social studies knowledge presented and the level of student skill development offered by the author or publisher. Of course, courseware specifications, such as target audience, hardware requirements, and cost, are a concern. Social studies teachers are expected to propose potential software for consideration and review. Therefore, Figure 1 is provided to offer a construct for evaluating social studies software.

Figure 1. Rubric for Evaluating Social Studies Software

Software Title:					
Author/Publisher Information:					
Category (Indicate Primary Only): _____ Drill and Practice _____ Simulation _____ Tutorial _____ Utility	**Hardware/Software Requirements:**				
Grade Level:					
Cost:	N/A	Poor	Fair	Good	Excellent
Rate Each of the Following Areas:	0	5	10	15	20
• **Content**					
Objectivity, Bias, Accuracy					
Social Studies Knowledge					
Social Studies Skills					
Value to Social Studies Curriculum					
General Instructional Quality					
Total Content Points (100 Possible)					
• **Technical Presentation**					
Technical Quality					
General Quality of Content					
Efficiency					
Total Technical Points (60 Possible)					
• **Appropriateness**					
Interpersonal Skills					
Age Appropriateness					
Total Appropriateness Points (40 Possible)					
Total Points Awarded (200 Possible)					
Identify Negative Factors	**Recommendation (Indicate One):** _____ Excellent, recommend purchase _____ Good, satisfies most learning objectives _____ Fair, needs additional review _____ Poor, do not recommend				

Examples of Best Educational Software

The previous section gave some criteria for evaluating the potential effectiveness of computer software instruction in social studies education. The enhancement of student learning through software takes several forms. The most obvious uses of computer technologies are as enhanced information sources. Social studies software gives learners previously unimaginable amounts of materials to work with: maps, photos, woodcuts, diagrams, lesson plans, statistical data, articles, music, sound files, image files, animations, film clips, movies, interest groups, and professional associations. When offered using the medium of Compact Disk or Digital Video Display, the social studies learner finds unimaginable resources. Table 4 provides a listing of the best programs for social studies instruction available.

Table 4. Best Educational Software for Social Studies Classrooms

Title	Category	Discipline/ Target Age	Evaluation Score	Cost	Comments
Carmen Sandiego Junior Detective	Simulation	History/ Grades K–3	C = 90 T = 60 A = 40 Total = 190	$50	Introduction to the excitement of chasing Carmen Sandiego. Does not require reading. Helps young students develop memory matching skills, gain familiarity with maps and symbols, and piece together clues to solve mysteries.
Oregon Trail II	Simulation, tutorial	Geography/ Grades 5–12	C = 90 T = 60 A = 40 Total = 190	$60	Brings the geography of the Old West to life, providing a unique interactive experience of American history.
Amazon Trail 3rd Edition: Rainforest Adventure	Simulation, tutorial	History, Geography, Ecology/ Grades 5–12	C = 95 T = 60 A = 30 Total = 185	$60	Journey into uncharted rainforests, where intrigue lurks everywhere in the Rainforest. Along the way, students travel back through time, meeting people from previous centuries who may or may not help them complete their adventures.
Road Adventure USA	Simulation, tutorial	Geography/ Grades 4–8	C = 85 T = 55 A = 30 Total = 170	$60	As contestants on a road trip across the United States following clues to mystery destinations, students use math, reading, research, geography, and problem-solving skills in real-life situations.
Schoolhouse Rock America Rock	Drill and practice simulation	U.S. History, Geography, Government/ Grades 3–8	C = 95 T = 55 A = 40 Total = 190	$60	Discover important facts about U.S. history, geography, government, and culture.
Where in Time is Carmen Sandiego?	Drill and practice simulation	History/ Grades 4–8	C = 80 T = 60 A = 40 Total = 180	$55	This motivates students to experience history while traveling through time in pursuit of the legendary Carmen Sandiego.

Note. C = Content, T = Technical, and A = Appropriateness.

Internet Use in the Social Studies Classroom

Introduction

A well-designed Web page for social studies includes an introduction that clearly identifies its purpose and its audience. Information and ideas support approved social studies standards and the page is written to meet the needs and interests of the student. An important attribute of a good Web site is that it comes from original and primary sources that may not be readily available to the intended audience. These sources include first-hand observations, measurements, accounts and reflections, original letters, memoirs and diaries, personal observations, interviews, audio recordings and movies, photographs, original artwork and creative writing and poetry, period or historical newspaper and magazine articles, and other resources found within the local community. Sources are clearly cited and recently visited by the teacher prior to student access to validate credibility and authority of the information presented.

Evaluation Classifications

An excellent Web page for K–12 social studies includes an introduction that clearly identifies its purpose and its audience, is well organized, presents a pleasing appearance, and is technically sound.

Content

The information and ideas presented support social studies standards, and the Web page is written to meet the needs and interests of the target students. The majority of the Web site contents come from primary sources that are not readily available, including first-hand observations, measurements, accounts and reflections, original letters, memoirs, and diaries, personal observations, interviews, audio recordings and movies, photographs, original artwork and creative writing and poetry, period or historical newspaper and magazine articles, and other resources found within the local community. Sources of all information are clearly cited so the reader can determine the credibility and authority of the information presented and any terms of copyright ownership. Web pages include relevant information, anecdotes, graphics, and links organized to support and enrich the overall social studies theme. The content is clearly focused and consistent with social studies developmental abilities. Finally, it should be apparent that the authors of the page are masters of the content and ideas presented and capable of Web page design and development.

Organization

A social studies site must be well organized. Each page should be professionally written with interesting introductions, transitions, bodies, and conclusions that support social studies learning. The order, structure, or presentation of information makes navigation easy, while providing a logical and satisfying learning experience for the student.

Appearance and Presentation

Overall appearance of a social studies Web site must be pleasing and contribute to content understanding. A balance of easy-to-read titles, text, colors, and graphics results in an effective learning experience. Graphic elements must provide for uncluttered or unambiguous content.

Technical Elements

An excellent Web site works. Graphics load quickly, especially for users with slow connections. Pages are offered in text-only mode for students who disable graphics loading to speed. Pages work in a variety of Web browsers, including at least Netscape Navigator, Internet Explorer, and America Online. Links to other pages and to internal resources all work as expected.

Rubric for Evaluating Social Studies Web Sites

When using the Internet to acquire information, such as historical names and dates, geographical places, and government-related dates, events, titles, and references, teachers must assist students in evaluating the objectivity of the source. By fourth grade, students are skeptical enough to discriminate conventional information sources (e.g., Library of Congress, Statistical Abstract of the United States) from superfluous sites that supply or withhold factual information in order to promote a cause, issues, or political or religious agendas. Teach students that a little detective work helps them establish the degree of objectivity or bias presented in any electronic information source. Teachers who use newspaper editorials or magazine letters to the editor already demonstrate how to distinguish and evaluate primary and secondary source material. The conventional middle school lessons on propaganda also teach techniques often used in the printed media, hard copy or online. Using print sources to confirm electronic sources develops sophistication in evaluating print and Web sites.

A second criterion for using Web sites as information sources involves efficiency. Because schools are time-constrained organizations, the efficiency criterion would have teacher and students make some preliminary judgments about what information is actually needed and what the most convenient sources are to find that information. The "W" part of the KWL (What Do I Know, What Do I Want to Know, and How Do I Know I Learned) chart.

The third criterion for assessing the value of sites for use in social studies classrooms is age appropriateness. The need to sequester young children from inappropriate Web sites has been well discussed in the professional and popular media. The primary challenge is figuring out how. There is a major difference of opinion between those who would protect children from the harsh realities of the world and those who would teach them to make appropriate and ethical decisions. Age appropriate also refers to many other important factors, such as readability and comprehension levels, technical difficulty of navigating the Web site, its design and presentation, and the use of icons, graphics, maps, pictures, animations, and photos. All are important factors in determining how social studies learners will value a site's information.

The best Web pages include relevant information, anecdotes, graphics, and links organized to support and enrich the overall social studies curriculum. Content is clear and focused as well as consistent with student developmental abilities. Table 5 offers a rubric for assessing the quality of social studies Web sites using the key elements of content, organization, appearance, and technical elements.

Table 5. Rubric for Evaluating Social Studies Web Sites

Criteria	20 Points	10 Points	0–5 Points
Content: purpose	Clear statement of purpose, theme, or main idea that would promote significant social studies learning	The purpose, theme, or main idea of this site is not clearly stated or may be vaguely related to social studies	This site lacks a clear sense of purpose or central theme related to social studies
Content: supporting details	Rich variety of relevant supporting information that is useful adds interest and contributes to an understanding of social studies	A variety of supporting information, much of which is useful, adds interest and contributes to an understanding of social studies	Not enough detail, information, or variety in the information provided; or, there may be too much information that is not interesting or useful or relevant to social studies
Content: target audience	There is a clear description of the intended audience; all or most of the information and ideas presented are clearly written	There seems to be a target audience, but it is not always clear that the authors understood or met the developmental needs of their intended audience	It is not clear who the audience for this site is, or this site does not meet the developmental needs of the intended audience
Content: project "teaches something new"	Information and ideas come from a range of formal and informal sources; much of the information comes from primary sources	Ideas and information come from a limited variety of information sources, including some primary sources	Ideas and information come primarily from commonly available sources (books, library, magazines, other Web sites); not enough new information or variety is presented to hold student interest
Content: accuracy of information	Information presented appears to be accurate, complete, and current	Information presented may be accurate, complete, and current, but this is not always clear	Information is incomplete, out of date, or incorrect; or it is impossible to check the accuracy of the information
Maximum 100 Points			
Organization: project introduction	Opening page draws in the visitor and introduces the overall social studies purpose and structure of the site	The home page introduces the basic social studies purpose; however, the structure of the site is not as clear as it could be	The opening page does not adequately introduce the purpose of the project; it is not clear what this site will present
Organization: quality of writing	This site is interesting to read and holds the visitor's attention; writing is simple, clear, and direct	The writing is understandable, but in some places content is hard to understand; problems are noted with grammar and usage	The writing in this project is difficult to understand; errors in grammar and usage are very noticeable and affect meaning
Organization: navigation	Easy to navigate; use of links and menus make it clear how to continue to explore an idea or area	Sometimes difficult to determine which links are central to the main idea or purpose of the site and which provide supporting information	The structure does not give enough guidance to navigate through the content, or else the structure is so complex that it is confusing
Maximum 60 Points			

Table 5. Rubric for Evaluating Social Studies Web Sites (continued)

Appearance: effective overall design theme	Pages are easy to follow with a consistent design theme; colors, backgrounds, and text are easy to read and create a pleasant viewing experience	Most pages are easy to follow; the same or similar design theme is used; colors, backgrounds, and text could have been used more effectively	The layout is cluttered or confusing, or the layout is so simple that the benefits of hypertext are lost on this project
Appearance: graphic elements	Graphics make a valuable contribution, are used consistently, and contribute to the overall flow of the information	Graphics help in understanding the information but are sometimes inconsistent, confusing, unnecessary or distracting	Graphics do not serve any useful purpose other than decoration; they are confusing, clutter the site, and should be left out
Appearance: multimedia resources	Multimedia resources, such as sound, video, and images, contribute to objectives of the site and enhance student understanding of the information presented	Multimedia resources, sometimes do not add to the understanding or relevancy of the topic	Multimedia resources are often unrelated to the topic and add little value to the information presented
Maximum 60 Points			
Technical: pages load efficiently	Images and text load quickly, even with slow modem speeds; pages work in a variety of Web browsers		Images and text loads are too slow; site has been optimized for a particular browser and works poorly in others
Technical: links to other sites	All links to internal and external Web sites and files work properly		Too many internal and external Web sites have been lost
Maximum 40 Points			
Maximum 260 Points			

Examples of Best Web Sites for Teaching Social Studies

> Social studies is the integrated study of the social sciences and humanities to promote civic competence. Within the school program, social studies provides coordinated, systematic study drawing upon such disciplines as anthropology, archeology, economics, geography, history, law, philosophy, political science, psychology, religion, and sociology, as well as appropriate content from the humanities, mathematics, and natural sciences. The primary purpose of social studies is to help young people develop the ability to make informed and reasoned decisions for the public good as citizens of a culturally diverse, democratic society in an interdependent world. (NCSS Archive)

Reviewing social studies Web sites is much like asking an audience to review a new movie. What may constitute an important element of Web page presentation for the history teacher is likely to be different from the government teacher. In addition, social studies encompasses economics, geography, sociology, politics and law, philosophy, psychology, religion, and others. With this variety of social studies, it is only logical to expect teachers to have differing opinions when it comes to the most important characteristics of potential Web sites. Table 6 offers a starting point for locating and assessing the best Internet sites for the gamut of social studies resources.

Table 6. Best Web Sites for Social Studies Classrooms

Title/ URL	Focus	Content Area(s)	Evaluation Score	Comments
Ask Eric ericir.syr.edu/cgi-bin/lessons.cgi/ Social_Studies	Teacher	Psychology, sociology, economics	C = 100 O = 50 A = 50 T = 40 Total = 240	Ask Eric lesson plans for social studies include psychology, sociology, and economics. The lesson plans are evaluated before being published on the site.
New York Times www.nytimes.com/learning/teachers/lessons/archive.html	Teacher	Economics, psychology, sociology	C = 90 O = 50 A = 60 T = 40 Total = 240	Excellent resource for teachers: lessons use articles (available with the lesson plan) from the *New York Times*. Lesson plans include objectives, time allowance, standards, materials, activities, assessment, and extension ideas. Economics is a strand. Psychology and Sociology are not named, but general "Social Studies" lesson plans could be used.
Trinity University, Texas www.trinity.edu/~mkearl/index.html	Teacher	Psychology, sociology, economics	C = 70 O = 40 A = 40 T = 40 Total = 190	A resource for sociology teachers only. Some of the information can be used with high school students, but its graphics are dark, and text is sometimes hard to read.
APA www.apa.org	Teacher	Psychology	C = 70 O = 60 A = 60 T = 40 Total = 230	These are the national standards from the American Psychological Association for teaching high school psychology.
NCSS www.ncss.org	Teacher	Social studies standards	C = 80 O = 60 A = 60 T = 40 Total = 240	This is an information service for social studies educators from the National Council for Social Studies. It had good information on national standards, but I did not find it to be practical or easy to navigate or read.
Ad*Access Project scriptorium.lib.duke.edu/adaccess/	Student	Advertising, sociology	C = 100 O = 60 A = 60 T = 30 Total = 250	This site features ads from 1911 to 1955. Students could study the advertising techniques, chart the number of ads per subject to find what was important to the people of different time periods, etc.
APA www.intropsych.org	Student	Psychology	C = 100 O = 50 A = 50 T = 40 Total = 240	This psychology site has quizzes on memory. The material might be college level, but it would depend upon the curriculum.
New York Times www.nytimes.com/learning/students/index.html	Teacher	History, politics	C = 70 O = 60 A = 60 T = 30 Total = 220	This site includes news summaries, daily news quizzes, word of the day, test prep question of the day, ask a reporter, etc.
The Vatican Museum www.christusrex.org	Student	Religion	C = 100 O = 30 A = 30 T = 30 Total = 190	This religious site includes artifacts, documents, and additional Web links.
Gateway to African American History usinfo.state.gov/usa/blackhis/	Student	History, sociology	C = 90 O = 50 A = 60 T = 30 Total = 230	This site provides information on the rich and varied contributions of African-Americans to the culture and history of the United States and the world.

Note. C = Content, O = Organization, A = Appearance, and T = Technical.

Other Technology Considerations for the Geography Curriculum

Introduction

While social studies most certainly includes all the fields of interest noted earlier in this chapter, geography has recently suffered perhaps the greatest decline in recent years (Schuncke, 1988). For that reason, the following attention is placed on the subject matter area of geography and the potential applications of technology. Perhaps such attention will positively impact the revival of this precious academic practice in the K–12 classroom.

Geography Technologies

There are five themes that form the structure of contemporary geography education. The National Council promulgated these themes for Geographic Education and the Association of American Geographers in the 1980s. The algorithm for evaluating geography-based technologies includes measuring the content against five themes as well as the age of the prospective student user. The five themes are as follows:

- **Location:** This involves the absolute and relative locations of people and places.
- **Place:** This theme involves the identification of the physical and human characteristics of a place that distinguish it from all other places.
- **Relationships within Places:** This theme explores the relations between humans and the places they inhabit.
- **Movement:** This theme explores the movement of humans, products, technologies, and communication systems through the physical environment.
- **Regions:** A region shares something in common throughout its area. That something can be a common language, biodiversity, landforms, or governmental control.

The key text for geography education is the National Geography Standards book, *Geography for Life*. In addition to the five themes, it presents 18 standards and five additional developmental skill areas. The themes, standards, and skills are organized by grade level: Grades K–4, Grades 5–8, and Grades 9–12, and are available at www.nationalgeographic.com.

These skills include the following:

- Questioning
- Acquiring information
- Organizing information
- Analyzing information
- Generalizing

There are rich media resources for teaching geography at the elementary, middle, and high school levels. Many resources are free and are accessible through numerous lesson plan sites (e.g., see Kathy Schrock's 2000 link list at www.discovery.school.com). Others may be purchased online. One of the largest online social studies material vendors is Social Studies School Service, Culver City, California (www.socialstudies.com).

Map skill development is a standard part of geography in elementary and middle schools. One of the best Internet resources is Brad Bowerman's site, QUIA (www.quia.com), with its thousands of lesson plans organized and searchable by topic, grade, title, etc. Specifically, the geography plans available on this site include drill and practice games and simulation exercises for place recognition, absolute and relative location, estimating, and many other geography skills.

Conclusions

Most social studies educators love their discipline; they are information junkies. For many, the reality that students have electronic access to more information than the teacher frightens them. Many are literally people of the textbook. They learned and still teach in print-oriented times and have psychological difficulty with this cyberspace, hyperlink world of the 21st century.

A clear implication for training the new breed of social studies teacher is that they must be taught with computers as an integral tool in their model classrooms. Their multimedia mind (i.e., one that works in digital and print worlds) must be widely developed while they are still learners.

Technical issues involved in making district, school, and classroom-wide decisions about computers, software, and the Internet must be resolved. Financing technology often diverts scarce funds from other parts of the educational system. Hardware maintenance, software updates, network upgrades, teacher training, and technical support personnel almost always cost more than initial estimates. Social studies education does not carry the spotlight like math and reading instruction, and as a result, does not command the budget clout of other content areas. Perhaps this chapter will encourage social studies teachers to better integrate technology into their curriculum and make the cry for equal technology for social studies so loud it cannot be ignored.

References

Barr, R., Barth J., & Shermis, S. (1977). *Defining the Social Studies* (NCSS Bulletin 51). Arlington, VA: National Council of the Social Studies.

Biggs, M. L. & Shermis, S. S. (1992). *Learning Theories for Teachers*. New York, NY: HarperCollins Press.

Bloom, B. S. et al. (1956). Taxonomy of Educational Objectives: Handbook 1: Cognitive Domain. New York: David McKay Co.

Gilbert, G. N. & Troitz, K. G. (1999, May). *Simulation for the Social Scientist*. Open University Press, United Kingdom.

Lengel, M. G. (1987). Thinking Skills, Social Studies and Computers, *The Social Studies*.

Postman, N. (1979). *Teaching as a Conserving Activity*. New York, Delacorte Press, 1979.

Sanders, N. (1966). *Classroom Questions: What Kinds?* New York: Harper and Row.

Sanderson, G. & McDonald, F. (Eds.) (1989). *Marshall McCluhan: the Man and His Message*. Golden, CO: Fulcrum Press.

Schuncke, G. M. (1988). *Elementary Social Studies Knowing, Doing, Caring*. New York: Macmillan Publishing Co.

Social Education. (1997–2001). The Official Journal of the National Council for the Social Studies, Yearly Issues on Computer Resources for Social Education.

Trinkle, D. A. & Merriman, S. A. (2000). *The History Highway 2000*, 2nd Edition, M. E. Sharpe, Inc., Armonk, NY.

Williams, B. (1995). *The Internet for Teachers*. Chicago, IL: IDG Books.

TECHNOLOGY IN THE LANGUAGE ARTS CLASSROOM

6

Derek Whordley, PhD

Introduction

Technology is transforming how the language arts are taught. The language arts curriculum, designed and developed over the years, includes the content areas of reading, writing, speaking, listening, viewing, and visual expression. The transformation currently underway has been fueled by the enormous growth of the World Wide Web and educational software. Learning is no longer constrained by printed materials, as the language arts become more accessible across cyberspace. Electronic books from classical and contemporary authors are readily available. The application of theories and practices throughout the English-speaking world is dispensed for real-time consideration. Students entering online writing communities examine the virtual works of peers in other states and other languages. Numerous sources of information support the development of a more literate population.

Historical Evolution of Language Arts-Based Technologies

Classroom teachers historically follow the linear, rigid scope and sequence format of the language arts textbook, an approach often described as a scope and sequence system. The step-by-step regimen challenged early learners to explore new ways of spelling, building vocabulary, comprehending sentence and paragraph structures, communicating with authors, writing more effectively, and reading from an ever-growing array of resources.

The effect of evolving technologies on the study of language arts across grade levels has been exciting and thought provoking, and often formidable and chaotic. For the alert teacher, agile in making curriculum changes, willing to take new initiatives for the improvement of instruction, and open to new thinking, advances in technology have been extraordinarily positive.

Not so long ago, chalkboards, books, handouts, worksheets, and illustrative visual aids were primary vehicles supporting students in their journey toward fluency in reading and language arts. Veterans of the pre-1960s classroom remember their introduction to educational radio, touted to advance the listening and learning pleasures of children. Solid thinking skills were widely considered keys to good reading comprehension; a "truth" confirmed by researchers who claimed to measure such things.

Tape recorders revolutionized the 1960s classroom. They represented something close to sorcery, or at least mysticism, as they wheeled endless reels of captured voices and returned them to the anxious listener. Students thought their own voices sounded "funny." For teachers of the decade, technology literacy consisted of reading books onto audiotapes in an attempt to develop listening and reading stations for "read along" activities in order to help students achieve higher recreational or instructional reading levels. These new technical skills accommodated individual differences in reading achievement and interests and attitudes, improved the pronunciation of words, and practiced what teachers called "putting more expression into it." Neighborhood dialects and colloquialisms began to fade as one classroom language merged in phonological elegance.

In the 1970s, typewriters were integrated into secondary business or typing classrooms. Older students destined for the humanities or social services were introduced to a research regimen that called for library reference sections filled with microfilm, microfiche, and index cards. Now, of course, there are online search engines, CD-ROM-based journals, and digitized encyclopedias to speed our inquiries.

Technological change continued to evolve, as the ability of computers to convey and share information rapidly began to affect the classroom. After all, reading and English language arts, ultimately, are merely methods of receiving language through the spoken words of others, text processed by the act of reading, and speech and writing expressed via language.

James Burke in *The Knowledge Web* (1999) showed historical and contemporary examples of how issues, inventions, phenomena, and people are connected. He imagined that, ultimately, "agents," i.e., electronic tools, will be found to shape information to the needs of individuals. "Above all they will journey across the knowledge webs to retrieve information, then process and present it in ways customized to suit the user. In time, they will act on behalf of their user because they will have learned his or her preferences by learning from the user's daily requirements" (p. 22).

With the advent of word processing, writing research reports turned into a cut, copy, and paste operation. Available technology instantly converts the spoken word into digital media and then into print. Advanced spell checking and grammar correction eliminate misspelled words and passive voice (theoretically, at least). The end of writing in dialects is predicted, as future programs convert text automatically to standard American English. Reading, writing, speaking, listening, viewing, and visual expression become an extension not so much of a student's capacity to think but the ability to point and click.

Standards for Technology in Language Arts

The National Council of Teachers of English and the International Reading Association developed a background paper on technology in the language arts as far back as 1966. The document is still referenced by the International Society for Technology in Education in its National Standards for Technology in Teacher Preparation (2000). In cross referencing two of its standards, the ISTE document notes:

- Standard 7: "Students conduct research on issues and interests by generating ideas and questions, and by posing problems. They gather, evaluate, and synthesize data from a variety of sources (e.g., print and nonprint texts, artifacts, people) to communicate their discoveries in ways that suit their purpose and audience."

- Standard 8: "Students use a variety of technological and informational resources (e.g., libraries, databases, computer networks, video) to gather and synthesize information and to create and communicate knowledge" (p. 34).

ISTE also describes "Performance Indicators for Technology-Literate Students" and offers several examples of technologies for use across the K–12 curriculum. The technologies cited reinforce, supplement, and sometimes replace more traditional approaches to instruction. In the primary grades, ISTE proposes that students use a variety of technological and information sources to "gather in" knowledge. They assume a level of competency with respect to multimedia authoring and presentation, teacher-identified Web sites, plus video camcorders, television, videocassette recorders, and compact disks. At higher grades, students might also learn how to plan electronic meetings, contribute to online conferences, and post work on the school's Web site.

From Grades 3 to 5, ISTE anticipates that language arts students will build on a primary skill set through practical applications of Web sites, electronic encyclopedias, and e-texts. By Grade 5, the presentation of projects using multimedia is expected, as word processing, multimedia authoring, and video production are integrated into thematic projects.

Middle school students add digital cameras and scanners, hypertext, electronic journals, animations, graphic software, and rubrics for electronic presentations to their repertoire of technology competencies. High school students employ presentation software, produce films, compare qualities of visual representations, and burn personal CD-ROM portfolios.

Technology standards, in general, and literacy skills, in particular, continue to evolve as technologies change. The Province of Alberta, Canada, described a series of Guiding Principles for Information Technology (http://www.ednet.edc.gov.ab.ca/technology/) and lists as its standards: technology integration, student learning and instruction, staff supports, responsible use, technology planning, data and information, hardware and software, networking and telecommunications, and applications software and systems.

Already, there are struggles to determine how broad or narrow standards should be. Yet, for many schools, standards remain elusive because of the unevenness of funding technologies. In the *Digital Divide* (2000), Bolt and Crawford noted:

> The majority of public schools still don't have directly allocated funds for telecommunications and don't have adequate infrastructure to support the technology being touted and dispensed by the computer industry and the government. Of the remaining schools, most do not have adequate funds for the maintenance and support of the equipment that they have managed to obtain. Even if adequate provision has been made for this (and it rarely is), the seemingly insurmountable obstacle of integrating this mass of equipment into a meaningful curriculum—including the significant teacher training required—still looms large (pp. 26–27).

It also remains difficult to establish standards for technology for reading and the language arts until teachers become more familiar with technology. Bolt and Crawford continued:

The picture remains bleak. In 1999, the Department of Education published the results of a survey of over thirty-five hundred of the nation's educators that asked about their facility with computer technology. Of those interviews, only about 20 percent reported that they were "very well prepared" in using computer technology in the classroom, although approximately four-fifths of the educators indicated that they had some training in computers and related technology (p. 29).

Finally, the authors of the *Digital Divide* had a great deal to say about the absence of Internet access among American minorities:

Computer ownership among European-American households is 46.6 percent, while the rate for minority groups like Latinos is only 25.5 percent. African-American and Latino households are less than half as likely as European-American families to have Internet access anywhere—on the job, at home, or in school (p. 97).

From the perspective of social justice, equality, quality issues, economics, and politics, it is hard to imagine standards that foster exclusive rather than inclusive learning environments. Alternatively, the rate of technological change may make it impossible to develop acceptable standards for literacy across society as a whole. Derrick deKerckhove in *The Skin of Culture* (1997) explained:

Our one-way, frontal relationship with the TV screen ushered in mass culture. The computer screen, introducing two-way inter-active modalities, added speed. The effect of integrated hypermedia will be total immersion. We are at the brink of a new depth culture that is now taking shape during the nineties. Every time the emphasis on a given medium changes, the whole culture shifts (p. 123).

Perhaps notions of standards in literacy will emerge piecemeal. For example, there are attempts to standardize citations from electronic documents, format documents for online publication, and attend to variances in personal writing styles. Even here, Walker and Taylor, in authoring *The Columbia Guide to Online Style* (1998), begin their preface with the following:

> All standards and guides to style, whether aimed at print or other media, necessarily suffer from the problem of trying to regiment the intractable. This book, then, attempts to achieve the apparently impossible: to provide an authoritative guide to the world of online writing and publishing, a world that continues to morph at such a rate that establishing standards may seem impossible or even deplorable (Preface).

It is possible to gain a sense of standards from Bonine and Pohlman's *Writing for the New Media* (1998). They suggested that, to write for interactive media and the Web, certain "tools" are helpful, including flow charting, software, word-processing programs, drawing and painting programs, interactive authoring programs, presentation programs, and programs to help the writer organize (pp. 89–93).

Brunner and Talley (1999) proposed a middle ground in their text, *The New Media Literacy Handbook*. They posited several important points. First, in a section on language arts standards and the new mediate, they noted:

> It is becoming increasingly clear that a critical reading of a multimedia production requires new concepts and that competent multimedia hypertext writing requires a new set of authoring skills (p. 125).

Second, they examined online books and suggested that:

> Standards-based language arts instruction expects a relationship to these texts, a more authentic way of allowing students to engage with them. The nature of the digital medium itself — the fact that the texts can literally be manipulated (copies, pasted, excerpted, altered, revised, annotated, illustrated)—offers a range of new opportunities for constructive engagement with them (pp. 127–128).

Third, they considered digital writing, collaborative writing, and e-links:

> Computer programs now allow multiple users to connect to a shared set of virtual rooms and interact with one another in real time through a universal set of commands (p. 151).

Perhaps standards in literacy will emerge from a student viewpoint concerning how the language arts should be taught. Perhaps students should set the standards for technology in literacy. In *Growing Up Digital* (1998), Tapscott noted, "for the first time ever, children are taking control of critical elements of a communications revolution" (p. 26). And later, he noted:

> As children interact with each other and the exploding information resources on the Net, they are forced to exercise not only their critical thinking but their judgment. This process is contributing to the relentless breakdown of the notion of authority and experience-driven hierarchies. Increasingly, young people are the masters of the interactive environment and of their own fate in it (p. 26).

More than a few noted authors suggested that children continue to assume leadership roles in all aspects of technology; language arts has the potential of being affected as much as any other traditional school subject.

Educational Software for the Language Arts Classroom

Introduction

It is uncertain whether anyone really knows which electronic media is best, be it commercially prepared, shared, or free educational software. Even research in the language arts offers little help. Precious little software links to national or state standards for reading and writing (although a case can be made that some of it matches coincidentally). Teachers are often left to their own devices to locate, evaluate, and select appropriate educational software to advance reading, writing, speaking, listening, viewing, and visual expression in their classroom.

Evaluation Classifications

Evaluating language arts software includes the following important criteria.

> **Software Methodology:** This methodology includes the learning objectives of the package and its ease of use. Important questions embrace the following: What does the program claim to help learners achieve? Does the program facilitate or hinder instruction? Does the software address the learning strategies of most students? How easy is the software to use and troubleshoot (by student and teacher)?

> **Approach to Language Arts Instruction:** What linguistic assumptions does the software make, and are they valid for the target classroom? Does the software support one of the accepted methods of language teaching (e.g., Direct Approach, Audio-Lingual Method, the Natural Approach, etc.)?

> **Design:** Does the program integrate information about culture with literature and daily situations? Does the software

consider different educational psychologies of learning, such as behavioral (recognition, recall, comprehension), cognitive (experiential learning and constructive understanding), and humanistic (using technology as a tool for discovery)? How does the program track student progress?

Procedures: Does the software offer a range of activities? Does the software offer a selection of possible correct responses (where appropriate)? How much control does the software afford learners and instructors over the content of the lessons?

Language arts software is also represented by two of the four common forms of educational software: drill and practice and tutorials. Particularly useful for language competencies (reading and writing), drill and practice software offers students rehearsal lessons on skills such as the alphabet, vocabulary, spelling and grammar, and visualization skills. Designed primarily to increase reading and retention rates, some language arts tutorials offer interactive reading and diagnostic assessment tools to help teachers detect learning disabilities unique to language acquisition and development.

Rubric for Evaluating Language Arts Software

Educational software for the language arts runs the gamut from distinguished to advanced, from basic to novice, to unacceptable. Distinguished software includes lessons with rich development of topics and ideas, careful organization with respect to accepted standards, vivid and effective details, effective use of language and images, and sophisticated control of sentences, grammar, usage, and mechanics. Advanced software sports similar capabilities with a lesser degree of success. Novice packages evidence a more limited development of topics and ideas with a lack of supporting details; an unclear focus with random organization, frequent and serious errors in wording, sentence structure, and mechanics; and, grammatical use that sometimes interferes with student understanding. The following rubric (Table 1) considers these important components of language arts software. The rubric may be revised to reflect the language arts teacher's predilection for reading, writing, speaking, listening, viewing, and visual expression.

Table 1. Rubric for Evaluating Language Arts Software (10 = Outstanding; 8 = Very Good; 6 = Acceptable; 4 = Satisfactory; and 2 = Weak)

	10	8	6	4	2
Methodology (100 Points Possible)					
Software helps learners achieve success by making learning easier					
Software offers exercises that are supplementary to what is being taught in class already					
Software provides information the instructor cannot or lacks time to provide					
Software frees class time for new information by providing extra practice and enrichment opportunities outside class hours					
Package includes well-written instruction manual and documentation					
Software lessons open quickly and easily					
Learner moves from lesson to lesson easily while saving work					
Software functions are self-explanatory and based on an intuitive set of rules or user instructions					
Learner receives informative, immediate, constructive feedback from responses					
Software judges user responses according to content area standards and accepted scope and sequence of instruction					
Approach to Language Arts Instruction (40 Points Possible)					
Software is based on a structural/functional/interactive approach to language arts instruction					
Software approaches language arts learning as different from other types of learning					
Software supports an identified method of language teaching (the Direct Approach, the Audio-Lingual Method, the Natural Approach, etc.) that matches the instructor's teaching style					
Software is available on a variety of platforms (MS-DOS, Macintosh, Windows, Windows '95, others)					
Design (60 Points Possible)					
Software offers remedial and enrichment exercises geared toward or adjustable for any of these learner variables: • Age • Field-dependent/-independent reasoning • Sex • Deductive/inductive reasoning • Native language • Visual-graphic • Visual-textual learning • Student interests • Auditory or kinesthetic learning • Specific learning needs • Introverted versus extroverted learners • High and low tolerance of ambiguity					

Table 1. Rubric for Evaluating Language Arts Software (10 = Outstanding; 8 = Very Good; 6 = Acceptable; 4 = Satisfactory; and 2 = Weak) (continued)

Learning exercises are designed and arranged on a progressing scale of difficulty				
Software considers different educational psychologies of learning, such as behavioral (recognition, recall, comprehension), cognitive (experiential learning and constructive understanding), and humanistic (using technology as a tool for discovery)				
Software focuses on objective discourse/text, syntax, lexis, morphology, graphology/phonology, or a combination of any of these				
Exercises can be worked in pairs or groups of students as well as individually				
Color, graphics, and sound necessary or important to the efficiency of the exercises are appropriate for the learning environment				
Procedure (30 Points Possible)				
Identify the types of activities offered by the software. • Games • Text construction • Quizzes • Text reconstruction • Simulation • Problem solving • Tutorial • Drill-and-practice • Exploratory activities				
Software anticipates learner responses by offering information on commonly made mistakes, frequent misspellings, etc.				
The learner or instructor is provided some measure of control over the content and presentation of the lessons				
TOTAL POINTS AWARDED (230 Points Possible)				
Software package is rated as: ____ **Distinguished** ____ **Advanced** ____ **Basic** ____ **Novice** ____ **Unacceptable**				

Examples of Best Educational Software

The most appropriate educational software for language arts involves drill and practice; tutorial runs a close second. Particularly useful for language competencies, drill and practice software offers students trial lessons on skills such as reading, vocabulary, spelling, and visualization. Language arts, in particular, demands software that presents information appropriate for a particular audience, because its subject matter is so age dependent. The best educational software provides clear directions for the learner and uses content-appropriate vocabulary. It provides online help options and positive, corrective, and, again, age appropriate feedback. Practice involves repetition on a progressively more complex scale that assesses student learning at every turn.

The best in tutorial software is designed from its inception to fuse the language arts skills of reading, writing, speaking, listening, viewing, and visual expression. A solid tutorial provides appropriate instructional prompts and varies its responses to student efforts. Student control of the lesson enhances learning; assessment is paramount. A listing of some of the best programs for language arts is found in Table 2.

Table 2. Best Language Arts Software

Title	Publisher	Audience	Language Arts Category	Evaluation Score/ Rating	Comments
The Treehouse	Borderbund Software Inc.	Primary	Writing	M = 90 A = 40 D = 45 P = 25 Total = 200 **Advanced**	Package including computer programs and Teacher's Guide with lesson plans for language arts sentence-building skills
Grammar Games	Davidson & Associates, Inc.	Grades 4–7	Reading, writing	M = 100 A = 40 D = 55 P = 30 Total = 225 **Distinguished**	Package including computer programs and Teacher's Guide with lesson plans and writing activities; computer game offers five different forms of a 30-question diagnostic test to help place the student; has three levels of difficulty with four different games
Bailey's Bookhouse	Edmark Corporation	Grades K–3; also good for school's beginning ESL population	Reading, writing, and listening	M = 95 A = 40 D = 55 P = 20 Total = 210 **Advanced**	Package including computer programs and Teacher's Guide with language arts activities; five different games; word meaning and recognition; recognizing upper and lower case letters, builds vocabulary; creates stories, completes rhymes
The Writing Center	The Learning Company	Grades 4–7	Writing, visual, and expression	M = 90 A = 30 D = 40 P = 30 Total = 190 **Advanced**	Teaches how to create documents, including page setup, text, and graphics; this program shows sample documents, includes templates, and gives helpful hints for creating a properly organized and attractive document
The Rosetta Stone	Fairfield Language Technologies	ESL and those learning basic French, Spanish, or German	Reading, listening, and viewing	M = 70 A = 25 D = 30 P = 25 Total = 150 **Basic**	Each language is taught at two levels with 11 lessons in each level, with pictures, words, and voice
Stepping Stones 1, Stepping Stones 2	CompuTeach	Grades K–3 and ESL beginners	Listening, viewing, and visual expression	M = 60 A = 30 D = 30 P = 20 Total = 140 **Basic**	Each level has three categories in which to choose games from: Reading, Math, and Language; the program works with words spoken, written, and represented with pictures
Kids Works 2	Davidson & Associates, Inc.	Grades K–3 and ESP beginners	Reading, writing, listening, viewing, and visual expression	M = 100 A = 40 D = 60 P = 30 Total = 230 **Distinguished**	This program allows the user to choose from four options that write, think, and talk; it uses simple icons specifically designed for a younger audience; the four options include story writer, story illustrator, story player, and icon maker

Note. M = Methodology, A = Approach to Language Arts Instruction, D = Design, and P = Procedures.

Additional Software for the Language Arts

Numerous Web sites incorporate the judgments of language arts practitioners. For example, indexed reviews are available at http://www.superkids.com; the reviews of books, music, and videos rated by age and developmental levels at http://www.smarterkids.com; and analyses of special interest to children ages six to 12 at http://www.childrenssoftware.com. These sites reference software across the curricula of schools and are cross referenced to the Children's Software Review at http://www.childrenssoftware.com.

There are also sites that offer more specific assessments of language arts and reading software. From http://www.teachers.teach.nology.com, there are quick links of literacy software and specific references to English as a Second Language products. An extensive site from California links literacy and technology via http://www.campus.fortunecity.com/newton/40/literacy.html.

The World Wide Web gives educators access to thinking about language arts across the English-speaking world. Teachers in Canada, Australia, New Zealand, South Africa, and other nations that accept English as an official language face similar issues to those found in American schools. Two British sites are worthy of special notice. The Virtual Teacher Center identifies educational software databases across subjects and age groups at http://www/vgc.ngfl.gov.uk. The British Broadcasting Corporation has a magnificent site to explore literacy learning across age groups and content areas at http://www.bbc.co.uk/education/home. A number of school districts have incorporated the Accelerated Reader or Star Reading from Renaissance Learning Software found at http://www/renlearn.com/reading.htm. The Computer Curriculum Corporation provides software for literature-based reading in Grades 1 and 2 and may be reviewed at http://www.ccc.learn.com. Software products are demonstrated by EduHound at http://www.eduhound.com and downloaded at CNET.com at http://download.cnet/downloads.

Internet Use in the Language Arts Classroom

Introduction

One problem with Web sites is that they keep disappearing. Does anyone have an idea where they go? My surfing eccentricities were fueled by reading pieces of Shetlandic and Orcadian from the islands north of Scotland. Alas, many of these sites have sunk into the North Atlantic, and new ones have surfaced to take their place. In 1996, Nicholas Negroponte wrote that "Web sites are doubling every fifty days. A new home page comes online every few seconds." They are probably proliferating even faster now.

A Rubric for Evaluating Language Arts Web Sites

To be effective as language arts teaching and learning tools, Web sites should address not only content information pertaining to reading, writing, speaking, listening, viewing, and visual expression, but also how these areas integrate with other online material. For example, users expect a language arts site to provide instruction. The best Web sites also use reading, writing, speaking, listening, viewing, and visual expression to <u>present</u> the material. A home page must excite the student while simultaneously addressing the language arts standards targeted. Multimedia resources, such as sound, video, and images, are integrated into the best sites to enhance student understanding of the information presented. Table 3 suggests a rubric for assessing the best sites.

Table 3. Rubric for Evaluating Language Arts Web Sites

Category	Criteria	20 Points	10 Points	0–5 Points
Identify the Primary Content of the Web Site and Score Only the Major Focus of the Site				
Content: reading	Information presented appears to be accurate, complete, and current.			
Content: writing	Information presented appears to be accurate, complete, and current.			
Content: speaking	Information presented appears to be accurate, complete, and current.			
Content: listening	Information presented appears to be accurate, complete, and current.			
Content: viewing	Information presented appears to be accurate, complete, and current.			
Content: visual expression	Information presented appears to be accurate, complete, and current.			

	Rate the Following Criteria Separately			
Category	Criteria	20 Points	10 Points	0–5 Points
Content	Directed at students with only higher- or lower-level abilities			
Content	Little accommodation for varying ability levels			
Content	Simple recall required			
Maximum 80 Points				
Method: project introduction	Home page excites the student and introduces the overall language arts standards of the site.			
Method: quality	This site is interesting to read and holds the student's attention. Writing is simple, clear, and direct.			
Method: navigation	This site is easy to navigate. Use of links and menus makes it clear how to continue to explore language arts.			
Maximum 60 Points				
Structure: effective overall design theme	Pages are easy to follow with a consistent design theme. Colors, backgrounds, and text are easy to read and create a pleasant viewing experience.			
Structure: multimedia resources	Multimedia resources, such as sound, video, and images, contribute to objectives of the site and enhance student understanding of the information presented.			
Maximum 40 Points				
Technical: pages load efficiently	Images and text load quickly even with slow modem speeds. Pages work in a variety of Web browsers.			
Technical: links to other sites	All links to internal and external Web sites and files work properly.			
Technical: Internet browsers	Site tries to accommodate different browsers, platforms, and systems capabilities.			
Maximum 60 Points				
Maximum 240 Points				

Examples of Best Web Sites for Teaching Language Arts

The best Web sites for teaching language arts turn the tables on educational software, placing tutorials ahead of drill and practice in importance. There are probably as many language arts Web sites for teachers as there are for students. Collections of thematic units and online step-by-step lesson plans in reading, writing, listening, speaking, grammar, and other language arts areas represent the majority of Web sites found. Table 4 provides examples of some excellent Web sites for language arts content and tools.

Table 4. Best Web Sites for Teaching Language Arts

Title/ URL	Target/ Focus	Evaluation Score	Comments
Animate Your World learning.turner.com/animate/how.html	Student Reading, writing, visual expression	C = 75 M = 50 S = 40 T = 50 Total = 215	This provides a collection of thematic creative writing activities for middle grade students. These activities do not require elaborate materials or intensive preparation and can be used without the videos. Each activity includes a reproducible worksheet that can be printed and distributed for classroom use.
Biography Maker www.bham.wednet.edu /bio/biomaker. htm	Teacher Writing, speaking, listening	C = 60 M = 50 S = 35 T = 50 Total = 195	This provides online step-by-step lessons to help middle school students write biographies. The lessons include questioning, learning, synthesis, and storytelling activities, and a list of great explorers and other biography resources.
Classic Literature of the Western World CyberSchool.4j. lane.edu/People/ Faculty/Bragg/ CLWW1/ CLWW1.html	Students Reading, writing	C = 80 M = 50 S = 40 T = 30 Total = 200	This site provides 11 lessons in which students read and analyze classical literature, learning about important authors and their works from that historical period. Written assignments include literary analysis essays and college-preparatory research papers. These lessons can be used with any AP English class.
Creating a Classroom Newspaper www.calgaryherald.com/educa/ CACNINTRO.html	Students Writing, visual expression	C = 80 M = 60 S = 30 T = 50 Total = 220	This provides reading and writing activities for integrating journalism into the language arts curriculum. The site features an online "A Teacher's Guide" with lesson plans, student worksheets, a newspaper glossary, and other useful materials for creating a classroom newspaper in Grades 6–12.
Linguistics Lesson Plans humanities.byu.edu/linguistics/ henrichsen/ 577Syllabus/LessonPlans.html	Teachers Reading, writing, speaking, listening	C = 80 M = 50 S = 20 T = 40 Total = 190	This site contains a collection of over 45 plans in reading, writing, listening, speaking, grammar, and other language arts areas for Grades 6–12.
Write Site www.writesite.org/	Students Reading, writing, visual expression	C = 60 M = 55 S = 25 T = 30 Total = 170	This site, developed by Greater Dayton Public Television for the middle school language arts curriculum, has students take the role of reporters and editors to research, write, and publish their own newspaper. The site includes unit outlines, student handouts, exercises, how to write materials, and much more.
PIGS in Cyberspace cspace.unb.ca/nbco/pigs /modules/	Students Reading, writing, listening, speaking	C = 70 M = 60 S = 40 T = 60 Total = 230	This project features cooperative lesson plan modules developed by teachers for Grades 4–8. The language arts module contains plans for reading, writing, listening and speaking, rapid reinforcers, and novels. Each lesson provides activities, enrichment suggestions, and Internet activities that can be adapted to any classroom situation.

Note. C = Content; M = Method; S = Structure; and T = Technical.

Other World Wide Web Sites for Language Arts Educators

Given all of this coming and going, it is wise counsel to remain grounded in a global framework of the language arts. The following sites demonstrate how two different governments view the challenges of reading and language arts in their English-speaking worlds.

For the **United States**, the following sites offer a national picture:

- http://www/ed.gov/free/s-lamart.html describes federal resources for educational excellence in the language arts and includes links to the America Reads Challenge, the Alphabet Superhighway, the Center for the Improvement of Early Reading Achievement (CIERA), and the Campaign to Help Children with Learning Disabilities to Succeed.

- http://www/ed.gov/pubs/parents/Reading/Parents.htm offers endless suggestions of how parents may help their children to read.

- http://www/novel.nifl.gov/ describes an independent federal organization that is working toward a fully literate nation in the 21st century.

- http://PutmanValleySchools.org/standards.html proves that occasionally, the ultimate Web site can be found in an unexpected spot. Putnam Valley Schools in New York links the United States government, all 50 states, multiple standards by subject area in other nations, center clearinghouses and labs, and newspapers and magazines.

Moving across the Atlantic Ocean to the **United Kingdom**, alternative perspectives are found at the following sites:

- http://www.standards.dfee.gov.uk/literacy offers perspectives on national standards K–12 in reading and the language arts.

- http://www.yearofreading.org.uk/database is the National Literacy Trust's Web site and online database that covers a wide range of literacy issues and family literacy, research on literacy, children with special needs, and reading habits in the United Kingdom.

- http://www.literacytrust.org.uk considers the perspectives of pedagogy in its references to the Literacy Hour and Reading Recovery.

Other World Wide Web Sites for the Administration of Language Arts

At the next level of available Web sites, the administrative aspect of language arts is seen in the work of states, provinces, and counties. Of particular interest are the following sites:

- http://www.vcaa.vic.edu.au/ from **Victoria, Australia**, contains excellent ideas on the evaluation of writing.
- http://www.sdcoe.k12.ca.us/SCORE/stand/sbestd.html is the systematically organized language arts site for the state of **California**.
- http://www.tea.state.tx.us/technology is the site for the **Texas Education Agency**. They have developed one of the most comprehensive plans to integrate technology across all curricula, obviously including the English language arts and reading instruction.

From these administrative units, it is possible to move from macro to micro viewpoints via the school districts or local education authorities and toward the grassroots of individual school sites and the classrooms of individual teachers. Some favorites from around the world are as follows:

- http://www.langstone-jun.portsmouth.sch.uk/ is a comprehensive primary school site in England, which pays particular attention to literacy.
- http://ireland.iol.ie/~bmullets/ is the award-winning site of Inver National School in the Republic of Ireland, which pays close attention to reading and writing across the curriculum.

- http://www.ambleside.schoolzone.co.uk/ambleweb/local.htm is the site of another terrific English primary school, which is equally attentive to reading and writing across the curriculum.

Other Language Arts Web Sites from Professional Organizations

Of course, professional associations of teachers involved in literacy studies also provide theory, practice, standards, and research across age groups. Teachers are apprised of ongoing international activities at federal, state, and local levels. They also identify research leading to best practices in the language arts. These associations include the International Reading Association (http://www.reading.org), the National Council of Teachers of English (http://www.ncte.org), the National Center for Education and the Economy (http://ncee.org), special education groups interested in literacy as varied as the Coordinated Campaign for Learning Disabilities (http://www.ldonline.org/abcs_info/ articles-info.html) and the British Dyslexia Society (http://www.bda_dyslexia.org.UK) may also be identified.

Conclusions

The only element that is certain as technology becomes more embedded in literacy curricula is continued change. Hopefully, the opportunity to tailor curriculum to the needs, interests, and ability levels of children that technology makes possible, will continue to advance literacy standards. However, if technology is only used as an alternative method of delivering traditional work, significant changes in language arts standards is unlikely. Will teachers have the time, the courage, and the initiative to use what is best in technology to enhance the lives of their students and leave the rest?

References

Bolt, D., & Crawford, R. (2000). *Digital Divide: Computers and Our Children's Future.* New York: TV Books, LLC.

Bonime, A., & Pohlman, K. C. (1998). *Writing for New Media: The Essential Guide to Writing for Interactive Media, CD-ROMs, and the Web*. New York: John Wiley.

Brunner, C., & Tally, W. (1999). *The New Media Literacy Handbook: An Educator's Guide to Bringing New Media into the Classroom*. New York: Doubleday.

Burke, J. (1999). *The Knowledge Web: From Electronic Agents to Stonehenge and Back — Another Journey through Knowledge*. New York: Simon and Schuster.

DeKerckhove, D. (1997). *The Skin of Culture: Investigating the New Electronic Reality*. London: Kogan Page.

Derry, T.K., & Williams, T. I. (1961). *A Short History of Technology from the Earliest Times to AD 1900*. New York: Oxford University Press.

Eliot, V. (1971). *T.S. Eliot, The Waste Land: A Facsimile and Transcript of the Original Drafts Including the Annotations of Ezra Pound*. San Diego, CA: Harcourt Brace and Company.

Handy, C. (1995). *The Age of Unreason*. London: Random House Group, Ltd.

Henderson, B. (Ed.) (1996). *Minutes of the Lead Pencil Club: Pulling the Plug on the Electronic Revolution*. Wainscott, NY: Pushcart Press.

International Society for Technology in Education. (2000). *National Educational Technology Standards for Students: Connecting Curriculum and Technology*. Washington, DC.

Kelley, R. (1991). *The Power of Followership: How to Create Leaders People Want to Follow and Followers Who Lead Themselves*. New York: Doubleday.

Leadbeater, C. (1999). *Living on Their Air: The New Economy*. Harmondsworth, UK: Penguin Books, Ltd.

Luck, S. (Ed.) (1999). *Encyclopedia of Science and Technology*. New York: Oxford University Press.

Mulgan, G. (1997). *Connexity: How to Live in a Connected World*. London: Chatto and Windus.

Negroponte, N. (1996). *Being Digital.* New York: Vintage Books Division of Random House.

Phillips, R. (Ed.) (1997). *The Hand of the Poet.* New York: Rizzoli International Publications, Inc.

Postman, N. (1985). *Amusing Ourselves to Death: Public Discourse in the Age of Show Business.* New York, NY.

Rushkoff, D. (1999). *Playing the Future: What We Can Learn from Digital Kids.* New York: Penguin Putman.

Sale, K. (1995). *Rebels Against the Future: The Luddites and Their War on the Industrial Revolution: Lessons for the Computer Age.* Reading, MA: Addison-Wesley Publishing Company.

Sanger, J. et al. (1997). *Young Children, Videos, and Computer Games: Issues for Teachers and Parents.* London: The Falmer Press.

Shenk, D. (1997). *Data Smog: Surviving the Information Glut.* New York: Harper Collins Publisher.

Tapscott, D. (1998). *Growing Up Digital.* New York: McGraw Hill.

Walker, J. R., & Taylor, T. (1998). *The Columbia Guide to Online Style.* New York: Columbia University Press.

TECHNOLOGY IN THE FOREIGN LANGUAGES CLASSROOM

WILLIAM J. SWITALA, PhD

Introduction

The world is shrinking every day. Television, the Internet, and jet travel have put people from all over the globe in closer contact than ever before in history. Because of this close contact, customs, beliefs, and cultures are shared on a regular basis. The door has also opened for greater interaction and economic interdependence in the global economy. However, one of the major stumbling blocks in this globalization and cultural sharing is the fact that communication among people still depends on an understanding of each other's language, an understanding that entails the written, as well as, the spoken, word.

While English has become the *lingua franca* of today's business world, not everyone in the world speaks or understands it. One need only travel in a foreign land to realize that outside of tourist and business centers, few can carry on a conversation in basic English. Even those who have studied, or been required to study, English for many years cannot speak it with ease. Pronunciation of English words is a major problem when learning the language from nonnative speakers who, in turn, cannot pronounce English correctly. In addition, many English idioms and everyday expressions suffer greatly when translated into French, Japanese, or Russian. The same may be said for translating foreign idioms into English. Even among English-speaking foreign businesspeople, subtle nuances in contracts, or business deals, are sometimes misunderstood because of language inadequacies.

While many foreign countries require their children to study English, there is no such mandate in America. The study of foreign languages is woefully inadequate in the United States. In a recent survey conducted by the American Council on the Teaching of Foreign Languages (ACTFL), only 33% of the students in Grades 7 through 12 were studying a language other than English. This amounts to a little over 6 million students. Of these, 64.5% were studying Spanish, 22.3% were studying French, 6.1% German, 3.5% Latin, and only 1% were studying Japanese. In Japan, English is taught universally beginning in middle school. In the United States, although many begin taking Spanish, by their senior year of high school, the attrition rate is so great that only 8.6% are still in Spanish class (Schultz, 2001). This lack of skill in speaking a second language has put many American travelers and businesspeople at a disadvantage at times when going abroad.

Nothing pleases citizens of a foreign country more than a traveler who understands local customs and makes an attempt to communicate in the language of the place. As mentioned earlier, Spanish is second only to English as the major language spoken in the United States. Hispanic Americans are the fastest growing minority group in our country. Look north to Canada as evidence of the impact large linguistic minorities have on the culture of a country. It is not unreasonable to assume that in the not too distant future, the United States will officially become a bilingual nation in English and Spanish, similar to the case in Canada with English and French.

An examination of the current situation in the study of foreign languages in America leads one to conclude that much more needs to be done to encourage greater numbers of student to study other languages. In addition, much more work needs to be done in improving the way foreign languages are taught. Thirty years ago, the goal of foreign language study was to acquaint the student with enough vocabulary and grammar intricacies that they could have a degree of facility in reading a language. Speaking the language was secondary to reading it. The current philosophy in language instruction, however, is that learning to speak a language leads one to truly understand it. Typically, in a traditional classroom setting, the teacher calls on a student to respond to some query in the language being studied. For most students, classroom practice provides the sole opportunity to speak the language in the class. Projecting this approach over a 180-day school year results in the student being able to practice the language for less than 10 hours out of a total of 120 hours of instructional time. Clearly, every attempt must be made to increase the time of interaction using the language.

Historical Evolution of Foreign Languages-Based Technologies

Labs (1940), Computers (1980), and Distance Learning (1990)

Technology has been used to teach foreign languages for the past 60 years. Starting with the language labs of the U.S. military in World War II, the utilization of various technologies has increased steadily over that period of time. The period of 1950 to 1980 has been described as the "Age of Methods." The language labs with their interconnected tape recorders moved from the military setting to the high school language class. The approach known as "audio-lingualism," where the student imitated correct pronunciation by listening to native speakers on tape recordings, was commonly used in the 1960s and 1970s (Rodgers, 2001). During the 1980s, the development of language programs using videotapes came into vogue. The most famous of these was the Capritz series for learning the French language entitled "French in Action." Students learned how to speak French by watching a series of videos centered on the daily life of a French teenager in Paris. In the 1980s, we also witnessed the birth of the computer as a device to enhance the learning of foreign languages. Starting with simple vocabulary development programs, the application of this technology has grown into full-fledged learn-a-language programs, authoring programs for foreign language teachers, computerized language lab systems, and "smart classrooms," where the computer is combined with videotapes and videodiscs networked to provide language instruction in an effective manner (Earp, 2001). Finally, in the 1990s, the development and application of distance learning opportunities took place, with the advent of satellite dishes and language programs broadcast through this medium.

Today, there are numerous products on the market that support language labs, computers, and distance learning methodologies. Entire language acquisition programs are available through distance learning and computer-assisted instruction. It is possible to learn a host of new languages using such resources as satellite programming and CD-ROM technology. Contemporary publishers of textbooks, computer programs, online curriculum sites, and distance learning providers routinely provide ancillary computer disks. The impact of these technologies has been that most schools now claim verifiable increases in the effectiveness of their foreign language instruction.

Basic Instruction, Reinforcement, and Enrichment

The use of technologies in the foreign languages classroom has likewise evolved over the years to address basic language instruction, reinforcement of traditional teaching methods, and enrichment of advanced language programs.

Defined as the acquisition of a new language, basic instruction pertains to all of those technological possibilities through which students learn another language. The three most common technology methods for delivering instruction in a new language are via CD-ROM software, Internet Web site, and distance learning programs using broadband satellite transmission. Each of these has special requirements, advantages, disadvantages, and potentials.

Reinforcement addresses aspects of learning associated with review, reexamination, and establishing learned material to a greater depth. Its function is to increase the retention of the subject matter so that students perform better on examinations while developing a greater ability to apply the new knowledge in real-world situations. Reinforcement is especially important in the study of foreign languages where learning is cumulative. Student success in tomorrow's lesson depends on how the fundamentals of today's lesson have been mastered. Technology plays a major role in reinforcing material learned in standard foreign language courses. It focuses student attention and provides a greater degree of variety and excitement, which, in turn, helps retain important concepts and skills. Reinforcement via technology is exhibited in three major formats: software programs, including programs that accompany the basic textbook and those that are independent of the textbook series; the Internet; and satellite transmissions.

Enrichment is the technique of utilizing any device to make learning more vivid and interesting and, therefore, more likely to be retained longer. It goes beyond what is normally offered in the textbook or in class, often enriching a student's understanding of other cultures. There are an almost unlimited number of technological opportunities to enrich the teaching of foreign languages. Elements that discuss various cultural aspects of language often introduce the art, music, dress, and customs of people living there along with the history and geography of the land. Excursions and travelogues provide a vicarious experience and often engender a desire to know even more about the people and language. Enrichment opportunities prepare the student for the ultimate enhancement experience — a trip to the country under study. As in the case of using technology for basic instruction and reinforcement, these opportunities for enhancement include CD-ROM software, Internet sites, and satellite transmission.

Standards for Technology in Foreign Languages

Language and communication are at the heart of the human experience. The United States must educate students who are linguistically and culturally equipped to communicate success-fully in a pluralistic American society and abroad. This imperative envisions a future in which ALL students will develop and maintain proficiency in English and at least one other language, modern or classical. Children who come to school from non-English backgrounds should also have opportunities to develop further proficiencies in their first language (ACTFL Mission Statement, 2002).

Organizations such as the American Council on the Teaching of Foreign Languages (ACTFL) and the American Classical League have developed national standards for teaching foreign languages in the United States. The ultimate goal of these standards is to improve the quality of foreign language instruction. The standards are arranged into major strands known as the five "Cs": Communication, Cultures, Connections, Comparisons, and Communities. Summations of the key elements of the ACTFL (2001) standards are depicted in Table 1.

Table 1. National Standards for Teaching Foreign Languages

Strand	General Competency	Specific Standards	Suggested Technologies
Communication	Communicate in languages other than English	**Standard 1.1**: Students engage in conversations, provide and obtain information, express feelings and emotions, and exchange opinions.	Videoconferencing
		Standard 1.2: Students understand and interpret written and spoken language on a variety of topics.	Electronic mail
		Standard 1.3: Students present information, concepts, and ideas to an audience of listeners or readers on a variety of topics.	Video and graphic presentation
Cultures	Gain knowledge and understanding of other cultures	**Standard 2.1**: Students demonstrate an understanding of the relationship between the practices and perspectives of the culture studied.	Internet
		Standard 2.2: Students demonstrate an understanding of the relationship between the products and perspectives of the culture studied.	Graphic presentation
Connections	Connect with other disciplines and acquire information	**Standard 3.1**: Students reinforce and further their knowledge of other disciplines through the foreign language.	Internet
		Standard 3.2: Students acquire information and recognize the distinctive viewpoints that are only available through the foreign language and its culture.	CD-ROM software and listservs
Comparisons	Develop insight into the nature of language and culture	**Standard 4.1**: Students demonstrate understanding of the nature of language through comparisons of the language studied and their own.	Electronic mail and computer-assisted instruction
		Standard 4.2: Students recognize that cultures use different patterns of interaction and can apply this language to their own culture.	Digitized encyclopedias
Communities	Participate in multilingual communities at home and around the world	**Standard 5.1**: Students use the language within and beyond the school setting.	Internet
		Standard 5.2: Students show evidence of becoming lifelong learners by using the language for personal enjoyment and enrichment.	Newsgroups and desktop publishing

Note. Suggested technologies are taken from Table 4 ("Guide to Common Classroom Technologies," Chapter 1). From ACTFL, 2001.

In 1999, the ACTFL and other language-specific professional organizations expanded the initial 1996 publication of generic standards to include language-specific standards at the K–16 levels of instruction for nine languages. The *Standards for Foreign Language Learning in the 21st Century* (2002) build upon the original generic standards.

Table 2. Standards for Foreign Language Learning in the 21st Century

Standard	General Competencies	Specific Standards	Suggested Technologies
1. Language, linguistics, comparisons	**Standard 1a.** Demonstrating language proficiency	**Standard 1a.** Candidates demonstrate a high level of proficiency in the target language, and they seek opportunities to strengthen their proficiency.	Computer-assisted instruction
	Standard 1b. Understanding linguistics	**Standard 1b.** Candidates recognize the dynamic nature of language, they know the linguistic elements of the target language system, and they accommodate for any gaps in their own knowledge of the target language system by learning on their own.	Computer-assisted instruction
	Standard 1c. Identifying language comparisons	**Standard 1c.** Candidates know the similarities and differences between the target language and their native language, they identify the key differences in varieties of the target language, and they seek opportunities to learn about varieties of the target language on their own.	CD-ROM software
2. Cultures, literatures, cross-disciplinary	**Standard 2a.** Demonstrating cultural understandings	**Standard 2a.** Candidates demonstrate that they understand the connections among the perspectives of a culture and its practices and products, and they integrate this framework for viewing a culture into their instructional practices.	Video and video conferencing
	Standard 2b. Demonstrating understanding of literary texts and traditions	**Standard 2b.** Candidates recognize the value and role of literary texts and use them to interpret and reflect upon the perspectives of the target cultures over time.	Digitized encyclopedias
	Standard 2c. Integrating other disciplines in instruction	**Standard 2c.** Candidates integrate knowledge of other disciplines into foreign language instruction and identify distinctive viewpoints accessible only through the target language.	Graphic presentation
3. Language acquisition theories and instructional practices	**Standard 3a.** Language acquisition and creating supportive classroom	**Standard 3a.** Candidates demonstrate language acquisition and use this knowledge to create a supportive classroom learning environment that includes target language input and opportunities for negotiation of meaning and meaningful interaction.	Graphic presentation
	Standard 3b. Developing instructional practices that reflect language acquisition and learner diversity	**Standard 3b.** Candidates develop a variety of instructional practices that reflect language acquisition theories and models and address the needs of diverse language learners.	Graphic presentation, word processing, and World Wide Web

Table 2. Standards for Foreign Language Learning in the 21st Century (continued)

4. Integration of standards into curriculum and instruction	**Standard 4a.** Understanding and integrating standards in planning **Standard 4b.** Integrating standards in instruction **Standard 4c.** Selecting and designing instructional materials	**Standard 4a.** Candidates demonstrate an understanding of the goal areas and standards of the Standards for Foreign Language Learning, and they integrate the framework into curricular planning. **Standard 4b.** Candidates integrate the Standards for Foreign Language Learning into language instruction. **Standard 4c.** Candidates use standards and curricular goals to evaluate, select, design, and adapt instructional resources.	Problem solving, simulation, and tutorial instructional media
5. Assessment of languages and cultures	**Standard 5a.** Knowing assessment models and using them appropriately **Standard 5b.** Reflecting on assessment **Standard 5c.** Reporting assessment results	**Standard 5a.** Candidates believe that assessment is ongoing, and they demonstrate knowledge of multiple ways of assessment that are age and level appropriate by implementing purposeful measures. **Standard 5b.** Candidates reflect on the results of student assessments, adjust instruction accordingly, and analyze the results of assessments. They use success and failure to determine the direction of instruction. **Standard 5c.** Candidates interpret and report the results of student performances to all stakeholders and provide opportunity for discussion.	
6. Professionalism	**Standard 6a.** Engaging in professional development **Standard 6b.** Knowing the value of foreign language learning	**Standard 6a.** Candidates engage in professional development opportunities that strengthen their linguistic and cultural competence and promote reflection on practice. **Standard 6b.** Teacher candidates know the value of foreign language learning to the overall success of all students and understand that they will need to become advocates with students, colleagues, and members of the community to promote the field.	Electronic mail and newsgroups

Note. Suggested technologies are taken from Table 1.4 ("Guide to Common Classroom Technologies," Chapter 1). From NCATE, 2002.

Foreign Language standards have a technology strand that is interwoven throughout the other strands. In addition to the above applications, the National Standards for Foreign Languages specifically state that students should be instructed in the means of using new technologies in the learning of foreign languages. The standards say that students should develop the ability to use "interactive video, CD-ROM, the Internet, electronic mail and the World Wide Web." They are to use these technologies to learn languages, reinforce their knowledge of the languages they are studying, interact with peers, and enhance their understanding of the people, cultures, and countries of target languages (ACTFL, 1999).

Clearly, standards emphasize the acquisition of speaking and comprehension skills; understanding the language and culture that produced it is paramount. Technologies, as referenced in these standards, become a prominent vehicle through which students may acquire these skills.

Educational Software for the Foreign Languages Classroom

Introduction

One of the most common technologies methods for teaching foreign languages in the classroom is software, primarily CD-ROM based. There are a number of software programs on the market today that enable a student to learn a new language. There are a number of important criteria to consider when selecting software for foreign language instruction; five stand out as most important for preparing technology-based instruction.

Evaluation Classifications

Content, management, ease of use, general design, and mode of instruction provide the structure for assessing foreign language software. An examination of context ensures the software is accurate, appropriate to the age level and cognitive abilities of the students, and stimulates higher-order thinking. Management criteria include teacher support, integration of assessment, adjustment to ability levels, and additional learning support material. Ease of use centers on student interaction with the software and the ability to navigate within the content without returning to a main menu or using options appropriate for beginners. Even software containing excellent content material fails in light of poor construction. Software packages designed by language teachers are much more prone to success than those created by technical experts and computer curriculum designers. Finally, a solid software package provides detailed instructional material such as reviews, hard-copy study sheets, and teacher lesson plans.

Basic Instruction

There are two fundamental ways of using this resource to teach a new language. First, students are grouped in a lab setting and share instruction. A school district may choose to use this approach instead of purchasing a textbook series, in which case, a teacher certified in the language should always be available to supervise learning. This teacher should also know how to operate and troubleshoot the lab computers. A lab aide may be necessary to insure that the software operates properly and time is not wasted with computer malfunctions. The teacher must receive the required training in the operation of the software and the methodology employed in its instructional aims. A second possible way to use the software is for students to learn new language skills in an independent, self-paced environment. Students learn the language outside the school's existing curriculum. Teachers act as mentors using the software, meeting with these students on a regular basis to review progress and discuss difficulties. They also certify that the student has completed the program in a satisfactory manner and, in some states, validate credits toward graduation. In cases where students are studying foreign languages not offered in the school, mentors are appointed who act as general supervisors for the instruction. The mentor does not need to know the language, but rather insures that all the procedures have been followed, which is especially important when taking examinations. While it is preferred that the mentor be a foreign language teacher on staff who knows the cognitive processes for learning a language, this is not an absolute necessity. In some cases, where a gifted student as part of an Individualized Educational Plan studies a language, the coordinator of gifted education serves as the mentor. A key advantage to using educational software is the ability of students to proceed at their own pace, independent of other students. The major disadvantage for students studying alone is the lack of interaction during practice, especially while speaking the language. Some schools solve this dilemma by grouping several students together in small clusters.

Reinforcement

Today, most foreign language textbook series come with a well-developed package of ancillary materials. These materials typically come in a large plastic crate and range from reproducible masters to computer software. They are comprehensive and have increased in their ability to help teachers teach their subject more effectively and efficiently. Usually, software ancillaries address assessment and reinforcement. Frequently, a computerized test bank provides chapter, unit, and final summative examinations. In most cases, teachers select questions from the test bank to create questions correlated to classroom learning objectives. Scoring, test item analysis, and grading are processed in a remarkably short period of time.

The second type of ancillary includes reinforcement exercises, typically arranged by objectives that track student progress through the lesson. Almost invariably, they contain drill and practice exercises, vocabulary development, and reviews of grammar and idiomatic expressions as well as materials that require the student to manipulate objects or statements to accomplish the assigned tasks. Sound is inherent in good educational software and usually consists of the correct pronunciation of the foreign terms and phrases used in the activity as well as some indicator of success or failure as students complete the task. In some cases, reinforcement software includes a tutorial for those who do not respond sufficiently to the formative questions. A final feature includes a self-test component that allows students to check personal progress and determine how well they have mastered the material and how well they are prepared for the examination.

There are several techniques and options to consider when using software to reinforce a foreign language curriculum. Similar to the discussion earlier of using software programs for basic instruction, two possibilities exist for using software to reinforce what is taught in a traditional, textbook-oriented, foreign language classroom. Software may be used in a lab setting or on stand-alone computers. In the lab setting, the software would reinforce basic instruction material, perhaps with the entire class present.

Activities would become part of the instruction and include both types of reinforcement programs: those that come with the textbook, and those that are independent of the text. The teacher should be present in the lab to monitor student work and to offer help wherever needed. A computer lab aide is also recommended. The stand-alone computer option is an excellent way to reinforce students with particular needs or problems. Such software is best used to upGrade the skills or understandings of a student having deficiencies or with students who would benefit from the opportunity for acceleration.

Enhancement

Software programs make up the largest source of enhancement opportunities for the average foreign language teacher. There are a great number of packages on the market that present stimulating and attention-holding offerings. The general techniques for using software packages to enhance foreign language learning are similar to those discussed for basic instruction and reinforcement. If the material is of value to the whole class, a lab configuration with a file server, or a network, is recommended. Individuals, or small groups of students, might work on an individual computer to complete a research assignment that could be shared with the rest of the class. Gifted students in a foreign language class might use one of these programs for acceleration. If the choice is to use a lab setting, teacher supervision is a must. If the individual or small group approach is used, it is a good idea to require some type of written report related to the program being viewed to help focus student attention and keep students on task.

Rubric for Evaluating Foreign Language Software

Software for teaching foreign languages is discussed according to its application as basic instruction, reinforcement, and enrichment. To better judge the quality of educational software appropriate for foreign language classrooms, Table 3 offers an easy-to-use rubric containing criteria and suggested points for assessing the key elements of Content, Management, Ease of Use, General Design, and Mode of Instruction.

Table 3. Criteria for Evaluating Foreign Language Software

Criteria	0–10 Points	11–20 Points	21–30 Points
Content	Program has accuracy problems	Program has minimal errors in facts	Program is accurate and factual
	Student attention wanders	Holds student attention	Students display enthusiasm with program
	Does not fit age or level of students	Has some flaws in age or level appropriateness	Program is age and level appropriate
	Simple recall required	Stimulates lower levels of Bloom's taxonomy	Stimulates upper levels of Bloom's taxonomy
	Directed only at students with higher- or lower-level abilities	More narrow in addressing ability levels	Accommodates a wide range of abilities
	Audio lacks proper accents	Audio portrays proper accents	Audio spoken by a native speaker
Management	Has no testing component	Has posttesting ability	Has pre- and posttesting capability
	Does not adjust for student ability	Has to be adjusted for ability levels	Automatically adjusts for student ability level
	Does not address recording or storing of student performance	Performance records can be generated but not stored	Students records of performance can be stored and easily retrieved
	No support materials included	Some support materials included	Well-written support materials included for teacher
Ease of use	Students require regular assistance to operate program	Some assistance needed to operate program	Students can operate program with no or minimal assistance
	Students have difficulty exiting program	Students can exit program after performing a few procedures	Students can easily exit the program at any time
	Students must restart the program to review a previous page	Students can review a previous page after several operations	Students can easily review a previous page without restarting
	User must follow detailed direction at all times	Some directions may be skipped at the option of the user	Directions may be skipped at the option of the user
General design	Layout of screen has a confusing format	Layout of screen has variations in format	Layout of screen has a consistent format
	Screen has no or a limited accommodation for different platforms or systems capabilities	Screen has some accommodation for different platforms or systems capabilities	Screen tries to accommodate different platforms and systems capabilities
	Screens are written in ambiguous language	Screens have some language flaws	Screens are written in a clear, concise manner
	Images appear to be unrelated to the text	Images are related to the text but are not well done	Images are sharp and related to the text
Mode of instruction	The software does not address the goals of the instruction	The content of the software has lapses in relation to the instruction	The content of the software fits the purpose of the instruction
	The audio is spoken with a poor accent	The audio is spoken by a nonnative speaker, but the speaker has a reasonably good accent	The audio is spoken by a native speaker
	Little accommodation for varying ability levels	Software accommodates a narrow range of abilities	Software accommodates a wide range of ability levels
	Little match between grammar and vocabulary and target audience	Grammar and vocabulary do not match target audience at times	Grammar and vocabulary match the level of the target audience
	Software provides no feedback	Software provides limited feedback	Software provides ample feedback

Examples of Best Educational Software

A major source for information on foreign languages educational software is Applause Learning Resources (http://www.applauselearning.com). ALR acts as a clearinghouse for other publishers, with a broad range of available programs on a variety of media. A listing of the best programs for instruction purposes is found in Table 4.

Table 4. Selected Foreign Languages Software

Title	Category/ Platform	Languages	Evaluation Score	Cost	Comments
Instant Immersion	Instruction Windows	French, German Italian, Spanish	C = 21 M = 20 E = 25 Total = 66	$49.95	Designed for 7–12 beginning and intermediate stages
Cambridge Latin Courses	Instruction Mac/Windows	Latin	C = 25 M = 23 E = 25 Total = 73	$201.00	A basic two-year course in Latin; emphasis on drill and practice
Talk Now	Instruction Mac/Windows	French, German, Italian, Japanese, Russian, Spanish	C = 26 M = 25 E = 25 Total = 86	$49.95	Elementary language study for Grades 4–8; drill and practice
Complete Grammar Series	Reinforcement Mac/Windows	French, German	C = 24 M = 23 E = 21 Total = 68	French: $480.00; Spanish: $365.00	Comprehensive review of grammar; has a diagnostic test component; French — 15 disks, Spanish — 11 disks; each disk has 10 lessons
Vocabulary Builder	Reinforcement Mac/Windows	German	C = 26 M = 25 E = 24 Total = 75	$39.95	Reviews basic German vocabulary using illustrations and a game format
Latina: Centaur Latin Drills	Reinforcement Mac/Windows	Latin	C = 27 M = 26 E = 27 Total = 80	$225.00	Drill and practice reviews; disks can be tailored to fit all of the major textbook series
Mexico: History and Culture	Enhancement Mac/Windows	Spanish	C = 28 M = 24 E = 28 Total = 80	$225.00	Multimedia program depicting the culture and history of Mexico
LeTour De France	Enhancement Mac/Windows	French	C = 28 M = 24 E = 27 Total = 79	$85.00	Multimedia tour of France; quizzes accompany each place visited
Roman Life	Enhancement Mac/Windows	Latin	C = 28 M = 24 E = 28 Total = 80	$125.00	Covers the major aspects of Roman daily life

Note. C = Content, M = Management, and E = Ease of Use.

Internet Use in the Foreign Languages Classroom

Introduction

Travel to your favorite countries and visit parks, monuments, universities, or just about anywhere else of interest. Enjoy the scenery of the Antarctica, the Caribbean, or the Middle East. It is all in one place called the World Wide Web. Make foreign language come alive for students by planning a trip abroad, locating and describing pictures of favorite monuments in the target language. Assign students to be local travel agents and clients, creating a travel package to suit the interests of their clients. Ask students to develop computerized routes to museums and tourist attractions. Conduct journal writings in the target language on a travel portfolio by visiting several cities online. The possibilities are endless.

Evaluation Classifications

To the previous elements for educational software, two factors are deleted and another added for consideration. Content issues remain paramount to any educational material regardless of the media. Internet sites are perhaps most susceptible to errors in subject matter and substance; no practical substitute for personal teacher evaluation has been found. General design issues are similar in nature to software as is mode of instruction. Unique to the Internet, however, is the concern of site operation. Links to external sites notoriously disappear without warning. Directions are often unclear or even omitted, leaving the learner to guess the next course of action. Flashy graphics, sounds, and colors distract from the necessary learning that must occur. These issues are considered in the rubric for evaluating Web sites that follows.

Basic Instruction

The Internet is an outstanding source for basic instruction in foreign languages. The same practical considerations listed for using educational software apply to the use of the Internet. Computers able to access the Internet are a must to use this resource. They may be used in a lab setting for group instruction or as individual stations for one-on-one learning. In either case, the need for a teacher, or a mentor, remains the same.

Reinforcement

A technologically astute teacher will also consider using the Internet to reinforce the lesson. There are several Web sites that offer opportunities to increase student knowledge and skill in using a foreign language. The "best of the best" sites offer remedial and study opportunities on several levels simultaneously. For example, the following may comprise various levels: greetings, family, numbers, age, birthday song, house objects, colors, body parts, and questions and answers (Level 1); community workers, songs, everyday objects, colors and questions, rooms in a house, and questions and answers (Level 2); numbers, adding and subtracting, animals, adjectives, song, more body parts, extended family members, possessives, and questions and answers (Level 3); and table objects, food, commands, questions and answers about daily activities, extended sentences using prepositional phrases, time, places (locations), and days of the week (Level 4).

Enhancement

A final implementation of the Internet offers enhancing opportunities to learn about the culture and the countries of the languages under study. The Internet is an endless source of enrichment materials, such as sites that foster student awareness of foreign language requirements in college; allow students to learn colloquialisms in their native tongues; share cultural and ethnic events such as newspapers and magazines, movies, radio, and television shows in other languages; join native speaking pen pal clubs; and visit (virtually, of course) natural history and art museums of foreign cultures.

Rubric for Evaluating Foreign Language Web Sites

Table 5 offers a user-friendly rubric for assessing the quality of foreign language Web sites and the key elements of Content, General Design, Mode of Instruction, and Site Operation.

Table 5. Criteria for Evaluating Foreign Language Web Sites

Criteria	0–10 Points	11–20 Points	21–30 Points
Content	Site has accuracy and currency problems	Program has minimal errors in facts and is relatively current	Program is accurate, factual, and current
	Student attention wanders	Holds student attention	Students display enthusiasm with site
	Does not fit age or level of students	Has some flaws in age or level appropriateness	Site is age and level appropriate
	Simple recall required	Stimulates lower levels of Bloom's taxonomy	Stimulates upper levels of Bloom's taxonomy
	Directed only at students with higher- or lower-level abilities	More narrow in addressing ability levels	Accommodates a wide range of abilities
	Audio lacks proper accents	Audio portrays proper accents	Audio spoken by a native speaker
General design	Layout of site has a confusing format	Layout of site has variations in format	Layout of site has a consistent format
	Site has no or a limited accommodation for different browsers, platforms, or systems capabilities	Site has some accommodation for different browsers, platforms, or systems capabilities	Site tries to accommodate different browsers, platforms, and systems capabilities
	Site written in ambiguous language	Site has some language flaws	Site written in a clear and concise manner
	Images on the site appear to be unrelated to the text	Images are related to the text but are not well done	Images on the site are sharp and related to the text
Mode of instruction	The site does not address the goals of the instruction	The content of the site has lapses in relation to the instruction	The content of the site fits the purpose of the instruction
	Any audio is spoken with a poor accent	Any audio is spoken by a nonnative speaker, but the speaker has a good accent	Any audio is spoken by a native speaker
	Little accommodation for varying ability levels	Site accommodates a narrow range of abilities	Site accommodates a wide range of ability levels
	Little match between grammar and vocabulary and target audience	Grammar and vocabulary do not match target audience at times	Grammar and vocabulary match the level of the target audience
	Site provides no feedback	Site provides limited feedback	Site provides ample feedback
Site operation	There are problems with the navigation path	There are some minor problems with the navigation path	The navigation path is clear and logical, and all the links work
	Students need regular assistance to access and operate the site	Students need minimal assistance to access and operate the site	Students can access and operate the site independently
	Exiting the site is difficult	Exiting the site requires several operational steps	Students can easily exit the site
	Directions are difficult to read and follow	Directions have a few ambiguities in them	Directions are clear and easy to follow
	Students can easily find themselves on an inappropriate site	Links are loose, access to other sites is possible	Links are well controlled, and access to other sites is improbable

Examples of Best Web Sites for Teaching Foreign Languages

A list of the few of the best Web sites out of the many that exist for teaching foreign languages is provided below. This list is by no means comprehensive, with literally hundreds of new pages appearing each month. Rather, Table 6 aspires to lend a starting point for locating and assessing the Internet for foreign language specific resources.

Table 6. Selected Foreign Language Web Sites

Title and URL Address	Category	Language Addressed	Evaluation Score	Comments
About.com http://(Specify Language).about .com/homework/ (language)	Instruction, reinforcement, enhancement	Chinese, French, German, Italian, Japanese, Latin, Russian, Spanish	GD = 24 MI = 26 OS = 25 Total = 75	This site offers all levels of instruction in the languages listed; there are links to other sites related to the language being studied
Parlo www.parlo.com	Instruction, reinforcement, enhancement	French and Spanish	GD = 25 MI = 23 OS = 24 Total = 72	This offers a virtual immersion approach with strong visual and audio components; it is geared for high school students and beyond
World Languages Glenco Online www.foreign language.glenco .com	Reinforcement, enhancement	French, Latin, Spanish	GD = 28 MI = 27 OS = 27 Total = 82	This site provides reinforcement and enhancement activities that accompany each of their textbooks; it features many quizzes and self-progress evaluations
Holt Rinehart and Winston www.hrw.com	Reinforcement, enhancement	French, German, Spanish	GD = 27 MI = 26 OS = 24 Total = 77	This site supports their textbook series; it mainly consists of quizzes that accompany each lesson in the textbook being used; it also links to other Web sites that are culturally oriented
Prentice Hall www.phschool. com/ foreign_languages/i ndex.html	Reinforcement	French, German, Latin, Spanish	GD = 26 MI = 25 OS = 23 Total = 74	This site allows the teacher to author a Web site with activities geared to the textbook being used in the class

Note. GD = General Design, MI = Mode of Instruction, and OS = Operation of the Site.

Distance Education and the Foreign Languages Classroom

Introduction

Distance education is rapidly becoming the newest and perhaps most promising media for teaching foreign languages. While the term "distance education" is still being defined, in this chapter, distance education is synonymous with high-speed satellite-link transmission only. Goals for the virtual foreign language classroom include providing foreign language course opportunities to all levels of students in all locations without sacrificing quality of instruction. Distance education simulates traditional instruction using qualified faculty and up-to-date instructional technology.

Evaluation Classifications

A school or school district considering distance education should keep several factors in mind. The first factor is the external equipment needed for successful operation of the program. Satellite dishes are placed on, or near, the school building. Fortunately, the advances in this area have diminished the size of the dish. Whereas 10 years ago the dish would have to be up to 10 or more feet in diameter, today its diameter is measured in inches. The dish must be anchored firmly to the building or the ground, because wind and vibrations often alter the position of the dish and diminish program signals. A second consideration is protection from damage and potential vandalism; a fence or other security measure is recommended. The second factor to be considered is reception and in-house distribution equipment. A satellite receiver downloads the signal and transmits it throughout the building. Monitors (at least 27 inches in size) should be strategically placed, and dedicated phone lines for two-way communication between the students and the instructor provide the necessary interaction during the class sessions. The phone line should be connected to a speakerphone to better facilitate discussions between the instructor and students. The third factor to be considered is classroom hardware, such as monitors, which is critical for the success of the program. And, preferably, someone trained in the proper operation of the system should be in the classroom. Although there are definite advantages to using a trained foreign language teacher, this is not a necessity. Some schools use instructional aides for this purpose.

The fourth factor is that usually, students taking a course via distance learning tend to be highly motivated, but problems often arise when attempting to match instruction with the broadcast times and the school's daily schedule. Some schools videotape the program to show at other times during the day to better match their schedule. Unfortunately, a major drawback of this technique is loss of the interactive portion of programming. The fifth factor to consider is operation and maintenance costs. The final consideration when using the distance education approach is the cost. Not only is there an initial outlay to purchase the equipment needed, there is a periodic maintenance charge to realign the dish, and there is also a tuition charge for each student taking part in the program. While this fee is not exorbitant, it is almost always more than the cost of utilizing educational software or the Internet.

Basic Instruction

Many states provide grant money, enabling schools to obtain the equipment necessary to access interactive language experiences via distance education. Satellite programming enables real-time conversation with people all over the world. Two-way communication supports actual dialogues with native speakers about literally any topic. The interchange with speakers, guests, or instructors, is spontaneous, the feedback immediate, and the situation completely realistic. Compare basic instruction via satellite with antiseptic textbooks, language tapes, or classroom lectures. The use of distance education is not feasible in the classroom on a regular basis due to differences in broadcast time zones, bandwidth issues, sufficient hardware, and mismatches with specific learning objectives. Exposure to distance education in the foreign languages classroom has been found to encourage basic instruction, while making students lifelong learners of language and culture.

Reinforcement

Reinforcement via satellite takes on a markedly different presentation not found on the typical satellite venues mentioned earlier. Instead, they are derived more from actual commercial programming. Providers such as Direct TV and others transmit programs in many foreign languages, ranging in content from documentaries about particular countries to soap operas and commercials. Most of these programs are produced, acted, and narrated by native speakers. As reinforcement, students develop a keener ear for the language by watching and listening to the dialogue on these shows.

Commercials are of particular value to K–12 students. They are on a more simplistic level, using less complicated vocabulary. Students often enjoy watching the familiar format of soap operas, due, in large measure, to the popularity of the genre on American television. The programs also have a story line that promotes student attention and the desire to understand what is being said during the episode. Debriefings after each program allow the teacher to reinforce the concepts being studied in the course and portrayed by the broadcast.

Enhancement

Distance education via satellite also provides a viable method for enhancing foreign language instruction. Among the many foreign language programs broadcast commercially over satellite are a number of culturally oriented shows, including travelogues of a country or some area of a country and trips to museums and other cultural attractions. Distance education remains an excellent resource for enhancement activities and should augment the learning objectives of every foreign language course.

Rubric for Evaluating Foreign Language Distance Education Programs

The Satellite Downlink Rubric (Table 7) was adapted from the Distance Learning Rubric (Wojnar, 2002) and is intended to evaluate the effectiveness of the teaching and technologies used in satellite downlink programming. Strong debates rage concerning whether satellite programming and videoconferencing are a part of distance education or should be considered "teaching through distance." Opponents claim that satellite programming is simply another form of traditional didactic lecturing, with the main difference being that the teacher and students are separated by time and distance. "True distance or online learning" classes, it is argued, support the role of the teacher as a facilitator, emphasizing student-centered classes, individualized instruction, self-reflection and higher-level thinking, and a higher degree of interactivity from learner–learner and from teacher–learner. Teachers and students are the most important considerations when defining online learning; the technology is only the medium to project the teaching. Rich content, interactions, and assessment components must be the primary focus of the instruction. The technologies should be seamless, providing the most efficient and cost-effective method of instruction delivery.

Assessing the value of distance education programs in a foreign languages curriculum takes on special meaning in the rubric in Table 7. Because the issue of distance education is new, an outside expert in distance education was sought to prepare a rubric that combines aspects of teaching with the technology associated with distance education. Excellent offerings provide nontraditional, distance instruction to students in remote locations, a better variety of foreign languages, keener awareness of diverse cultures, and a responsiveness required by the business community and adult learner.

Table 7. Criteria for Evaluating Foreign Language Distance Learning (Generic Distance Learning Rubric Modified for Teaching Using Satellite Downlinks)

Criterion	Below Average	Average	Above Average
Technologies	**0**	**10**	**20**
Connectivity	Unable to remain connected; lessons often interrupted by connectivity problems	A rare problem with connectivity; lesson objectives met	No problems with connectivity; able to remain online without any interruptions in service
Quality of projected images	Fuzzy or unclear images most or all of the time	An issue on occasion, but not distractive	No problems with clarity of images
Content/technologies balance	Technologies overpower the content in the lesson	Average integration of technologies into the lesson	Technologies are presented in a seamless manner, used as the medium and not the primary focus of the lesson
Supporting resources	No handouts, manuals, or supporting documents to augment the teaching lesson	Handouts, manuals, or supporting documents provided	Handouts, manuals, or supporting documents address several of the following: learning styles, multiple intelligences, pedagogical issues; and, they are rich in text, graphics, and audio (CD-ROM included)
Teaching	**0**	**10**	**20**
Back-up instructional plan in the event of technology problems	No back-up plan provided	Back-up plan provided for routinely encountered problems	Comprehensive back-up plan, periodically tested, and appropriately funded and staffed
Student engagement and active learning	Teacher-centered dialogue is from the teacher to the student only; students are seldom engaged in the learning process	Exchange of dialogue between students and the teacher; learning clearly engaging the student	Two-way exchange of dialogue between the students and the teacher defines the learning environment
Auditory responses	Problem with the audio (voice recognition — too soft, too loud, frequently asked to repeat content)	Average audio reception	Eloquent speaker providing clarity of intonation and correct pronunciation and diction
Presentation skills	Inappropriate use of peripheral technologies (e.g., speaks to chalkboard instead of to the audience, inappropriate use of handheld devices causing learning distractions, etc.)	Effective use of peripheral technologies (e.g., adequate presentation skills)	Motivating integration of peripheral technologies and presentation skills; model speaker
Allowing for "wait time" for student responses	Teacher answers own questions frequently; seldom attentive to distance learner responses	Allows adequate time for students to think before responding to questions	Teacher anticipates and appears comfortable allowing for adequate "wait time" for student responses; encourages students to repeat their question to the class if needed; and receptive to distance learner responses

Table 7. Criteria for Evaluating Foreign Language Distance Learning (Generic Distance Learning Rubric Modified for Teaching Using Satellite Downlinks) (continued)

Challenges thinking	Students are not challenged to think	Some challenging of thinking in the class noticed	Teacher raises the bar for learning, and individualizes instruction for all students
Lesson objectives	Objectives covered are taught below or above the level of the learners in the class	All objectives covered and taught to the level of the learners in the class	All objectives covered, enhancement to the lesson provided and higher-level thinking encouraged; all learning objectives were addressed at the level of each learner
Affective Learning			
Feedback from the teacher	Teacher provides below average feedback when using distance education	Adequate amount of helpful feedback is provided when using technology	Above average feedback is provided and is extremely helpful during technology-based learning
Teacher enthusiasm	Teacher enthusiasm for teaching the subject is viewed below average when using technology	Average enthusiasm for teaching the subject using technology	Teacher passionate about teaching the subject; technology supports this passion
Learner enthusiasm	Technology barely increases excitement for learning the subject	Technology creates enthusiasm for learning the subject	Technology generates passion for learning the subject
Building communities of learners (cooperative learning)	Students routinely work alone without interacting with other students	Class is representative of a mixture of individual and group activities	Students supporting one another, taking a lead role in learning, and helping their peers learn

Note. From *Distance Learning Course Design: A Comprehensive Program of Instruction for Online Educators,* by L. C. Wojnar, 2002, Boston, MA: McGraw-Hill Primis Custom Printing.

Examples of Best Distance Education

The Satellite Educational Resources Consortium (SERC) is by far the most experienced provider of basic instruction in foreign languages utilizing distance education via satellite transmission. Most distance education providers offer a full range of programs in math, history, science, and English, in addition to languages. Generally, programs offered via distance are affiliated with a college or university, and instructors tend to be professors at these institutions of higher learning. A list of better distance education programs is found in Table 8.

Table 8. Selected Foreign Language Distance Education Programs

Title/Provider	Category	Languages	Evaluation Score	Cost	Comments
SERC	Instruction	Spanish	Tech = 15 T = 20 A = 10 Total = 45	$540 (per site for members)	Two levels of beginning Spanish instruction are offered for kindergarten, first, or second Grades
SERC	Instruction	Japanese, Latin, German, Spanish	Tech = 15 T = 20 A = 10 Total = 45	$500.00 per student	Interactive satellite-link course designed to engage students in mastering the basic skills of speaking, listening, writing, and reading
United Star Distance Learning Consortium	Instruction, enhancement	French, Latin, German, Spanish	Tech = 18 T = 16 A = 15 Total = 49	$500 per student (1–10 students)	Distance learning technologies use live, interactive satellite broadcasts with CD-ROM and Web-based integration Target is primarily high school students
International Channel Networks	Enhancement	Various European and Asian languages focus	Tech = 10 T = 10 A = 15 Total = 35		Provider and marketer of multicultural, multilingual television programming in the United States

Note. Tech = Technologies, T = Teaching, and A = Affective Learning.

Other Technology Considerations in the Foreign Languages Curriculum

Some special considerations are in order to address the needs of foreign language students with disabilities. While there may be a limited number of such students in the typical foreign language classroom, the legal ramifications of educating special needs children demand that teachers adapt their instructional techniques when necessary. And, technology provides an excellent tool for these curricular adaptations.

Special needs students fall into three general categories: physical, learning, and emotional. Each challenge requires special accommodations. Students with auditory and visual impairments require special adaptations, usually involving additional technologies. Additional equipment, such as Braille keyboards or keypads, is available from organizations devoted to educating students with these challenges. Care must be taken to insure that students can access all the components of the computer, including the keyboard, disk drives, printers, and any other ancillary pieces of equipment.

Learning challenged students range from mild to profound learning disabilities. It is rare that a student with a profound disability would be found in a foreign language class. However, many students with moderate to mild learning disabilities enroll in foreign languages during their middle and high school years. Remedial and enhancement technologies, in particular, allow students to progress at their own pace, commensurate with their learning abilities. Educational software aids in meeting the adapted goals for challenged students by permitting the teacher to design activities that concentrate on strengthening skills that an individualized learning prescription has identified as desirable. Finally, an instructional aide is recommended to assist a learning-challenged student to use technology to the optimal advantage.

Emotionally challenged students often possess average, or above average, intelligence. They seldom need the type of accommodations required for physically or learning-challenged students. Unlike the typical classroom situation, the computer screen often fixes the attention of these students and helps to minimize distractions. However, frustration associated with poor technologies may lead to outbursts of inappropriate behavior in some of these students. Technologies must be clear and easy to operate, and equipment must be in good operating order.

Conclusions

The potential applications of technology in the foreign languages classroom are limited only by the imagination of the teacher. The classroom teacher draws from many diverse sources to instruct, reinforce, and enhance the teaching of a language. As with any new teaching device, the teacher must be familiar with the products before using them. Teachers must preview all materials, and develop their own set of competencies and skills necessary to correctly operate the equipment. In-service training before use is encouraged.

Technology has proven to be a valuable asset for effectively teaching a foreign language to students in the 21st century. Following the guidelines, recommendations, and considerations provided in this chapter will help ensure successful integration into the foreign languages classroom.

References

American Council for the Teaching of Foreign Languages. (1999). *National Standards for Foreign Language Education,* (www.actfl.org).

American Council for the Teaching of Foreign Languages. (1999). *Standards for Foreign Language Learning: Preparing for the 21st Century,* (www.actfl.org).

Earp, S. (2001). "More than just the Internet: Other Technology for Language Teaching," *ERIC Review, K–12 Foreign Language Education, 6,* 1, (www.eric.ed.gov/resources/ericreview/vol6no1/tech.html).

Rodgers, T. S. (2001). "Language Teaching Methodology," *ERIC Digest,* September 2001, (www.cal.org/ericcll/digest/rodgers.html).

Schultz, R. A. (2001). "Foreign Language Education in the United States," *ERIC Review, K–12 Foreign Language Education, 6,* 1,(www.eric.ed.gov/resources/ericreview/vol6no1/trends.html).

Wojnar, L. C. (2002). *Distance Learning Course Design: A Comprehensive Program of Instruction for Online Educators,* Boston, MA: McGraw-Hill Primis Custom Printing.

Technology In The Fine Arts Classroom

Marilyn J. Narey, MSEd

8

"What do you mean she wants to order computers for her classroom? Why she's the art teacher!"

"My son is very talented in art, but I want him to take courses that will prepare him for a successful future. How can he make a living as an artist? He'll starve!"

"I wanted my history students' work to be more "creative," so I taught them how to insert clip art."

"Why are you using all that video and computer stuff with your students — that's NOT ART! Let the tech department handle that, we art teachers should stick to the paint and clay!"

Introduction

Any arts educator who enters the realm of technology has most likely encountered comments similar to those above. The attitudes and perceptions of a large portion of the educational community regarding art and technology are often reflected by the larger American society. Art to many conjures romantic images of a bearded and bereted artist passionately lunging with loaded brush at a canvas propped in the corner of a crowded garret. Technology, on the other hand, induces visions of shiny metal and plastic humming with modern efficiency and usually manifested by a bank of glowing computers.

Administrators who are only marginally acquainted with art and technology too easily dismiss the probability of any connection between the two. Subsequently, they reserve computer hardware and software purchases for the math and science departments, rather than for art or music. Parents, unaware of the demand for talented artists in the technology-based design and entertainment industries, discourage their sons and daughters from taking arts courses. Teachers often fail to see the value that art and technology hold for their students. Or worse, they misunderstand how to effectively integrate art and technology into their subject area and actually create lessons that employ inappropriate uses of each. Fellow arts educators often add to the clamor of opposition, claiming, "Technology has nothing to do with 'true' art."

Unfortunately, all of these stakeholders in our children's futures are missing an extraordinary opportunity to meet the needs of a large portion of students, many of whom are visual or kinesthetic learners born into today's "techno-culture." Many in government, education, and the media speak out with concern over the barrage of images encountered in our culture and caution that education must begin to provide our children with skills to translate this "visual language." Schools should provide a balanced education to help students acquire meaning beyond the literal. Computer technology and interactive media rely heavily on images, sounds, colors and movements: the language of the artist. Therefore, administrators, educators, and the community must realize that the most effective means of addressing our students' present and future needs is through a marriage of arts and technology and the integration of the two across all disciplines.

This chapter of *Teaching With Technology Across the Curriculum* assists the educator in understanding the valuable role of art and technology in the classroom and seeks to convey the potential of this "dynamic duo" to motivate, instruct, and inspire students and teachers. It also explores the long history of technology in the fine arts discipline and introduces past and current uses of instructional technology in the classroom. Several evaluation rubrics are included to determine appropriate fine arts software and Web sites as well as provide criteria for lesson design when incorporating art and technology into a subject area.

Defining Art

Art often defies labeling or definition, yet everyone categorizes and qualifies it according to their own experiences, beliefs and education. Consider your personal definition of art, the criteria that makes it distinctive, and how you respond to it.

The question, *"What is art?"* is difficult to answer because of the variety of individual aesthetic and philosophical viewpoints. Like all philosophical questions, the answer is culturally rooted and is both logical and emotional. Responses to the question, "what is art?" can be supported but not proven. However, this is certainly not a reason to ignore the study of art in the curriculum.

Learning is not about collecting facts; rather, it is a search for understanding. Therefore, the question *"What is art?"* is one that should be pondered, discussed, and argued in the classroom. In many states' standards, such as those in Pennsylvania and in the National Visual Arts Standards, aesthetics is included as a required strand, developing student understanding of the issues associated with investigating the meaning of art. Art teachers are encouraged to begin aesthetic discussion even in the elementary grades (National Standards for Arts Education, 2002).

Defining Technology

Technology, as it applies to the fine arts classroom, also has a controversial definition. At its roots, technology is the "process by which human beings fashion tools and machines to increase their control and understanding of the material environment." However, in contemporary culture, "technology" is often limited to computers.

Established Definitions

For the purposes of this chapter, the following definitions are provided: *Art is the creative exploration of an idea, and the communication of that idea through one or more media* (Narey, 2001). The definition of technology is informally divided into "traditional" technologies, including all tools and machines invented before the widespread use of electricity, and "current" technologies from the so-called digital age. With these definitions in hand, the chapter explores the dynamic interdependence between the artist and technology that has existed throughout history.

Historical Evolution of Fine Arts-Based Technologies

Traditional Technologies

Brushes, chisels, and pencils might be the tools that most people associate with the visual artist. The instrument is the musician's "tool." The dancer seems to have no "tool" other than the body. Yet, the arts are labor intensive. Throughout history, artists have sought tools and technologies to make the job easier, quicker, or better. Artists, particularly visual artists, have used, improved, designed, and created new technologies to attain their artistic goals.

Since the prehistoric humans blew pigments through hollowed reeds to leave an outline of a hand on a cave wall, tools have been used to make marks of mankind's existence on the Earth (Russell, 1993). The early cave dweller used fur and grass to paint animal images in the high, unlit recesses that could have only been reached by scaffolds built from branches that were drug into the cave. The light of burning moss and animal fat in hollowed stone lamps illuminated dark walls as these people drew mysterious images and symbols. From these earliest of times, artists have relied on and advanced technology to create their art.

In ancient Greece, artists devised a technology for firing their pottery to take advantage of the country's iron-rich clay, creating the thousands of black and red-figure vases, remnants of which have provided archeologists with so much information about their culture. Medieval artists developed the pointed arch and the flying buttress in order to make their cathedrals "reach to the heavens." In the mid-15th century, the invention of the printing press impacted all of Europe. Words, pictures, and newly invented musical notation no longer had to be painstakingly created by hand, one manuscript at a time.

Many artists of the past used the camera obscura, a device that projected the view from outside onto the interior through a pinhole in its wall (Crary, 1998). This technology was an indispensable tool for painters to solve problems of perspective. Many found it easier to simply trace the two-dimensional image projected onto the glass, rather than work out the geometric details of creating the illusion of depth. The principles behind the camera obscura, which had been known for centuries, eventually led to the invention of the camera and later to the moving picture.

The camera allowed artists such as Matthew Brady, Ansel Adams, and Dorthea Lange to document history, to capture the beauty of the landscape, or to impact social change; all traditional roles of art. Edward Muybridge conducted early experiments with motion photography and established the groundwork for the development of the moving picture. As other artists and inventors continued exploring and developing his ideas, the new art technologies of film and cinema began to grow (Feldman, 1985).

Current Technologies

Today, artists use technologies in new and exciting ways. Andy Warhol applied photo-silk screen technology to manipulate images from popular media and print them on canvas. He also made films and experimented with other emerging technologies to comment on the self-absorbed, consumer culture of America in the 1960s.

Contemporary artist, Tony Oursler, combines art, drama, and technology by projecting videotaped performances onto a variety of objects, such as animal organs in jars of formaldehyde, or onto suspended spheres to communicate his perceptions of human interaction and society (Arnason, 1998).

Nam June Paik often uses video monitors like constantly changing mosaic tiles to communicate his cultural vision. Paik's contribution, *Megatron,* in the National Museum of American Art, utilized 150 monitors that operated independently but shared multiple random combinations of rapidly moving video and animation. The work was set to audio that ranged from ceremonial chants to rock and roll. Orchestrated by a complex system of laser disk players, computers, and digital sequencers, the piece demonstrated the highly integrated technology and art creations typical of this artist's work (Bolz, 1997).

Chuck Close, no stranger to technology in his art, relies on assistive technology in his artistic work. In his early career, the Polaroid Corporation provided him with a huge camera to experiment with his large-scale portraits. Because a spinal cord disease resulted in the artist's inability to move his arms and legs, he depends on the technology of a hydraulic lift to move him into position to work on his canvases.

Music technologies include synthesizers, MIDI keyboards, and MP3s. Musical instruments are now designed with the aid of a computer. Dancers incorporate video and computer images in performances. Technology assists in designing ballet shoes and equipment. Choreography is sometimes created on the computer. The creation of works for the stage has evolved into a highly integrated relationship between technology and all of the art forms.

These are only a few of the ways that artists have used and are using technology. Artists need technology to help them to continue to break down barriers of time, space, and other limitations of the physical world, and technology will keep evolving, as these creative individuals reach forward into the infinite potential of the human mind. The relationship of the artist and technology is one that is destined to last.

Technology in the Arts Classroom

Teachers, like artists, need technology to make their jobs more efficient and effective. Analysis of how arts teachers have used technology in the past will likely reveal examples such as slide, overhead, and opaque projectors, record players and tape recorders, filmstrip and film projectors, and cameras of various sorts. Interestingly, most of this technology was employed naturally and, for the most part, effectively within the rhythm of the school day. Teachers of visual art, music, and dance used these technologies as easily and freely as most teachers use a chalkboard, because these devices facilitated their instruction.

Occasionally, a teacher's own creativity inspires use of technologies in a less traditional manner, such as placing a glass dish of swirling food coloring, oil, and water on an overhead projector to create the mood for an elementary class "under-the-sea" painting lesson. Teachers might also employ presentation tools as student production and performance devices, designing lessons in which students draw scenes and characters on acetate. They place these scenes on an overhead projector and move the acetate characters to project simulated puppet shows.

It would seem a simple task then for arts teachers to integrate newer educational technologies into their classrooms. Yet, many teachers staunchly refuse to have anything to do with video cameras or computers. Reasons for this may vary, however teachers must remember that artists have always worked in the latest media. Implementation of the new computer- and video-based media in the classroom is not a rejection of the old tools and technologies. Rather, it is an important expansion of one's creative armamentarium. Art teachers, like all artists, should be on the front line of change if it leads to a higher level of student understanding.

Standards for Technology in Fine Arts

Arts education benefits student and society. It benefits the student, because it cultivates the whole child, gradually building many kinds of literacy, while developing intuition, reasoning, imagination, and dexterity into unique forms of expression and communication (The National Standards for Arts Education, 2002). Arts education standards make a difference, because in the end, they speak powerfully to two fundamental issues that pervade all of education: quality and accountability. Standards help define what a good education in the arts should provide: a thorough grounding rooted in the individual skills of visual arts, dance, music, and the visual arts.

The standards that follow describe the cumulative skills and knowledge expected of students upon graduating high school. They presume that the students have achieved the standards specified for Grades K–4 and 5–8.

[Specific standards for these grades are available on the NSAE Web site at: http://artsedge.kennedy-center.org/professional_resources/standards. Note: Suggested technologies were taken from Table 4 ("Guide to Common Classroom Technologies," Chapter 1).]

Table 1. Standards for Technology in the Fine Arts Curriculum

General Competency	Specific Standards	Suggested Technologies
Dance (9–12)	**Standard #1**: Identifying and demonstrating movement elements and skills in performing dance	Video and graphic presentation educational software
	Standard #2: Understanding choreographic principles, processes, and structures	
	Standard #3: Understanding dance as a way to create and communicate meaning	Audio/video
	Standard #4: Applying and demonstrating critical and creative thinking skills in dance	Audio/video
	Standard #5: Demonstrating and understanding dance in various cultures and historical periods	World Wide Web
	Standard #6: Making connections between dance and healthful living	
	Standard #7: Making connections between dance and other disciplines	Audio/video
Music (9–12)	**Standard #1**: Singing, alone and with others, a varied repertoire of music	Audio/video
	Standard #2: Performing on instruments, alone and with others, a varied repertoire of music	MIDI interfaces
	Standard #3: Improvising melodies, variations, and accompaniments	Music synthesizers
	Standard #4: Composing and arranging music within specified guidelines	Music synthesizers
	Standard #5: Reading and notating music	MIDI interfaces
	Standard #6: Listening to, analyzing, and describing music	Music synthesizers
	Standard #7: Evaluating music and music performances	Audio/video
	Standard #8: Understanding relationships between music, the other arts, and disciplines outside the arts	World Wide Web
	Standard #9: Understanding music in relation to history and culture	Tutorial instructional Media

Table 1. Standards for Technology in the Fine Arts Curriculum (continued)

Theatre (9–12)	**Standard #1**: Script writing through improvising, writing, and refining scripts based on personal experience and heritage, imagination, literature, and history	Word processing, desktop publishing
	Standard #2: Acting by developing, communicating, and sustaining characters in improvisations and informal or formal productions	Video
	Standard #3: Designing and producing by conceptualizing and realizing artistic interpretations for informal or formal productions	Video
	Standard #4: Directing by interpreting dramatic texts and organizing and conducting rehearsals for informal or formal productions	Video
	Standard #5: Researching by evaluating and synthesizing cultural and historical information to support artistic choices	World Wide Web
	Standard #6: Comparing and integrating art forms by analyzing traditional theatre, dance, music, visual arts, and new art forms	Audio/video
	Standard #7: Analyzing, critiquing, and constructing meanings from informal and formal theatre, film, television, and electronic media productions	Audio/video
	Standard #8: Understanding context by analyzing the role of theatre, film, television, and electronic media in the past and the present	
Visual Arts (9–12)	**Standard #1**: Understanding and applying media, techniques, and processes	Graphics presentation
	Standard #2: Using knowledge of structures and functions	
	Standard #3: Choosing and evaluating a range of subject matter, symbols, and ideas	Graphics presentation
	Standard #4: Understanding the visual arts in relation to history and cultures	Graphics presentation
	Standard #5: Reflecting upon and assessing the characteristics and merits of their work and the work of others	Word processing
	Standard #6: Making connections between visual arts and other disciplines	List servers, electronic mail

Note. From *What Every Young American Should Know and Be Able to Do in the Arts, The National Standards for Arts Education*, Consortium of National Arts Education Associations, 2002.

Educational Software for the Fine Arts Classroom

Introduction

Teachers must explore the variety of resources for integrating technology into a fine arts program. Along with utilizing a variety of technology hardware, commercial software is a resource for informational or interactive production, presentation, enrichment or remediation purposes.

Evaluation Classifications

Examples of excellent classroom integration of arts and technology abound. Arts teachers who use technology usually apply the same creativity to their instruction as they infuse into their art. Classroom applications for this content area are often divided into categories, including the following: direct instruction, student production, assessment and evaluation, performance and exhibition, and interpersonal communication.

Direct Instruction

Technology provides a variety of formats for direct instruction. Visual arts teachers collect images and works of art from the Internet to supplement a limited supply of graphic reproductions. Photographs taken with a digital camera offer still more resources. An LCD (liquid crystal display) projector enlarges images for optimum classroom viewing, a feature definitely appreciated by any arts instructor who has attempted to teach artwork from a textbook to a crowd of 30 art students. A Smart Board enables freehand drawing on projected images and enhances a teacher's ability to demonstrate design and composition. Processes such as calligraphy are also more easily viewed when videotaped. Teachers with access to a computer with a video card often insert video clips into *Power Point* presentations or interactive Web sites.

The ability to custom design instructional materials is extremely attractive to the arts teacher. A proliferation of materials for arts education does not exist in the quantity available for other subject areas. Further, many arts teachers prefer to create their own materials that support their own curriculum. Custom-made materials include classroom presentations and interactive lessons (using graphics presentation software); online hand-outs, study guides, and text-based workbooks (products of word processing); and virtual field trips (courtesy of Web page design software); and digital instructional videos (using video design software).

Student Production

In the arts, technology also functions as a primary student production tool. Creative visual arts applications include design graphics and artwork from word-processing programs such as *Apple Works* or *Microsoft Word*, or more professional packages such as *Adobe PhotoShop* or *Macromedia Flash*. Visual art students venture further into multimedia applications by creating their own Web pages or video clips. Digital cameras for still shots and short length video open new creative horizons.

Music students produce works using music composition software and MIDI keyboards. Dance does not rely as much on technology as the visual arts and music, however, an innovative model of student production was developed at a middle school in North Carolina (Cuper, 1999). There, dance students worked with the Macromedia software, *Poser*, in their dance class. Initial experiments involved recreating their movements on the dance floor with digitized figures on a laptop computer. The uses of technology for student production are limited only by teacher and student imagination.

Assessment and Evaluation

Technology is an excellent assessment tool for the fine arts. Videotaping formative and summative assessments in the performance aspects of the arts disciplines helps students learn self-evaluation skills. Students review tapes of their dance or music performances with their teacher to discover weaknesses or to refine their work. They are encouraged to look and listen more deeply to aspects of their performance and the subtle variances in movement or expression affecting the quality of their performance.

An excellent visual arts assessment practice for middle school students involves taping individual student critiques. As students discuss the artistic goals of their art pieces and point out specific qualities in their work, they also assess how well they achieved their objectives or what is needed to make the piece more successful. Students who may at first have difficulty writing independently about their work often find it easier to talk about their ideas during a videotaped critique. Interactions with the teacher who can guide the reflective experience can later result in deeper, more meaningful written reflections.

Performance and Exhibition

A major component of arts education is performance or exhibition. Creation of a virtual arts gallery or classroom exhibition is an excellent means of demonstrating fine arts work. Once created, the virtual show linked to the school Web site, reaches local and universal audiences. Sculptures and other three-dimensional work can be videotaped from a variety of angles. With more advanced skills and equipment, interactive 360° virtual views can be created and video clips combined with highly integrated multimedia productions. In addition, student reflections or artist statements are added to a presentation using text and sound, and teachers contribute helpful comments or sound bytes of appreciation to supporters.

Interpersonal Communication

A final classification of arts technology takes the form of interpersonal communication. In addition to using the Internet to communicate with parents and students or to partner students with their counterparts in other countries, technology aids in communicating with other arts educators. Bulletin boards, list-servs, and e-mail are extremely important to the lone arts teacher in a small rural district. Often, these teachers have no one around to advise them on grant writing, managing that unruly 10th period music class, or commiserating over an annual art supply budget cut (again). With a click of the mouse, art teachers are connected to colleagues throughout the world.

Rubric for Evaluating Fine Arts Software

The first step in implementing software for the Fine Arts curriculum is to investigate any packages already owned by your school. The technology coordinator, principal, department chairperson, school librarian, or media specialist usually provide this information. Excellent software may already be available to meet the needs of students while avoiding costly duplication.

Some schools and school districts require prior approval of software purchases and provide specific request forms. An example Software Request Form is provided at Appendix A. A description of the curricular area, lesson goals and objectives, system requirements, and identified software packages comprise the key elements of the form to be completed by the teacher. Most reputable software providers encourage a designated trial period to determine if the software is appropriate.

The following rubric has been designed to comprehensively examine various components of fine arts software. Points are assigned and serve mainly to demonstrate a relative value for that criterion. A minimum total score has not been established to specify whether or not the software should be purchased. It is highly likely that a specific software package might score very low in some areas and still meet learning objectives.

Table 2. Fine Arts Software Evaluation Rubric

INSTRUCTIONAL CRITERIA (51 Max Points)	3	2	1	0	N/A
Meets goals and objectives					
Age/developmentally (cognitively — reading, visual art) appropriate					
Age/developmentally (technical skill) appropriate					
Age appropriate (emotionally, socially) to targeted group of learners					
Content is accurate, free from error					
Content is free from stereotype/bias					
Representative of wide community/inclusive of a variety of ideas, beliefs					
Maintains student interest/attention throughout the lesson					
Provides/maintains appropriate levels of challenge					
Provides reasonable opportunities to be successful					
Provide a level of student control					
Stimulates sensory and cognitive curiosity/encourages exploration					
Demonstrates relevance of content/skills to student					
Appropriate/adequate feedback					
Offers a variety of display and student response (keyboard and mouse)					
Utilizes information mapping					
Appropriate length					
NAVIGATION (24 Max Points)					
Loads easily					
Is reliable and free from system errors					
Good orientation information					
Directions are clear					
Allows easy movement throughout the program					
Can be exited at any time					
Can be restarted at point left off, without going through entire program					
Consistent tools for navigation					

Note. 3 = Outstanding, 2 = Satisfactory, 1 = Weak, 0 = Extremely Poor, and N/A = Not Applicable.

Table 2. Fine Arts Software Evaluation Rubric (continued)

QUALITY OF DESIGN (27 Max Points)	3	2	1	0	N/A
Screens are a well laid-out combination of text and graphics					
Effective use of color and design elements					
Graphics make information more attractive					
Graphics help visualization of a particular event, person, place, or object					
Graphics help memorization of key information					
Graphics organize information into coherent structure					
Graphics, animations, sounds work together with text to make a particular point clear					
Sound adds to the understanding of the teaching point					
Graphics and music are consistent with the nature of the content					
ASSESSMENT (6 Max Points)					
Appropriate formative assessment is offered					
Appropriate summative assessment is offered					
UNIQUE PRODUCTION SOFTWARE ISSUES					
TOTAL POINTS AWARDED (108 Max Points)					

COMMENTS

Identify Category of Fine Arts Software:

o   **Direct Instruction**

o   **Student Production**

o   **Assessment and Evaluation**

o   **Performance and Exhibition**

o   **Interpersonal Communication**

RECOMMENDATION
Category:

o   **Recommend Purchase**

o   **Do NOT Recommend Purchase**

Note. 3 = Outstanding, 2 = Satisfactory, 1 = Weak, 0 = Extremely Poor, and N/A = Not Applicable.

Examples of Best Educational Software

When it comes to locating educational software, the classifications of dance and theater are limited. Music and visual arts, as might be expected, represent the majority of educational software in the fine arts curriculum. The packages in Table 3 represent some of the best in educational fine arts software.

Table 3. Fine Arts Educational Software

Title	Fine Art/ Category	Evaluation Score	Cost	Comments
Learn to Dance Instruction Videos	Dance (No software found; videos substituted)	I = 45 N = NA D = 20 A = NA Total = NA	$19.95	Reasons to buy instructional videos: 1. Learn to dance from the experts in their field 2. Use videotape many times 3. Learn at your own pace 4. Increase retention 5. Use as a valuable aid with lessons
	Direct instruction			
Practica Musica	Music	I = 48 N = 20 D = 25 A = 6 Total = 99	$125.00	A complete music theory/ear training tutor for Macintosh and Windows computers
	Direct instruction			
Songworks	Music	I = 40 N = 18 D = 25 A = 6 Total = 89	$125.00	Music composition software; compose, play back, and print out music quickly and easily
	Direct instruction			
Little Kidmusic and Big Kidmusic	Music	I = 50 N = 20 D = 25 A = 5 Total = 100	$75.00	Help kids learn to read music by focusing on pitch and rhythm skills; very nice package
	Direct instruction			
Dolphin Don's Music School	Music	I = 50 N = 15 D = 25 A = 5 Total = 95	$39.95	CD-ROM featuring 10 music education lesson games that teach ear-training, reading of notes, rhythms, key signatures, intervals, and chords
	Performance exhibition			

Note. I = Instructional, N = Navigation, D = Design Quality, and A = Assessment.

Table 3. Fine Arts Educational Software (continued)

Musition	Music Direct instruction	I = 50 N = 20 D = 25 A = 5 Total = 100	$119.00	Interactive drill-based teaching of fundamental areas of music theory, note reading, and rhythm for beginners to advanced scales, jazz chords, clefs, and instrument keys and range for experienced students of music theory
Arts Management Systems	Theatre Assessment evaluation	I = 25 N = 20 D = 25 A = NA Total = NA		Hands-on management of people who buy tickets, provide donations, volunteer, sales of reserved tickets, donations, adding people to mail lists for subsequent follow up, word merge, ticket printing; useful for arts class discussing the real-world aspect of managing the arts
KidPix	Visual arts Student production	I = 50 N = 22 D = 25 A = 4 Total = 101	$59.95	Draw/paint program for young grades; good intro to *Power Point*
Adobe Pagemaker	Visual arts Student production	I = 45 N = 24 D = 27 A = 2 Total = 98	NA	Page layout — desktop publishing, very basic; not necessarily educational software, but very effective as a visual arts presentation system
Fireworks	Visual arts Student production	I = 40 N = 24 D = 27 A = NA Total = NA	$99.00	Web graphic generator; not necessarily educational software, but also effective as a Web design system
Corell Painters Classic	Visual arts Student production	I = 40 N = 24 D = 27 A = NA Total = NA	$99.00	Apply range of visual effects (color, texture, etc.) with a variety of drawing and painting tools; highly engaging; highly recommended

Note. I = Instructional, N = Navigation, D = Design Quality, and A = Assessment.

Internet Use in the Fine Arts Classroom

Introduction

Web sites are another resource that can bring technology into a fine arts curriculum. There are countless numbers of sites of varying qualities and for almost any instructional purpose imaginable.

Evaluation Classifications

A listing of recommended fine arts Web sites with brief descriptions is included here along with an evaluation rubric with instructions to rate the example sites. Web site applications for this content area are divided into categories including: lesson planning, thematic units, student sites, and teacher sites. Lesson plans are available from such renowned institutions as the Getty Institute for the Arts and the National Endowment for the Arts. Thematic units combine multiple subject matter area lesson plans, resource pages, book activities, books, and professional resources organized by theme. Themes can include the four seasons, holidays, animals, and patriotic resources, to name a few. And, they typically require some cooperation among the content area teachers, especially at the secondary level. Student and teacher sites continue to be divided into direct instruction, student production, assessment and evaluation, performance and exhibition, and interpersonal communication.

Rubric for Evaluating Fine Arts Web Sites

The following rubric suggests an assessment scheme applying much the same criteria used for software; namely, instructional content, navigation, quality of design, and infusion of assessment. Use the rating system in Table 4 to evaluate prospective Web sites for integration into the fine arts curriculum.

Table 4. Fine Arts Web Site Evaluation Rubric

INSTRUCTIONAL CRITERIA (39 Max Points)					
	3	2	1	0	N/A
Meets the following art objective:					
Age/developmentally (cognitively — reading, visual art) appropriate for this age level					
Age/developmentally (technical skill) appropriate for this age level					
Age appropriate (emotionally, socially) for this age level					
Content is accurate, free from error					
Content is free from stereotype/bias					
Represents the community/inclusive of a variety of ideas, beliefs					
Maintains student interest/attention throughout the lesson					
Information is current					
Information is documented, author of site is listed					
Provides a level of student control					
Stimulates sensory and cognitive curiosity/encourages exploration					
Demonstrates relevance of content/skills to student					
NAVIGATION (15 Max Points)					
	3	2	1	0	N/A
Site loads well					
Good orientation information					
Directions are clear					
Allows easy movement throughout the site					
Provides consistent tools for navigation					

Note. 3 = Outstanding, 2 = Satisfactory, 1 = Weak, 0 = Extremely Poor, and N/A = Not Applicable.

Table 4. Fine Arts Web Site Evaluation Rubric (continued)

QUALITY OF DESIGN (27 Max Points)					
	3	2	1	0	N/A
Site displays a well laid-out combination of text and graphics					
Effective use of color and design elements					
Graphics make information more attractive					
Graphics help visualization of a particular event, person, place, or object					
Graphics help memorization of key information					
Graphics organize information into coherent structure					
Graphics, animations, sounds work together with text to make a particular point clear					
Sound adds to the understanding of the teaching point					
Graphics and music are consistent with the nature of the content					
UNIQUE WEB SITE ISSUES					
TOTAL POINTS AWARDED (81 Max Points)					

COMMENTS	Identify Focus of Student/Teacher
Identify Category of Fine Arts Web Site:	**Web Site:**
o Lesson Planning	o Direct Instruction
o Thematic Units	o Student Production
o Student Site	o Assessment and Evaluation
o Teacher Site	o Performance and Exhibition
	o Interpersonal Communication

RECOMMENDATION
Category:

o **Implement Web Site into Fine Arts Curriculum**

o **Do NOT Implement Web Site into Fine Arts Curriculum**

Note. 3 = Outstanding, 2 = Satisfactory, 1 = Weak, 0 = Extremely Poor, and N/A = Not Applicable.

Examples of Best Web Sites for Teaching Fine Arts

Significant resources are available on the Internet for the Fine Arts curriculum. Lesson plans and thematic units abound. Student sites provide instruction and enrichment, while teacher sites provide additional resources for classroom instruction, student production, assessment, and exhibitions. The following sites in Table 5 represent some of the best.

Table 5. Fine Arts Web Sites

Title and URL Address	Category and Focus (If Applicable)	Evaluation Score	Comments
ARTSEDNET www.artsednet.getty.edu/Arts EdNet/Resources/index.html	Lesson planning NA	I = 35 N = 15 D = 27 Total = 77	The Getty Institute Arts Education Site
ArtsEDGE artsedge.kennedy-center.org/teaching_materials/curricula/artsedge.html	Lesson planning NA	I = 37 N = 10 D = 25 Total = 72	National arts and education network developed through a cooperative agreement between the JFK Center for the Performing Arts and the National Endowment for the Arts
STArt www.open.k12.or.us/start/tasks.ncgi	Lesson planning NA	I = 32 N = 14 D = 25 Total = 71	STArt provides support for K–8 art teachers; look to their site for fine arts lessons (dance, drama, music, visual arts) and resources; links to the National Visual Arts Standards and Oregon Standards

Note. I = Instructional, N = Navigation, D = Design Quality, and A = Assessment.

Table 5. Fine Arts Web Sites (continued)

GraphicsDEN www.actden.com/grap_den/ index.htm	Student site Direct instruction	I = 36 N = 14 D = 25 Total = 75	Teach students to use a computer graphics program to create unique digital art; excellent interactive art–technology site for students in Grades 9–12
How to Read a Painting www.kcsd.k12.pa.us/~project s/critic/	Student site Assessment and evaluation	I = 37 N = 14 D = 26 Total = 77	Learning Art Criticism Skills to Enrich the Museum Experience for students in Grades 6 and up; excellent assessment module
New York Philharmonic Kidzone www.nyphilkids.org	Student site Student production	I = 32 N = 12 D = 18 Total = 62	Sound unit in science; great interactive site for kids; students can learn about instruments, orchestras, etc., as well as create their own virtual instrument; Grades 3 and up
Eyes on Art www.kn.pacbell.com/wired/ art2/	Student site Interpersonal communication	I = 39 N = 15 D = 27 Total = 81	Excellent interactive site for students in Grades 6 and up
Drawing Development in Children www.learningdesign.com/Port folio/DrawDev/ kiddrawing.html	Teacher site Assessment and evaluation	I = 30 N = 10 D = 25 Total = 65	Provides an overview of the stages of children's artistic development; helpful for teachers in designing age/developmentally appropriate lessons; despite low score, well suited to purpose
National Arts Standards http://artsedge.kennedy- center.org/professional_resour ces/standards/natstandards/	Teacher site Assessment and evaluation	I = NA N = 10 D = 25 Total = NA	National Arts Standards for visual art, dance, music, and theatre

Note. I = Instructional, N = Navigation, D = Design Quality, and A = Assessment.

Other Technology Considerations in the Fine Arts Curriculum

A more comprehensive list of additional Fine Arts Web sites is provided in Appendix B.

Conclusions

This chapter provides an overview of the history of art and technology as well as the standards for incorporating technology into the fine arts curriculum. It suggests evaluation rubrics for educational software and Web sites and offers the best in software and sites for further consideration. Hopefully, arts teachers gained further insight into implementing or expanding technology use in the classroom, while teachers in all disciplines discovered a wider perspective of art and technology applications in their own subject area.

References

Arnason, H. (1998). *History of Modern Art*. NewYork: Harry N. Abrams, Inc.

Bolz, D. (1997). A video visionary. *Smithsonian Magazine, 28*(7) 38-9.

Crary, J. (1998). *Techniques of the Observer*. Cambridge, MA: MIT Press.

Cuper, P. (1999). Getting there from here: One teacher's dance with technology. *Meridian: A Middle School Computer Technologies Journal, 2* (2), 1-5. Retrieved June 8, 2001 from URL: http://www.ncsu.edu/meridian/jul99/dance/index.html.

Feldman, E. (1985). *Thinking about Art*. Englewood Cliffs, NJ: Prentice Hall.

Narey, M.J. (2001). *K-12 visual arts curriculum*. (Available from Canon-McMillan School District, Canonsburg, PA 15317).

National Art Education Association. (1994). The national visual arts standards. Reston, VA: NAEA.

The National Standards for Arts Education. (2002). *What every young American should know and be able to do in the arts*. Consortium of National Arts Education Associations.

Russell, S. P. (1993). *Art in the World*. Fort Worth, TX: Harcourt Brace Jovanovich College Publishers.

Shlain, L. (1991). *Art & Physics: Parallel Visions in Space, Time, and Light*. New York: William Morrow.

Appendix A
Software Request Form

1. GENERAL INFORMATION

Faculty name:	**Date of request:**
Subject(s):	**System requirements:** *(What hardware do you need to run the software?)*
Grade level:	
Art goal/objectives:	
Selected topic:	
Category: o **Direct Instruction** o **Student Production** o **Assessment and Evaluation** o **Performance and Exhibition** o **Interpersonal Communication**	

2. DEFINE THE INSTRUCTIONAL NEEDS

Why do you need the software? What kind of software? Who will use it?

3. IDENTIFY POSSIBLE SOFTWARE PACKAGES

Title 1: **Title 2:** **Title 3:**	**Publisher 1:** **Publisher 2:** **Publisher 3:**
Catalog 1:	**Contact information 1:**
Software objective *(as described in catalog or package — these should match the objectives that you stated above)* **Cost:**	**Address:** **Phone:** **Fax:** **E-mail:** **Distributor offers preview: Yes ___ No ___**
Catalog 2:	**Contact information 2:**
Software objective *(as described in catalog or package — these should match the objectives that you stated above)* **Cost:**	**Address:** **Phone:** **Fax:** **E-mail:** **Distributor offers preview: Yes ___ No ___**
Catalog 3:	**Contact information 3:**
Software objective *(as described in catalog or package — these should match the objectives that you stated above)* **Cost:**	**Address:** **Phone:** **Fax:** **E-mail:** **Distributor offers preview: Yes ___ No ___**

Appendix B
Additional Fine Arts Web Sites (Not Evaluated)

Title and URL Address	Category and Focus (If Applicable)	Comments
Artswire www.aaae.org/lesson/lessplan.html#art	Lesson planning NA	Small collections of fine arts lesson plans
Sandford www.sanford-artedventures.com/teach/gen_lessons.html	Lesson planning NA	Sandford's site for general curriculum lesson plans incorporates art into a variety of subjects like science, social studies, math and reading
Chicana and Chicano Space mati.eas.asu.edu:8421/ChicanArte/index.html	Thematic units NA	Resource for teachers, students, and others interested in Chicano and Chicano art and culture; some considerations in selecting the artworks and its relevance to significant themes, gender balance, geographic breadth, and historical range
Smithsonian American Art Museum nmaa-ryder.si.edu/collections/exhibits/posters/	Student site	Brings together some of the great graphic images made in the United States over the past century; it views the American poster through its early examples, peculiar slogans, and visual devices, which incorporate a diverse vocabulary of symbols with broad appeal for Americans
National Gallery of Art www.nga.gov/feature/watson/watsonhome.html	Student site Student production	John Singleton Copley's "Watson and the Shark" was inspired by an event that took place in Havana, Cuba, in 1749; excellent guide to the many aspects in a visual work of art; for students in Grades 6 and up
Face to Face: Portraits From the Past www.sanford-artedventures.com/play/portrait2/a1.html	Student site Assessment and evaluation	Carmine Chameleon has accidentally set off a time machine, pulling five people out of the past; your task is to identify them using only their portraits as a guide so they can be returned to their time period
A. Pintura, Art Detective www.eduweb.com/pintura/	Student site Direct instruction	Outstanding, clever, and stimulating site using a Dashiell Hammett detective style to explore art in some depth; for students in Grades 4 and up

Note. I = Instructional, N = Navigation, D = Design Quality, and A = Assessment.

Inside Art	Student site	What if you were trapped inside a painting and had to solve a mystery to get out? An adventure inside art history; for students in Grades 4 and up
www.eduweb.com/insideart/index.html	Performance and exhibition	
Leonardo's Workshop: An ArtEdventure	Student site	Travel back in time to the Renaissance and explore Leonardo da Vinci's workshop to solve this interactive mystery; for grades 4 and up
www.sanford-artedventures.com/play/leonardo/index.html	Direct instruction	
WebMuseum, Paris	Student site	Images of paintings and artists' biographies covering a broad range, including Gothic, Renaissance, Impressionist, and 20th century paintings; includes a section on Japanese art
www.southern.net/wm/	Direct instruction	
Ancient Egyptian Art	Student site	Egyptian art and its central role in Egyptian civilization; browse the 4000-year time line to explore the information chronologically, or the index of 40 objects featured from the Museum's collection
www.metmuseum.org/explore/new egypt/htm/a_index.htm	Direct instruction	
Maya Adventure	Student site	A photographic exhibition of ancient and modern Maya culture, including Maya textile design, clothing, and other artifacts; part of The Science Museum of Minnesota's Maya Adventure Web site; for students in Grades 7–12
www.sci.mus.mn.us/sln/ma/top.html /	Direct instruction	
Origami	Student site	Clear instructions and elegant models in the traditional Japanese art of paper folding from Joseph Wu in Japan; contains links to many other origami sites, including "How to Make an Origami Crane"; for grades 4 and up
www.origami.vancouver.bc.ca/	Direct instruction	
Oatmeal Box Pinhole Photography	Student site	An entertaining site teaching children how to make their own pinhole camera as well as outlining the processes involved in producing their own photographs; for grades 4 and up
www.nh.ultranet.com/~stewoody/	Student production	
Piano on the Net	Student site	Educational site teaches students piano skills; the instructor for the course is film composer and jazz musician, Clinton Clark; each lesson takes about 35 minutes to complete; students may work at their own pace; for students in Grades 4 and up
www.pianonanny.com/	Direct instruction	

Note. I = Instructional, N = Navigation, D = Design Quality, and A = Assessment.

New York Philharmonic Kidzone	Student site	Students can see photographs of instruments and hear how they sound on this educational Web site; for students in Grades 2 and up
www.gspyo.com/	Student production	
Student Work and Accountability Web Site	Teacher Site	Document and develop models of how the examination of student work can be used in the various contexts of a school system to inform practice and policy
www.annenberginstitute.org/accountability/lswA/lswframe.html	Assessment and evaluation	
Looking at Student Work Collaborative	Teacher site	This Web site offers protocols for looking at student work, with a special focus on the professional development aspects of this process; it provides an interactive component that explores issues relevant to the advanced users of protocols and research in the field
www.lasw.org/	Assessment and evaluation	
Project Zero	Teacher site	Offers information on the project's history and its research, and lists current and upcoming studies in the theories of children and adult learning processes; included is information on workshops, symposia, and publications
pzweb.harvard.edu/	Interpersonal communication	
The Rainy Day Resource Page	Teacher site	Assists in search for additional fine arts Web sites
www.cp.duluth.mn.us/~sarah/rdr010.html		

Note. I = Instructional, N = Navigation, D = Design Quality, and A = Assessment.

Technology In The Technology Classroom

9

Lawrence A. Tomei, EdD

Introduction

Technologies in the classroom are now the norm in schools equipped with multimedia, graphics and animation, access to the Internet, and handheld and remote devices. Students use these technologies as once they used pencils, books, and manipulatives to learn content in all subject areas. Learning is surpassing mere skills and facts; students are thinking and solving problems using these new skills. Literally, the world has become their classroom. Technologies help students master content aided by the fastest Internet connections at home as well as school. Technologies are the norm rather than the exception as tools for learning and content to be taught and mastered in school.

Technologies are transforming how teachers teach and how their students learn, making it possible for both to attain the demands of ever-increasing standards. To meet these demands, educators have come to consider technology as a content area to be learned and as tools to be mastered.

Technology as a Content Area

The competent student uses technology to access, generate, and manipulate data and to publish results; to evaluate performance of hardware and software components of computer systems and apply basic troubleshooting strategies as needed; to enhance professional growth and productivity, communicate, collaborate, conduct research, and solve problems, and promote equitable, ethical, and legal use of technology resources.

The competent teacher applies technologies that support instruction in their grade level and subject areas. The teacher plans and delivers instructional units that integrate a variety of software, applications, and learning tools. Lessons reflect effective grouping and assessment strategies for diverse populations. The competent teacher also understands the changes in instructional technologies, their effects on workplace and society, their potential to address lifelong learning and workplace needs, and the consequences of their misuse; integrates advanced features of technology-based productivity tools to support instruction, extend communication outside the classroom, enhance classroom management, perform administrative routines more effectively, and become more productive in daily tasks; and uses computers and other technologies in research, problem solving, and learning development. Finally, the competent teacher develops information literacy skills to access, evaluate, and use information to improve teaching and learning and engage in collaborative planning and teaching with other educator colleagues and the larger school community.

A summary of some general and specific technology awareness issues presented in leading schools throughout the country is depicted in Table 1.

Table 1. General and Specific Technology Competencies for Grades K–12

Appropriate Grade Level	General Competency	Example Specific Competencies
Grade level K–3	The student demonstrates an understanding of what technology is	• The student can start, restart, and shut down classroom technology (e.g., a computer). • The student demonstrates an understanding of how classroom technologies operate and how their medium (e.g., floppy disk, videotapes, etc.) works. • The student demonstrates an understanding of the rules for using technology.
Grade level 4–8	The student demonstrates an understanding of what technology is and the different technologies available in the classroom	• The student demonstrates an understanding of how various classroom technologies work and how they are used for learning. • The student can identify active and nonactive commands and locate menus (e.g., computer pop-down menus, PLAY/START/STOP/REW/FF options from a VCR remote, etc.). • The student can prepare various technologies for presentation (e.g., load software applications, load videocassettes, etc.). • The student can communicate with teachers and peers using a proper technology vocabulary.
Grade level 9–11	The student demonstrates an understanding of what technology is, the different technologies available in the classroom, and how they operate	• The student can apply classroom technologies to their own learning requirements (e.g., use educational software appropriate for learning teacher-selected academic content, use a camcorder for videorecording, etc.). • The student can create, move, delete, copy, and back up educational resources prepared using technology. • The student can communicate with teachers and peers using a proper technology vocabulary. • The student can use technologies for self-learning and personal development.
Grade level 12–college	The student demonstrates an understanding of what technology is, the different technologies available in the classroom, how they operate, and their impact on lifelong learning	• The student can apply to his/her learning environment, one or more of the following instructional technologies: multimedia computers, CD-ROM (Read/Write) drives, color printers, videocassette (read/write) recorders, camcorders, digital cameras (including downloading and editing images), and digital and handheld scanners. • Students implement a sound personal understanding of the proper use and care of technology, including safety rules, school policies and guidelines, respect for property, a code of fair use and discipline, and a proper code of ethics in the application of technology for learning. • The student will master the following technology tools: word processing, multimedia design and presentation, spreadsheets, paint and draw (digital imagery), and database design and implementation.

Technology Tools for Learning

Technology tools often focus on questions of a student's skill in manipulating a diverse range of technologies and raises reservations about whether those skills are put to use to their best advantage in classroom settings. For example, technology tools can be used to deliver content, to promote experiential learning, to support collaborative learning, to demonstrate knowledge, to assess learning, etc. As schools prioritize their technology resources, a broad vision for the uses of technology is called for to embrace the promise of flexible, customized teaching and learning that takes advantage of a wider range of media, learner preferences, and teaching approaches.

Figure 1. Study of Student Use of Technology Tools, 1999

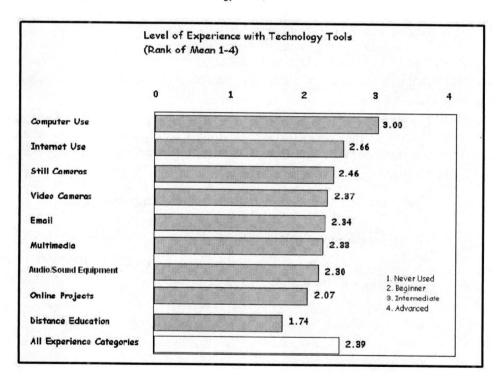

In a 1999 study conducted in the state of Utah (Figure 1), students were surveyed about their level of mastery in key technology tools, including general computer and Internet use, cameras, electronic mail, multimedia, audiovisual equipment, and online learning (including distance education). In summary, students placed themselves between beginner and intermediate levels of experience in their overall use of technology hardware (2.39). Students reported that they are most skilled at computer use with a solid intermediate (3.0) mean score, followed by Internet use at 2.66. Students were rated closer to beginners in the more interactive uses of the Internet, such as the use of email (2.34), multimedia (2.33), and online projects (2.12). And, most students reported that they have "never used" distance education, with a score of only 1.74. Again, most students assess themselves as beginners/novices with respect to their mastery of technology tools for learning.

Another study conducted by the ERIC Clearinghouse on Information and Technology identified several trends toward student mastery of technology tools in schools. Sources for the analysis included five leading professional journals in educational technology; papers given at annual conventions of three professional associations; dissertations from five universities that have a high level of doctoral productivity; and the educational technology documents that have been entered into the ERIC database. Here are some of those results that add a few additional technology tools to the growing list of minimum student competencies:

- Computers are pervasive in schools and higher education institutions. Virtually every student in a formal education setting has access to a computer.

- Networking is one of the fastest growing applications of technology in education.

- Educational technology is increasingly available in homes and community settings. Some of the newest technology tools include scanners, CD-ROM burners, desktop video, and video/sound capture.

- New delivery systems for educational technology applications have grown in geometric proportions.

- Educational technology is perceived as a major vehicle in the movement toward education reform.

In summary, research contributes a growing knowledge base about technologies in the classroom. As educators, we must continue to remind ourselves that, unlike other academic areas, technology must be viewed as content to be studied and as a tool for lifelong learning.

Historical Evolution of Technology-Based Technologies

The Apple II 1978

Steve Jobs and Steve Wozniak's Apple II was really the beginning of the personal computer boom. It debuted at the first West Coast Computer Faire in San Francisco in 1977. With a built-in keyboard, graphics display, and BASIC built into ROM, the Apple II was actually useful. In its original configuration with just 4 KB of RAM, it cost $1,298. A year later, this was increased to 48 KB of RAM with the floppy disk drive release in 1978.

VisiCalc 1979

VisiCalc spreadsheet software was released in 1979 for the Apple II. Many experts attribute VisiCalc as the first software package that made teachers look at personal computers as educational and business tools, not just toys. If the Apple II was the father of all personal computers, VisiCalc was the father of all personal productivity software.

The IBM PC 1981

In 1981, the landmark announcement of the IBM PC stunned the computing world. People had always thought of IBM as a high-end mainframe player. Even the chairman of IBM is supposed to have looked at the original PC and said that it would never fly, that mainframes would dominate forever. Despite its weaknesses, IBM did get one critical thing right with the PC. It was based on an open architecture so that it could grow into the future. This strategy, combined with IBM's huge influence and the release of Lotus 1-2-3 a year later, made business people sit up and take notice. The PC and its descendants went on to dominate the computing industry, although its entry into the educational marketplace was slower in materializing.

Lotus 1-2-3 1982

VisiCalc on the Apple II may have sold Wall Street on the idea of electronic spreadsheets, but Lotus 1-2-3 was the spreadsheet that Wall Street adopted. When the IBM PC took over the business world in the early 1980s, Lotus 1-2-3's simple but elegant grid was without question the best spreadsheet available. It added simple chart-style graphics and data retrieval functions to the paradigm established by VisiCalc. By the early 1990s, Lotus could brag that Lotus 1-2-3 was the best-selling application of all time. Lotus's period of dominance finally ended when *Microsoft Excel* came out with a graphical user interface for Microsoft Windows.

The Apple Macintosh 1984

In January 1984, the educational world took note of the introduction of Apple's Macintosh computer, with its graphical user interface that generated even more excitement than the IBM PC had 3 years earlier. It was the Macintosh product that changed the way people used computers. The Macintosh (lovingly called simply the Mac) was introduced in the famous "1984" TV commercial broadcast during the Super Bowl. It featured a small built-in high-resolution monochrome display, the wonderful Macintosh operating system with its graphical user interface, and a clunky looking single button mouse. Apple included several key applications that made the Macintosh immediately useful. *MacPaint* showed people what a mouse was good for, and *MacWrite* demonstrated that WYSIWYG (What You See Is What You Get) word processing really worked. The Macintosh redefined "user-friendly."

Microsoft Windows 1985

Originally released in 1985, Windows finally gave PCs the chance to run large graphical applications. Multiple programs could be run simultaneously, and although this was not true preemptive multitasking, it was a big step forward. Virtual memory was also provided. An impressive lineup of major software vendors with applications ran under Windows. Among these were versions of *Microsoft Word* and *Microsoft Excel*, which went on to dominate the personal word-processing and spreadsheet markets on both Microsoft Windows and the Apple Macintosh. The bottom line was that a PC running

Windows was now almost as easy to use as an Apple Macintosh. Because of this, Windows swept through the PC world like wildfire, and within a year, nearly everyone was running it on their PCs.

HyperCard 1987

In August 1987, an Apple engineer introduced a new type of software development tool — HyperCard. HyperCard was unlike any previous software development tool in two key respects: it was interactive rather than language based, and it was geared toward the construction of user interfaces rather than the processing of data. As such, HyperCard made an ideal tool for rapid prototyping and the development of in-house educational applications.

Virtual Reality 1990

In the early 1990s, the availability of high-powered 3D graphics worksta-tions allowed interactive 3D graphics to be developed. Computer-aided design (CAD) and 3D animation for special effects were two relatively obvious uses, but a more interesting and exciting use was the concept of virtual reality (VR). Virtual reality allows a user to be placed within a virtual world that could be explored from an arbitrary point of view. Early uses of VR included walkthroughs of buildings that had not yet been con-structed, simulations of environments that were too expensive or too dangerous to perform normal training within (e.g., outer space), and multiplayer virtual reality games. Other more sophisticated uses were found within existing scientific visualization fields, such as chemical engineering. In a sense, virtual reality had actually been around for ages in the form of flight simulation.

To make the virtual world convincing to the user, a number of special devices were invented. The most important of these was the stereoscopic head-mounted display, which tracked the position and orientation of the user's head and displayed a different image to each eye to trick the user's binocular vision into perceiving depth in the 3D scene. The head-mounted display also fed separate audio signals to each ear to produce stereo sound. When driven by appropriate software running on a computer with fast enough 3D graphics, the user could become totally immersed in a realistic virtual environment.

The Apple Newton 1993

The Apple Newton, released in August 1993, was the first popular handheld personal digital assistant (PDA). The Newton's primary input device was a stylus pen, and it relied heavily on printed handwriting recognition and pen-based navigation for its user interface. It was aimed squarely at mobile business professionals, and had a built-in notepad, calculator, to-do list, calendar, and address book for organizing personal and business affairs. Using an optional wired or wireless modem, it could send faxes or hook up to the Internet to send and receive email. Unfortunately, the first generation of Newtons was received poorly.

The Intel Pentium 1993

The Intel Pentium processor began shipping in late 1993, and it swept through the PC industry faster than any of Intel's previous processors. The Pentium contained the equivalent of 3.1 million transistors and initially ran at 60 MHz. Today's speeds approach 600 MHz and have literally made multimedia computer technology affordable in school computer lab and student homes.

The Multimedia Computer 1995

In contrast to previous computer technology, today's classrooms and labs have multimedia equipment available, including video projection systems, large-screen monitors, VCR/DVD hookups, DVD players, scanners, CD-R and CD-RW drives, digital cameras, and so forth. Although the Internet had been around for many years, it was the introduction of the multimedia computer that made the World Wide Web possible and, in turn, made the Internet popular.

The World Wide Web 1996

The Web offered a simple, friendly, graphical way of browsing for information or entertainment. Millions of electronic storefronts suddenly sprang up for the tens of millions of Web "surfers" to look at. Suddenly the Internet boomed, and just about everyone who owned a computer wanted to connect.

The World Wide Web was based on the original hypertext idea. Information was stored as formatted hypertext that browser tools such as Netscape could fetch from across the Internet and display to the user. HTML was soon augmented to allow pictures, then video and audio, and even 3D graphics and virtual reality. Users loved the Web, because the user interface was a simple point and click style, much easier than ftp and telnet. The user base, particularly in the field of education, grew very rapidly, doubling every few weeks. Current opinion is that the Web started the next big boom in the computer industry — the widespread use of networking for entertainment and education.

Standards for Technology in a Technology-Based Curriculum

Introduction

The International Society for Technology in Education (ISTE) and its Accreditation and Standards Committee established the de facto guidelines for evaluating computing and technology programs in the United States. In their National Educational Technology Standards (http://cnets.iste.org/pdf/nets_brochure.pdf), ISTE and the National Council for Accreditation of Teacher Education (the official body for accrediting teacher preparation programs), stated, "To adequately prepare our students for adult citizenship in the Information Age, computer related technology must become a tool that students and teachers use routinely."

As part of the NETS, ISTE and NCATE released a set of Technology Foundation Standards for Students in pre-kindergarten through 12th grade. They also published guidelines of fundamental concepts and skills for applying information technology in educational settings. It is those standards for technology that are discussed now.

Technology Standards for Students

Technology standards for students are divided into six broad categories that provide a framework for planning technology-based activities in which students achieve success in learning, communication, and life skills. These categories include the following:

- **Basic operations and concepts:** Students must demonstrate a sound understanding of the nature and operation of technology systems and become proficient in the use of technology.

- **Social, ethical, and human issues related to technology:** This standard infuses an understanding of the responsible uses of technologies, information, and software and encourages positive attitudes toward technology uses that support lifelong learning, collaboration, personal pursuits, and productivity.

- **Technology productivity tools to enhance learning:** Included in this standard are technologies to increase productivity and promote creativity; collaborate in constructing technology-enhanced models, prepare publications; and produce other creative works.

- **Technology communications tools:** The fourth category concentrates on telecommunications technologies, preparing students to collaborate, publish, and interact with peers and experts, and communicate effectively to multiple audiences.

- **Technology research tools:** This category involves student use of technologies to locate, evaluate, and collect information from a variety of sources; process data and report results; and evaluate and select information resources appropriate for specific tasks.

- **Technology problem-solving and decision-making tools:** The final category prepares students to use technology resources for solving problems and making informed decisions in the real world.

Technology Standards for Teachers

ISTE's Technology Performance Profiles for Teacher Preparation suggest ways to prepare teachers to use technology in the classroom. The Profiles offer a series of guidelines for creating a program in instructional technology. As with student standards, the Society settled on six key categories:

- **Technology operations and concepts:** Teachers are expected to demonstrate a sound understanding of technology operations and concepts, including knowledge of concepts related to technology and current and emerging technologies.

- **Planning and designing learning environments and experiences:** Teachers are expected to design, implement, manage, and assess their own appropriate learning situations incorporating technology-enhanced instructional strategies to support the diverse needs of learners.

- **Teaching, learning, and the curriculum:** Teachers are expected to infuse technology into their curriculum to maximize student learning, address the diverse needs of students, and develop higher-order skills and creativity.

- **Assessment and evaluation:** Teachers are expected to apply technologies effectively. To accomplish this standard, teachers must be able to evaluate technology-based instructional strategies and the subject matter content to be taught

- **Productivity and professional practice:** Teachers must use technology to enhance their own productivity and professional practice, especially to communicate and collaborate with peers, parents, and the larger community in order to nurture student learning.

- **Social, ethical, legal, and human issues:** As their students, teachers must understand the social, ethical, legal, and human issues surrounding the use of technology in schools and apply those principles in practice.

Educational Software for the Technology Classroom

Introduction

All software is not created equally. Some is much better than others. Some programs might be good for some things but not for others. The job of an educator is to distinguish what is appropriate for the classroom — what works for the teacher and the student and what does not.

Evaluation Classifications

To become a discriminating user of educational software for technology, begin by discerning the six types of educational software and their primary goals. Drill and practice provides students with practice on concepts they have already learned. Good drill and practice provides feedback and explains how to get the correct answer. Tutorials present a new concept, where text illustrations, description, and simulations are provided to teach a specific task, skill, or application. Simulations can be great tools for integrating various disciplines into a specific unit. Most simulations have math, science, social studies, and language arts aspects. Educational games are generally in a drill and practice format with a winner or top score option. Good problem solving and simulations can have a game appearance. Students are required to use strategy and input. Most simulations and games have some problem-solving aspect. Problem-solving programs can be great classroom discussion starters for exploratory learning. Productivity software is also known as tool software. This includes any software used as a tool to produce documents, spreadsheets, a database, or other instructional materials.

There are many different reasons to evaluate software. As the amount and variety of educational software grows, there is a commensurate need for it to be assessed for suitability for its intended purpose. Teachers need to know whether and how an item can be used to improve classroom instruction. Learners need to know how the software might impact their learning experience. Technologists may have to recommend which of several software alternatives should be purchased. Finally, developers of educational software need to define criteria against which their products can be assessed.

To meet the demands of classroom teacher, student, technologist, and designer, educational software must offer multiple instructional designs and address several pedagogies. Educational software with a balanced approach should deliver basic skill instruction as well as critical thinking exercises and opportunities for student collaboration. It should offer language arts instruction that incorporates whole language and phonics instruction, for example.

A second key facet of educational software is flexibility, in terms of purchasing options and implementation models. Educators need numerous purchasing options for integrating technology, from the district's wide area network, to a school site implementation or a classroom focus on mathematics software, for example. In addition, for the configuration or scope, the software must be flexible enough to allow educators to select and tailor lessons to each student's learning needs. It should also offer flexibility in terms of classroom implementation for use as a presentation tool, as well as individual student or group workstations.

Last, and most certainly not least, is results of the learning experience. Educators must have a way to measure student learning and ensure that educational goals are being reached. This can be accomplished with software that incorporates a management system, and administrators have this capability. Today's educational software can track a student's performance individually and modify instruction accordingly. Software should provide a variety of assessment tools for skills and open-ended instruction, including management system reports, assessment rubrics, and student portfolios.

A Rubric for Evaluating Technology Software

Recent advances in instructional software have been dramatic, in quantity and quality. Producers of software have made large strides toward creating software that serves specific educational goals instead of directing those goals. A second major advance has been in the degree of learner interactivity offered, thereby providing greater learning for students and taking greater advantage of the capabilities of the computer. The selection and evaluation criteria provided by the rubric in Table 2 are designed to aid practicing educators in dealing with the dilemma created by the proliferation of quality instructional software available today.

Table 2. Rubric for Evaluating Technology Software

Criteria	0–10 Points	11–20 Points	21–30 Points
Instructional design	Interface is hard to understand and is frustrating; no indication of where to start; graphics are confusing; slow loading	Interface is somewhat easy to understand; it occasionally causes confusion but helps more than it hinders; apparent where to start; graphics are somewhat helpful; slow loading	Interface is attractive and very easy to understand; it makes sense and feels good to use; obvious where to start; graphics are very helpful, fast loading
	Navigation is difficult; it is easy to get lost and hard to retrace steps; there are many unnecessary layers	Navigation is somewhat easy; user gets lost occasionally but can retrace steps; there are few unnecessary layers	Navigation is easy; it is hard to get lost and easy to retrace steps; there are no unnecessary layers
	Software has a tendency to crash	Software occasionally crashes	Software rarely crashes
	Software is not user friendly	The software is user friendly in some aspects, not in others	Software is user friendly
Flexibility	Students can use program but it requires a great deal of teacher assistance	Students can use program with teacher help	Students can use program with minimal teacher help
	On-screen directions are obtuse, requires teacher guidance and reference to documentation	On-screen directions often require teacher explanations	On-screen directions are clear
	Directions are critical to using this software and cannot be skipped at option of user	Directions cannot be skipped but can be turned off by the teacher	Directions can be skipped at option of user
	Directions are linked entirely to the documentation: no onscreen assistance	Directions can be reviewed at certain times throughout the instruction	Directions can be reviewed at any time.
	Students are not permitted to review previous screens unless they exit and re-start the program	Students can review some previous screens at the discretion of the software	Students can review previous screens without restarting program
	Student must complete a unit of instruction before exiting the program	Student can exit at certain locations within the program at the discretion of the software	Student can exit the program at any time
	Student must restart the program from the beginning whenever they exit early	Student can restart components of the program once they have exited the software.	Student can restart the program where they stopped.
Results of the learning experience	Software does not state its objectives and gives no way of evaluating user experience	Software is sketchy or unclear about its objectives; it is difficult to evaluate user experience	Software is clear about its learning objectives; gives a clear way to evaluate user experience
	Content not applicable to the curriculum standards	Content applicable to the curriculum standards in some ways	Content applicable to the curriculum standards
	Content makes no connection to the learner's experience	Content makes some connection to the learner's experience	Content makes connections to the learner's experience
	Content has no source	Difficult to trace content to a source	Content comes from a credible source

Examples of Best Educational Software

The best educational software appropriate for technology content is to be found in the drill and practice, tutorial, and productivity categories. For drill and practice software, some of the most important instructional factors to be considered include presenting information appropriate for particular audience, providing clear directions for the learner, and using age and content appropriate vocabulary. To properly guide the student through the software content, the best educational software has an availability of online help options and feedback that is positive and corrective. Good software provides an opportunity for practice by the student with items ranging in difficulty on a progressive continuum with appropriate learning theory and pedagogy for the desired instructional goals. Finally, a solid drill and practice software package assesses student learning by providing a reporting mechanism suitable to track student progress.

Determining instructional factors for presenting information in tutorial software begins by stimulating a student's prior knowledge of the content material followed by a lesson designed with appropriate content scope and sequence. A sound tutorial guides the student with an appropriate use of instructional prompts and varied responses to student inputs. Practice is encouraged via feedback that is positive and corrective, and learner control of the lesson is a paramount consideration. Finally, assessment of student learning is automatic, reportable to the student and instructor, and contains valid pre- and posttests.

Productivity software presents information employing a methodology appropriate for the content (linear or branching). It guides the student by using prompts and help menus, both online and hard-copy documentation. Practice is not necessarily encouraged, however, when addressing complex features and options of the tool, is provided via online examples and demonstrations. Assessment of student learning as well is not often provided as part of the product; rather, evaluation of student understanding of productivity software is most effective using authentic, project-based learning events.

With these considerations in mind, Table 3 provides some examples of the best educational software in the drill and practice and tutorial categories for technology content and tools.

Table 3. Best Technology Software

Title	Category/ Platform(s)	Evaluation Score	Grade Level	Cost ($)	Comments
HyperCard	Productivity Mac	I = 28 F = 30 R = 30 Total = 88	6–8	99.00	Organizes information into easy-to-use "stacks" of cards for navigation and searching; clicking on a button, students view related text, graphics, sounds, and movies
KidsSpiration Inspiration	Productivity Mac/Windows	I = 25 F = 25 R = 25 Total = 75	K–3 4–12	104.50	Helps students K–12 see, organize, and develop great ideas using the proven principles of visual learning; for young readers and writers
Kid Pix Studio	Productivity Mac	I = 20 F = 22 R = 26 Total = 68	3–12	29.95	Imaginative art tools that inspire creativity and offer endless hours of fun
Kid Works Deluxe	Productivity Mac/Windows	I = 20 F = 22 R = 24 Total = 66	6–12	59.95	Integrated application with word processing that prints stories in a variety of fonts; art program with paintings, stickers, and animation; and, multimedia
PageMaker Plus	Productivity Mac/Windows	I = 24 F = 30 R = 28 Total = 82	6–12	800.00	Helps students create high-quality documents, templates, illustrations, photos, etc., simply and reliably; very pricey.
Read, Write, and Type	Drill&Practice Mac/Windows	I = 18 F = 16 R = 22 Total = 56	1–3	39.00	Merges the teaching of phonics-based reading skills, with an introduction to typing
Grammar Fitness	Tutorial Windows	I = 16 F = 14 R = 16 Total = 46	6–10	79.00	Helps students improve their grammar skills, including usage, diction, idioms, grammatical relationships, and punctuation.
Mavis Beacon Teaches Typing	Drill&Practice Mac/Windows	I = 24 F = 24 R = 28 Total = 76	3–12	59.95	Learn to type with this keyboarding program; works individually with beginners or advanced typists; provides appropriate instruction, practice, feedback, and information based on student performance
Kid Keys	Tutorial Mac/Windows	I = 22 F = 16 R = 30 Total = 68	K–2	63.95	Teaches young learners the alphabet, the computer keyboard, and how to use a mouse
Typing Tutor	Drill&Practice Mac/Windows	I = 30 F = 28 R = 28 Total = 86	5–12	59.95	Introduces students to the keyboard and familiarizes them with the look and feel of e-mail and Internet web pages as they increase their speed and accuracy on the keyboard
Dr. Seuss's ABC	Tutorial Mac/Windows	I = 28 F = 20 R = 20 Total = 68	K–3	44.95	More than 400 alphabetically inspired surprises hidden within 26 pages make learning words and letters fun through an illustration

Note. I = Instructional Design, F = Flexibility, and R = Results.

Internet Use in the Technology Classroom

Introduction

Many instructors and professors tell their students not to use pages from the World Wide Web in their projects or papers because of the many issues with finding authoritative and accurate information, as discussed earlier in this document. Usually, they are referring to use of pages found on the "surface web" and not databases of journals, newspapers, books, or data purchased by libraries and delivered to readers using the Web.

Evaluation Classifications

It is estimated that the Internet is composed of over 552.5 billion Web pages or documents and is growing by 7.3 million pages a day (The How Much Information Project, 2000). Web pages consist of those which are freely available to any user and currently composed of some 2.5 billion documents and proprietary pages (some 550 billion of them) often only accessible by members of organizations that produce or purchase them, organizations such as businesses, professional associations, libraries or universities. For educational purposes, there are nine basic types. Reference/research sites include pages containing online resources suitable for supporting student investigations, studies, and explorations. Examples of such sites include Internet search engines, online encyclopedias, online library resources, etc. School sites involve home pages of educational institutions depicting mission, history, development, awards, curriculum/academics, and, of course, sports. Sites often contain email addresses of faculty and links to showcase activities within the school. Content sites provide an educational forum, bringing together the people, events, photographs, documents, art, literature, music, movies, timelines, activities, and classroom resources for a specific instructional topic. Entertainment sites include links to educational entertainment featuring sports and game software, strategy games, action adventure, music creation software, simulation software, role-playing software, and trivia software, often used for enrichment activities following a successful mastery experience in the classroom. Shared/collaborative sites take in today's world of instant communication and global economic society. There is a need to examine and understand how cultural differences and behaviors influence collaboration and collaborative learning among institutions and individuals. Shared/collaborative sites provide the forum for examining, understanding, and sharing cultural differences, even if a difference is simply between regions of the United States. Assessment sites report on student performance with comprehensive information about what students know and what they can do in various subject areas. They provide descriptions of students' strengths and weaknesses in basic and higher-order skills; comparisons of achievement by race/ethnicity, gender, type of community, and region; longitudinal trends in performance; and relationships between achievement, student backgrounds, and classroom instruction. Tutorial sites consist of online lessons, white papers, quicksheets, tips and tricks, frequently asked questions (FAQs), "how to's" and other sources of technical information. There appears to be a tutorial covering what seems like every possible topic of interest to educators, including productivity applications, computer security and troubleshooting problems, Internet basics, graphics software, Web page design and programming, operating systems, and more.

The vast majority of WWW sites are designed and authored by nonexperts. The quality or accuracy of the information found on the World Wide Web is primarily nonrefereed material. Teachers are ultimately responsible for evaluating the information found on Web sites for content, accuracy, and currency.

A Rubric for Evaluating Technology Web Sites

With over a half trillion Web sites to assess, teachers must quickly home in on key characteristics that separate possible sites of educational benefit from "net litter." For example, teachers might consider format: the Web site should be user friendly with a clear intent, yet be easy to understand with appropriate, clearly labeled links. A Web site should be aesthetically considerate with graphics and text that are quickly downloaded, relevant to the content, and age appropriate. The site should be appealing with a creative use of graphics and colors. Teachers are interested in sites that promote higher-order thinking skills and challenge their learners to think, reflect, discuss, hypothesize, compare, classify, etc. But by far, the most important characteristic of a good Web site concerns content; it must be credible, accurate, complete, and current. If it engages the learner and addresses multiple intelligences and learning styles in the process, so much the better. The evaluation rubric provided in Table 4 is designed to aid the educator in locating, analyzing, and selecting the best Web sites for classroom use from among the abundant sites available on the Internet.

Table 4. Rubric for Evaluating Technology Web Sites

Criteria	0–10 Points	11–20 Points	21–30 Points
Web site analysis	Layout has little or no structure or organization	Structure consistent; headings and style consistent within pages; text and links reliable and logical	Consistent format found on all pages; design is intentional and well thought out for target audience; attempts made to accommodate different Web browsers, platforms, and system capabilities
Web site design and development	Difficult to understand, spelling and other errors Images are unrelated to page/text; most images were recycled from other pages on the Internet; images are too big/small in size or resolution; images poorly cropped or have color problems	Site easy to understand; perfect spelling; one or two grammar, syntax, or semantic problems Images have sound relation to text; some images are student-produced; images have proper size, resolution, colors, and cropping	Clear, concise, well-written; images are from three or more sources (scan, CD-ROM, QuickCam, Photoshop, PhotoDeluxe or Illustrator, etc.) Images have strong relation to text; student-produced, and are proper size, resolution, colors, and cropping
Web site implementation	Navigation between pages difficult for students; links missing and redirected to new addresses Credible information is erroneous, incomplete, insignificant, and out of date Information is inferior and not likely to be revisited Integrates only one content area or discipline	Navigation between pages clear; all links work Credible information is suspect, complete, trivial, and poorly maintained Information is modest and not likely to be revisited Integrates content areas or disciplines, but poorly Loads quickly without significant delays	Navigation path is clear and logical, all links work Credible information is accurate, complete, meaningful, and maintained Information is rich and likely to be revisited Integrates several content areas or disciplines Visually appealing for students Information is verifiable, reliable, and consistent
Web site evaluation	No analysis of learning outcomes; site contains formative or summative assessment but not both Neither engaging nor particularly interesting	Integrates multiple sources of information to assess student learning; balances intrinsic and extrinsic motivation for learning Relies on technology to interest the learner	Meets the standards or objectives of the curriculum Uses highest levels of Bloom's taxonomy and the Taxonomy for the Technology Domain Engages the learner throughout

Examples of Best Web Sites for Teaching Technology

The best Web sites for teaching technology are likely found in the categories of content, tutorials, and shared/collaborative. For content-specific sites, the most important instructional factors to be considered include organization; an inviting opening page which draws the visitor inside, logical and effective page layout, clear connection among sections, and easy navigation. The content must be accurate, current (has the site been updated within the last two months?), and relevant to student's present level of understanding. Presentation issues include whether the Web site is clearly identified and easy to find, its layout is clear and easy to follow, and the background and text colors work well together. In addition, graphics, icons, images, and sounds must be used consistently. Finally, a content site must be designed so that all the links work properly, the graphics are optimized (reduced in size for speedy loads yet large enough for required details), and work in all major browsers (Netscape, Explorer, and America Online at a minimum).

The best tutorial sites reflect many of the same characteristics of the content site; the primary distinction concerns the attention to detail. While content sites are delivered for a particular topic to particular students, tutorials must allow for a greater range of diversity in presentation. Offering a tutorial on word processing, for example, requires several instructional modes to ensure that many student learning styles as possible are addressed. Some additional issues include full compliance with copyright guidelines, student interaction, built-in assessment with guided remediation if necessary, and more attention to grammar, punctuation, and spelling.

Finally, the best shared/collaborative sites disclose the institution's philosophy and academic standards. The site relates school community, location and type of school, personnel and contact information, academic calendars, and school policies (for example, attendance, discipline, or grading). For academic matters, a shared/collaborative site might provide a general electronic mail address for communication with teachers and students and a bulletin board system so that visitors can post and reply to messages from fellow students.

Table 5 provides some examples of the best content, tutorials, and shared/collaborative web sites for technology content and tools.

Table 5. Best Technology Web Sites

Title	Description	Evaluation Score	Site Type	URL Address
Tutorialfind — find tutorials on absolutely anything	Tutorialfind is the largest tutorial directory on the Web; it features over 300 categories of tutorials and currently more than 3000 links; categories include everything from 3D software to Web development	A = 28 DD = 30 I = 30 E = 30 Total = 118	Tutorial	www.tutorialfind.com/tutorials/
Power Point in the Classroom	Introduction, creating slides, making changes, adding images, adding motion and sound, timing and rehearsal, and taking a presentation on the road	A = 28 DD = 30 I = 30 E = 20 Total = 108	Tutorial	hwww.actden.com/pp/
Teaching Through Technology	Teaching Through Technology is a professional development resource for teachers from the Wisconsin Educational Communications Board	A = 30 DD = 30 I = 25 E = 10 Total = 95	Tutorial	www.ecb.org/ttt/index.htm
Word Processing Tutorial Secondary Students	Basics of word processing created for the high school student level	A = 25 DD = 25 I = 28 E = 15 Total = 93	Tutorial	http://www.uwf.edu/coe/tutorials/technolo/wordproc/wordproc.htm
Teaching Keyboarding to Elementary-Age Students	A team approach for teaching elementary educators how to teach proper keyboarding skills to their students	A = 22 DD = 20 I = 20 E = 15 Total = 77	Tutorial	http://biseben.bus.usu.edu/papers/keyboarding/keyboarding.htm
The Portage School Grade 4 Spreadsheet Lessons	Two lessons that introduce Grade 4 students to spreadsheets	A = 25 DD = 15 I = 15 E = 20 Total = 75	Shared/collaborative	http://www.plpsd.mb.ca/resources/introduc.htm
Internet Primer	A primer on the Internet including the World Wide Web (WWW), ftp, Gopher, and Telnet; email, listservs, and newsgroups; and netiquette	A = 25 DD = 15 I = 20 E = 15 Total = 75	Students	http://www.mhhe.com/socscience/intro/santrock/primer.htm
Keyboarding Online @ Crews Middle School	Everything to teach keyboarding including rules and tools, finger positioning, and drill sheets	A = 20 DD = 15 I = 15 E = 20 Total = 70	Content	http://www.crews.org/curriculum/ex/compsci/keyboarding/index.htm
Paint Shop Pro 5 Tutorials	Twenty-four online tutorials covering all aspects of Paint Shop Pro	A = 25 DD = 10 I = 15 E = 15 Total = 65	Tutorial	http://www.grafx-design.com/psp_tut.html
Mr. Hallett's 7th Grade Online Computer Basics Class	Everything a 7th grader wanted to know (needed to know) about computers but was afraid to ask	A = 15 DD = 15 I = 15 E = 15 Total = 60	Shared/collaborative	www.aptosjr.santacruz.k12.ca.us/computers/computers.html
Our Lady of the Sacred Heart High School	Home page with mission, history, faculty, curriculum, and, of course, sports	A = 15 DD = 10 I = 10 E = 10 Total = 45	School	www.olsh.org/

Note. A = Analysis, DD = Design/Development, I = Implementation, and E = Evaluation.

Other Technology Considerations in the Technology Curriculum

Many educators accept teaching with technology as perhaps the most important instructional strategy to impact the classroom since the textbook. A Taxonomy for technology in the technology content area offers a view for designing learning objectives using technology.

A Taxonomy for the Technology Domain

Research shows that teachers who use a classification scheme to prepare instructional learning objectives tend to produce successful student learning outcomes (Kibler, Barker, & Miles, 1970; Krathwohl & Bloom, 1984). The classification proposed in Table 6 includes literacy, collaboration, decision making, discrimination, integration, and tech-ology. Each step offers a progressive level of complexity for teaching technology-based content material and should be considered when incorporating technology into an integrated thematic unit.

Table 6. Taxonomy for the Technology Domain

Taxonomy Classification	Action Verbs that Represent Intellectual Activity on this Level
Literacy **Understand technology and its components**	• **Understand** computer terms in oral and written communication • **Demonstrate** keyboard and mouse (click and drag) operations • **Use** basic computer software applications. • **Operate** computer input and output devices
Collaboration **Share ideas, work collaboratively, form relationships using technology**	• **Make use of** communications tools for individual writing and interpersonal collaborations • **Share information** electronically among students • **Communicate** interpersonally using electronic mail
Decision Making **Use technology in new and concrete situations**	• **Apply** electronic tools for problem solving • **Design** effective solutions to practical real-world problems • **Develop** new strategies/ideas with the help of brainstorming software • **Prepare** an electronic spreadsheet • **Create** calendars, address books, and class schedules
Discrimination **Select technology-based instructional materials appropriate for individual students**	• **Appraise** educational software and determine its effectiveness with respect to individual student learning styles • **Discriminate** multimedia resources appropriate to student development, age, gender, culture, etc. • **Assess** various Internet environments for their strengths as possible student learning tools • **Employ** electronic media to construct new research and investigate lesson content
Integration **Create new instructional materials using various technology-based resources**	• **Design, construct,** and **implement** teacher-made Internet-based materials for learning subject content • **Design, construct,** and **implement** teacher-made text-based materials for learning subject content • **Design, construct,** and **implement** teacher-made visual-based classroom presentations for learning subject content • **Consider the uses** of technology to address the strengths and avoid the weaknesses inherent in multiple intelligences • **Focus** student learning using integrated instructional materials
Tech-ology **The study of the value and uses of technology**	• **Defend** copyright and fair use laws for using technology • **Debate** the issues surrounding legal/ethical behavior when using technology • **Consider the consequences** of inappropriate uses of technology

Level One: Technology for Literacy

Technology literacy is defined as the minimum technical competencies expected of students. The first rung on the ladder establishes the most fundamental literacies for the technological learner. At this lowest level of intellectual activity, learners demonstrate varying degrees of basic computer skill mastery at each level of elementary, middle, secondary, and postsecondary education. Teachers should use learning objectives that promote an understanding of computer terms and concepts, the operation of computer hardware, and the use of basic computer applications. Teachers should use action verbs that involve general awareness and use of simple technology. Here are two learning objectives grounded in technology literacy:

> "Following a hands-on demonstration from the teacher, students will access their computers, enter their passwords, and complete the first online session within 45 minutes."

> "Using a mouse and keyboard, students will locate three Internet sites provided by the teacher."

Level Two: Technology for Communication

Level two addresses the ability to use technology to interact with others. Effective uses by the learner include technology for written and oral communication, the professional exchange of information, and interpersonal collaboration. Teachers should ask students to share information in written form (word processing, desktop publishing), participate in and interpret interpersonal dialog (via newsgroups, list servers, and chat rooms), and respond to direct interchange (electronic mail). Some example learning objectives in communications include:

> "Using email, the student will send at least two messages and reply to another four messages from their electronic pen pals during the first 2 weeks of the semester."

> "Students will use the chat room at least weekly during the grading period to share ideas with fellow classmates about assigned readings."

Level Three: Technology for Decision Making

Decision making refers to an ability to use technology in new and concrete situations, including those of the previous two levels. Helping the learner acquire decision-making skills via technology includes such important tools as spreadsheets, brainstorming software, and statistical analysis packages. Making decisions using technology requires greater student understanding than the previous stages. Therefore, teachers at this level should design, develop, and apply various technologies as practical tools for student self-learning. Here are a few example objectives that reflect this level's strength.

> "After recording the quantitative results of a 2-week observation period, students will capture the resulting weather data in electronic format and use the 'what if' features of spreadsheets to forecast the next day's weather."

> "Prospective college applicants will use the resources of CD-ROM catalogs to research and identify at least three potential colleges based on area of the country, programs desired/offered, cost and financial assistance opportunities, and reputation and personal interest."

Level Four: Technology for Discrimination

Technology is a potent tool for exploring and discovering academic content. At this level, it centers on identifying appropriate classroom instructional resources. Teachers are finding a growing cache of educational software, electronic journals, and Internet sites appropriate for student use. Teachers should analyze available technology resources and select those that match student learning strategies with specific lesson objectives. A few learning objectives that demonstrate technology for learning include:

"Students will assess four Internet sites concerning the Holocaust and select the site that best reflects their feelings and emotions about the Nazi's 'final solution.'"

"Students will construct a comprehensive outline using online brainstorming software in support of their senior classroom research project."

"Students will employ advanced math software and complete the first four lessons on algebra attaining at least a 90% on the online quiz at the conclusion of each lesson."

Level Five: Technology for Integration

Integration asks the teacher to take several technologies and develop new (i.e., previously nonexistent) materials to help students better understand the current lesson. For example, Internet sites are clearly becoming the media of choice for hosting lesson content. Unfortunately, due to immature knowledge of Web interface design principles, they are often disjointed, redundant, sometimes flawed, and often confusing to the student. At this level of the taxonomy, teachers should identify content-rich hyperlinks and combine this information with visual and auditory presentations, textual matter, and other technologies to create entirely new lesson materials.

In his landmark research, Howard Gardner (1993, 1999) developed the idea that there is not a single "intelligence," but rather seven: visual/spatial, musical, verbal, logical/ mathematical, interpersonal, intrapersonal, and body/kinesthetic intelligence. Classroom teachers, using various technologies at this level, benefit from his investigations by selecting a format that best suits their students' individual learning styles. Example objectives at the integration level include:

"Using a teacher-prepared workbook created from online Internet resources, students will explore the possible theories of dinosaur extinction and select their favorite theory."

"Using a teacher-developed visual presentation, students will examine the skeleton of the human body and correctly identify 8 out of 10 major bones."

"Students will use teacher-made Web pages containing a photo digital image, email address, and summary of personal interests to present a synopsis of books read this semester."

Level Six: Tech-ology

The hyphenated word, tech-ology, suggests that the highest level of the taxonomy deals with the study of technology; perhaps it would be best to entitle this level as "technologyology;" the study of the value and uses of technology. Social issues surface whenever thinking students consider the implications of technology use. At this level, teachers should introduce technology-related issues for students to appraise, argue, assess, choose, compare, and defend. For example, journals and newspapers expose the disparity of computer access between the wealthy and poor (May, 2000). Teachers might initiate classroom debates about the availability of information between the computer "haves" and "have-nots." Other potential topics include copyright and fair use laws and their impact; censorship on the Internet; or legal and ethical behavior when using information and technology. This top level of the taxonomy asks learners to judge the value of technology and predict how it affects society as a whole. Here are some examples:

"Students will locate a publication, journal, or newspaper article which reflects an aspect of the legal/ethical use of technology and prepare a grammatically correct, three-page, double-spaced report critically analyzing the premise of the work."

"Learning groups will locate the U.S. Copyright Office online and use their information to prepare a 25-minute presentation on the topic, 'United States Copyright Laws and Fair Use for Educators,' to be given to the class."

"Class members will join an online chat room to debate the benefits and drawbacks of a Microsoft monopoly. After the discussion, four salient points must be used by the student to prepare a point paper describing the effects of any proposed government action against the corporation on individual computer users in America."

As mentioned in Chapter 1, taxonomies are tools for the teacher and the learner. Research by a team of graduate students in an instructional design course documented how objectives prepared in the technology domain produced more consistently successful learning outcomes. Each member of the class was responsible for a different graduate-level course hosted in the WebCT online environment. They readily identified learning objectives written without benefit of the Taxonomy for the Technology Domain and rewrote those objectives using appropriate action verbs. Then, they presented both sets of objectives (a "before and after," if you will) to students enrolled in that course. Without exception, learners preferred the more specific taxonomy-based objectives. Conditions for learning were less ambiguous, student outcomes were demonstrable and verifiable, and criteria for successful mastery of the objectives were indisputable (Tomei, 2001).

Recap of the Technology Taxonomy

The bottom line for teachers: match teaching strategies with student learning styles using the taxonomy. Literacy, collaboration, decision making, discrimination, integration, and tech-ology objectives offer a new perspective for immersing technology into classroom teaching.

Conclusions

After nearly three decades of technology in classrooms, many noticeable advancements have been chronicled. Most schools have computer labs; many have computers in every classroom. Over 90% of schools are connected to the Internet, and over one-third of teachers have access to technology in their classrooms. Most teachers and students use word-processing programs, spreadsheets, simulations, and multimedia software.

This chapter considers how technologies are transforming the way in which teachers teach and students learn. Distinct from other discussions, technology is viewed from the perspectives of subject matter content area and as tools for learning. From a content area viewpoint, students must learn to use technology to access data, operate hardware and software, grow professionally, and use technology to benefit mankind. As a tool, students must become technologically literate — users of these latest apparatus for lifelong learning.

As with every content area, a teacher must know and understand the history of the subject matter to be taught. Likewise, a recognition of the minimum competencies (in education, we call them standards) required to succeed is compulsory. Such appreciation of how technology began, how it matured into a viable teaching strategy, and how it has become a literacy for students in the 21st century will hold the instructional technologist of the future in good stead.

On the practical side, teachers are bombarded with countless catalogs of educational software and an almost limitless number of Internet sites purporting to sustain education and the classroom. In this chapter alone, a dozen software packages and Web sites were offered as the best the discipline has to offer. Certainly, each reader of this book would have examples of such materials and most would likely be better examples. So, hopefully, the rubrics for evaluating software and Web sites offered in the chapter will serve to help the educator assess, compare, select, and, most importantly, match the very best educational technologies to the individual learning objectives deemed important to the teacher and to the best learning style of the learner.

References

Bloom, B. S., Englehart, M. B., Furst, E. J., Hill, W. H., & Krathwohl, D. L. (1956). *Taxonomy of Educational Objectives: The Classifications of Educational Goals*. New York: Allyn & Bacon/Longman/Pearson Publishers.

Content Area Standards for all Teachers. School District #54, Schaumburg, IL, web54.sd54.k12.il.us/district54/lts/dmoore/techstandards/ILLtech.htm.

Gardner, H. (1993). *Frames of Mind: The Theory of Multiple Intelligences*. Boulder, CO: Basic Books, Inc.

Gardner, H. (1999). *Intelligence Reframed: Multiple Intelligences for the 21st Century*. Boulder, CO: Basic Books, Inc.

Goldman, S., Cole, K., & Syer, C. (1999). *The Technology/Content Dilemma,* Institute for Research on Learning, Menlo Park, CA, www.ed.gov/Technology/TechConf/1999/whitepapers.

Kibler, R. J., Barker, L. L., & Miles, D. T. (1970). *Behavioral Objectives and Instruction*. New York: Allyn & Bacon/Longman/Pearson Publishers.

Krathwohl, D. L., & Bloom, B. S. (1984). *Taxonomy of Educational Objectives. The Classifications of Educational Goals. Handbook I*. New York: Addison-Wesley Company/Pearson Publishers.

Lyman, P. & Hal, R. V. (2000). How Much Information? Project, University of California, Berkeley, www.sims.berkeley.edu/research/projects/how-much-info/.

May, M. (2000, January 18). Push on to get home computers to poor students. *San Francisco Chronicle*, p. A-13.

Plotnick, E. (2000). *Trends in Educational Technology*, ERIC Clearinghouse on Information and Technology, ERIC Digest, www.ed.gov/databases/ERIC_Digests/ed398861.html.

Ronan, J. (2001). *Tips for Evaluating a World Wide Web Search*, University of Florida, www.uflib.ufl.edu/hss/ref/tips.html.

Tomei, L. A. (2001). *Writing Learning Objectives Using a Taxonomy for the Technology Domain*. Duquesne University, School of Education. Unpublished manuscript.

Tomei, L. A. (2001). Using a Taxonomy for the Technology Domain. *Technology: Applications to Teacher Preparation*, Pennsylvania Association of Colleges and Teacher Educators, Monograph III, October.

Tyner, K. (1999). *Student Uses of Educational Technology in Rural Utah*, State of Utah Resources Service Center, www.wested.org/tie/surweb/welcome.shtml.

Technologies For Students With Disabilities

Linda M. Lengyel, PhD

10

Introduction

Computers and other technologies are powerful tools supporting students with disabilities. Students with visual impairments access written text through auditory output devices or print magnification devices, students with learning disabilities who have difficulty organizing thoughts use software as a visual organization tool, students with physical disabilities write papers using adaptive equipment attached to a computer or voice recognition software, students who cannot use their voice speak using an alternative communication device.

Historical Evolution of Technologies for Students with Disabilities

Technology has a long history of assisting persons with disabilities; dating as far back as Alexander Graham Bell in the early 1800s, when he worked on devices for people with hearing impairments, beginning with the phonoautograph, a device to "see speech." If you consider the medical advances that have been made for people with disabilities, technology is traceable as far back as the 1500s, when Ambrose Pare began manufacturing metal limbs and corrective devices for people with physical disabilities. Currently, technology provides access to curriculum and activities that in the past were not accessible to students with disabilities. As cited by the National Council on Disability (1993), Radabaugh so aptly stated, "for Americans technology makes things easier; for Americans with disabilities, technology makes things possible."

With the passing of Public Law 19-142 in 1975 and recent enactments of that law with the Individuals with Disabilities Education Act (IDEA), there has been an even greater focus on supporting students with disabilities in the general education curriculum and activities. It must be stressed that the use of technology by students with disabilities is not unique to special education classrooms. Technology is of possible benefit whenever there is a mismatch between the demands of the environment and the skills and abilities of the student. For example, students need to demonstrate understanding and the learning that takes place in the classroom; however, not all students are able to talk. A mismatch between the environment and the student exists. However, using technology, students communicate using an augmentative communication device, effectively removing the barrier.

When discussing students with disabilities, it is helpful to understand the distinction between a disability and a handicap. A disability is defined by what a person "has" or is living with, for example, a student may have a learning disability, or a student may be blind. A handicap is the result of the interaction between the student and the environment. Handicaps are barriers imposed by what is in (or not in) the environment. For example, if a student is blind (the disability) and in an environment that offers text only through visual reading, the student is also handicapped. If that same student is in an environment that provides the text on audiotape or in

Braille, the handicap is removed. Perhaps then, the primary purpose of technology for students with disabilities is to remove or diminish the handicap and provide a means to by-pass the disability and offer access to curriculum and activities.

Another purpose of technology is to provide remediation activities, opportunities for repeated review of challenging content. Technology can offer the same learning outcomes for students with disabilities as they do for students without disabilities. Each of the preceding chapters presents invaluable information that can and should be applied to students with disabilities.

Assistive Technology refers to technology that assists students with disabilities. This chapter reviews some of these technologies that support and assist such students. Assistive technology is defined in the Individuals with Disabilities Education Act as "any item, piece of equipment, or product system, whether acquired commercially off the shelf, modified, or custom-ized, that is used to increase, maintain, or improve the functional capabilities of a child with a disability" [20 U.S.C. 1401(1)]. The list of Web sites located in Appendix A provides a description of the agencies, federal statutes, and assistive technologies available for Students with Disabilities. An abridged inventory of assistive technology products for Students with Disabilities is in Appendix B.

Technology Standards for Students with Disabilities

The use of technology for students with disabilities is well grounded in legislation and professional standards. A brief discussion of how these standards have evolved in the United States is provided below.

The Uses of Technology and Legislation

The use of technology for persons with disabilities was first referenced in legislation in 1954 in the Vocational Rehabilitation Act Amendments of 1954, Public Law 82-565 (Flippo, Igne, & Barcus, 1995). Because assistive technology has been such a historical part of supporting people with disabilities, a complete review of the legislative history is beyond the scope of this chapter. A summary of the four major pieces of legislation that refers to the use of technology with persons with disabilities is depicted in Table 1.

Table 1. Major Legislation for Technology and Persons with Disabilities

Individuals with Disabilities Education Act (IDEA) as amended in 1990 and 1997 **Definition**. The term "assistive technology device" means any item, piece of equipment, or product system, whether acquired commercially off the shelf, modified, or customized, that is used to increase, maintain, or improve functional capabilities of a child with a disability.
The Rehabilitation Act Amendments of 1986 (P.L. 99-506) and 1998 **Definition**. Rehabilitation technology: "the systematic application of technology, engineering methodologies, or scientific principles to meet needs of individuals with handicaps in areas which include education, rehabilitation, employment, transportation, independent living, and recreation."
Developmental Disabilities Assistance and Bill of Rights Act, Amended 1987 (PL 100-146) **Definition**. The Developmental Disabilities Assistance and Bill of Rights Act requires that all funded services be aimed at providing opportunities and assistance for persons with developmental disabilities to allow them to "achieve their maximum potential through increased independence, productivity and integration into the community."
Technology Related Assistance Act 1988 (PL 100-407), Amended 1994 (PL 103-218) **Definition**. Assistive technology (AT) is defined as any item, piece of equipment, or product, whether acquired commercially, off the shelf, modified, or customized, that is used to increase, maintain, or improve the functional capabilities of individuals with disabilities.

Technology and Professional Standards Related to Students with Disabilities

Professional standards also address the use of assistive technologies in the classroom. The Council for Exceptional Children (CEC) publishes the Standards for the Preparation and Licensure of Special Educators. The use of technology in designing and implementing supports for students with disabilities is infused throughout these Standards. In 1999, Lahm and Nickels published a separate set of standards related specifically to the use of technology in the Council for Exceptional Children journal, *Teaching Exceptional Children*. These standards are presented in Table 2.

Table 2. Essential Knowledge and Skill Competencies

Standard 1: Philosophical, Historical, and Legal Foundations of Special Education

Essential Knowledge
- Legislation and regulations related to technology and implications for special education

Skills
1. Articulate a philosophy and goals for using technology in special education
2. Use technology-related terminology appropriately in written and oral communication

Standard 2: Characteristics of Learners

Essential Knowledge
- Characterize exceptional learners that influence the use of technology
- Impact of technology on exceptional learners
- Impact of technology on exceptional learners with moderate disabilities

Skills
3. Identify the academic and physical demands placed on the student by computer software and related technology materials

---

Table 2. Essential Knowledge and Skill Competencies (continued)

Standard 3: Assessment, Diagnosis, and Evaluation

Essential Knowledge
- Analyze, summarize, and report student performance data to aid instructional decision making regarding technology
- Identify functional needs, screen for functional limitations, and identify if the need for a comprehensive assistive technology evaluation exists
- Refer for additional evaluation regarding technology if adequate data are not available for plan development
- Recognize the need for further evaluation regarding technology, and refer to other professionals when appropriate
- Recognize poor outcomes regarding technology needs, and reevaluate and reinitiate the process as needed
- Work with assistive technology team members to identify assistive technologies, both hardware and software, that can help individuals meet the demands placed upon them in their environments
- Define measurable objectives to monitor progress toward achieving stated goals regarding technology
- Observe and measure consumer's performance with the assistive technology after a period of initial use
- Compare actual performance with anticipated performance and the goals stated in the intervention plan
- Interview the consumer, the family, and caregivers to determine if the technology solution meets their present and future needs

Standard 4: Instructional Content and Practice

Essential Knowledge
- Procedures for evaluating computer software and other technology materials for their potential application in special education program

Skills
4. Identify elements of the special education curriculum for which technology applications are appropriate and ways they can be implemented
5. Design, deliver, and assess student-learning activities that integrate computers/technology for a variety of student populations
6. Design student-learning activities that foster equitable, ethical, and legal use of technology by students
7. Identify and operate software that meets educational objectives for students in multiple educational environments
8. Use computers to support various stages of the learning process and to facilitate student reporting of educational achievements
9. Use technology to compensate for learning and performance barriers
10. Identify and use assistive technologies that can provide access to educationalmaterials that are otherwise inaccessible to some individuals
11. Use computer-based productivity tools to develop classroom materials
12. Teach special education students to use productivity software programs to perform tasks such as word processing, database management, graphics, production, and telecommunications
13. Teach special education students to operate equipment and run associated educational programs
14. Use productivity tools for word processing, database management, and spreadsheet applications
15. Solicit accurate feedback from end-users, and others having experience with technology
16. Understand proper mechanical and electrical safety practices, or direct their use in the assembly and integration of the technology at a defensible level of competence

Table 2. Essential Knowledge and Skill Competencies (continued)

Standard 5: Planning and Managing the Teaching and Learning Environment

Skills
17. Demonstrate the proper care of technology systems and related software, use simple diagnostics to determine problems that arise, and perform routine maintenance
18. Arrange and manage the classroom environment to facilitate the use of technology

Standard 6: Managing Student Behavior and Social Interaction Skills

Skills
19. Organize computer activities to promote positive social interactions

Standard 7: Communication and Collaborative Partnerships

Essential Knowledge
- Roles that related services personnel assume in providing technology services to special education students

Skills
20. Recognize the need to refer a consumer to another professional regarding technology
21. Identify assistive technology team members and their roles
22. Design and implement integrated technology classroom activities that involveteaming and small group collaboration
23. Collaborate with consumer and other team members in planning and implementing the use of assistive and adaptive devices
24. Communicate effectively, including listening, speaking, and writing on technology issues
25. Use electronic mail and Web browser applications for communication and for research to support instruction
26. Advise general education teachers about the use of technology systems with special education students who are mainstreamed into their classes

Standard 8: Professionalism and Ethical Practices

Essential Knowledge
- Confidentiality of information
- Limits of expertise — recognize and seek outside expertise

Skills
27. Recognize own skills and knowledge regarding technology, and limit individual practice accordingly
28. Maintain a professional development program to ensure the acquisition of knowledge and skills about new developments in technology as they become available
29. Identify activities and resources to support professional growth related to technology
30. Demonstrate knowledge of equity, ethical, legal, and human issues related to technology use in special education

---

Educational Technologies for Students with Disabilities

Introduction

Technologies to support students with disabilities are categorized in several different ways. This section reviews technologies that support student communications; provide environmental control; provide access to computers; and assist in listening, seeing, and writing. In addition, technology is further defined as high tech, medium tech, low tech, and no tech (Flippo, Inge, & Barcus, 1995). This chapter focuses on high and medium technology solutions.

There are many other uses of technology, for example, technologies that assist in mobility, adaptive equipment that assist in dressing and eating, and home and vehicle adaptations. A complete review of all available assistive technologies is beyond the scope of this chapter. Therefore, this chapter focuses on the technologies seen most often in classrooms. However, school personnel should be aware of all technologies appropriate for students with any level of challenges, whether they are considered to have "severe disabilities" or "mild disabilities."

Communications Technologies that Support Students with Disabilities

Communication is needed in every school, in every classroom. Christy Brown illustrates the importance of communication in the following quote from his book, *My Left Foot*, written in 1954:

> Speech has always been one of the biggest obstacles in my endeavor to make ordinary contact with people. It has been the one aspect of my handicap that has caused me the bitterest pain, for without speech one is practically lost, curtained off from other people, left wishing to say a million things and not able to say one. Writing is all very well, but there are some emotions that cannot be conveyed, that cannot be "felt" through the written word alone. Writing may be immortal, but it does not bridge the gap between two human beings as the voice may, and oh, I would

rather have an hour's fierce argument with a pal or a few moments of soft chatter with a girl than write the greatest book on earth. (as cited in Tanchak & Sawyer, 1995)

Students who do not communicate well verbally can use communication devices to express themselves. Such devices are generally referred to as augmentative or alternative communication devices. Although the devices may look the same, there are significant distinctions between alternative and augmentative communication devices. Using a device in addition to or to support their verbal communication is considered augmentative communication. Using a device instead of human speech is alternative communication. Many students use augmentative communication; however, students with more severe communication disorders use alternative communication devices.

Either set of devices can be high technology or low technology. High technology communication devices allow for input and output of information. In the more complex devices, the student typically types in a thought that is communicated through display or auditory output, or both. The amount of information stored in the device varies. The more complex devices may also serve as computers, allowing users to create and edit file documents through a word-processing program.

Figure 1. Dynavox Alternative Communications Device

Examples of multipurpose devices are the RealVoice, the Touch Talker/Light Talker, the Liberator, and the Dynavox (Figure 1) (Tanchak & Sawyer, 1995). The Crespeaker is a smaller, handheld talking device that stores up to 100 characters, or about 18 words, and has 402 built-in phrases. The Crespeaker "speaks" the message and displays a corresponding message on its small screen. Less complex communication devices rely less on the traditional keyboard and more on a series of buttons that display the message when pressed. The Big Mack (Figure 2) is one large button with a removable cover, so images may be placed under the cover. The Big Mack repeats a single recorded message when the button is pressed.

Figure 2. Big Mack Button

The selection of the right communication device is essential. As stated earlier, assistive technologies lessen the gap between student abilities and the demands of the environment. A match between what the student needs and what the environment demands must be made. The selection of the right communication device often demands the talents of an individual with expertise in augmentative and alternative communication. Such an expert is found in speech and language departments or by contacting the Department of Education for a referral.

Teachers in classrooms play an important role on the team. Selecting the appropriate communication device requires an understanding of the child and the features needed most. Such student-focused considerations include motor, sensory, and cognitive–linguistic abilities as well as the ability to encode information using symbols (Tanchak & Sawyer, 1995). A thorough assessment to identify the appropriate augmentative or assistive communication device is essential.

Environmental Control Devices that Support Students with Disabilities

Many students with physical disabilities benefit from technological support to control their environment. Environmental controls are "devices with the capacity to regulate aspects of a person's physical surrounding" (Sprigle & Lane, 1995). Environmental control devices give a student access to a computer, a communication device, or other objects in the classroom.

Typically, switches enable a student to control another object or activate an object. For example, the Control Center Latch Switch controls three adapted items simultaneously. A single touch turns an adapted tape recorder on, while another touch turns it off. Single-button switches are also available to operate single items or to record messages. Some of the considerations in the selection of an environment control device include the following (Inge & Sheperd, 1995):

- Student's use of the body to control the device
- Amount of energy required to control the device and the fatigue factor that results
- The student's range of motion

- The portability of the device
- Student reaction to the device
- Operating techniques (i.e., direct selection, visual scanning)
- Student feedback from the device
- Flexibility of the device
- Use with augmentative or alternative communication devices

Access to Computers

Computers are standard tools in schools and homes. Some students with disabilities cannot readily access information from the computer; they may need the help of additional technologies. Access here is defined as much more than turning on the computer with an environmental control switch. Some students have challenges seeing or hearing, which limits their access to software and the Internet. Other students may have difficulty using the keyboard or mouse to manipulate information. Microsoft and Apple operating systems provide built-in options that support students with disabilities. For example, Microsoft offers an "accessibility wizard" that guides the user through accessibility options and configurations. Table 3 provides a summary of available accessibility features.

Table 3. Accessibility Options in Windows and Macintosh Operating Systems

Accessibility Option	Microsoft www.microsoft.com/enable/	Apple www.apple.com/disability/
Magnification	• Adjust the magnification level of text and images in the magnification window. • Change the size and location of the magnification window. • Change the position of the magnification window on the desktop. • Invert the screen colors. • Use a high-contrast scheme. • Magnifier tracking options are as follows: • Following the mouse pointer as it moves on the screen • Following the keyboard focus, which centers on the location of the cursor • Following text editing	• CloseView is a screen enlarger; it magnifies all screen images (including text, graphics, menu bar, and the mouse cursor) up to 16 times the normal size
Pointers/cursor	• Three sizes available for pointer • Several colors • Enlarged cursor	
Color schemes	• High-contrast schemes available	• CloseView can inverse the Macintosh display (text appears white on a black background)
Keyboard options	MouseKeys: navigation with the numeric keyboard as opposed to the mouse • StickyKeys: repeats simultaneous keystrokes • On-screen keyboard • Keyboard access to the taskbar • FilterKeys: adjusts the keyboard response so that repeated keystrokes are ignored • ToggleKeys: emits sounds when certain "locking" keys are pressed	• MouseKeys • StickyKeys • SlowKeys: enable the user to change the length of time it takes for a keystroke to be registered on the screen
Mouse options	• ClickLock: highlights or drags without continuously holding down the mouse button • SnapTo: automatically moves the pointer to the default button in a dialog box • Mouse Pointer Visibility Options: shows pointer trails, hides pointer while typing, shows location of pointer when you press the CTRL key	
Auditory output	• "Narrator," a text-to-speech utility built directly into the operating system • SoundSentry provides visual cues for system sounds • ShowSounds makes applications display captions for the speech and sounds they make	• Text-to-Speech allows your computer to speak the alert messages that appear on the screen • Speakable Items: recognizes the built-in commands (the commands that came with your speech software) and the names of each file in the Speakable Items folder on your hard disk
Visual output		• Visual Alerts: enables a user to be alerted to errors and alerts that are given via sound feedback by the menu bar blinking
Keyboard/mouse alternatives	• SerialKeys allow the use of alternative input devices instead of a keyboard and mouse	

More information on these features is available at www.microsoft.com/
enable/ for Microsoft and www.apple.com/disability/ for Apple systems.
Some Internet service providers (ISPs) add their own accessibility features
for greater access for their clients. For example, in the recently released AOL
6.0, a range of accessibility options has been added (www.corp.aol.com/
access_policy.html). There is a call for "universal design" in the creation
of software and Web sites. Architects who design accessible buildings for
persons with physical disabilities coined the term. Visit www.cast.org/udl/
for more information.

Educational Technologies for Teaching Students with Disabilities

Technology that Assists Teachers

The technologies discussed thus far are for the student as user. Technologies can also be invaluable for teachers who must modify and adapt
curriculum for their students with disabilities. Special education teachers
are often given responsibility to adapt written materials used in general
education classrooms; preparing materials using word processing makes the
task easier. Some publishers are now providing materials (tests, worksheets,
handouts) on disk, which allows teachers to quickly modify them for all
students. Graphic programs such as *Inspiration* are useful to create story
webs and other graphic organizers for the visual learner. Additionally,
software for tracking student progress is particularly useful for special
education teachers.

Teaming and Collaboration

Any discussion regarding students with disabilities should include the
importance of teaming and collaboration. The 1997 Reauthorization of IDEA
provided even greater emphasis on the inclusion of students with
disabilities in general education classrooms. The intent of IDEA was always
to promote the coeducation of students with disabilities in environments
with their nondisabled peers. For any inclusive efforts to be successful,
collaboration is essential.

School teams supporting students who can be assisted by technology are typically comprised of several different players. Membership of these teams is driven by the needs of the individual student. Students with speech and language challenges have a speech and language pathologist as part of the team. Students with motor challenges have occupational and physical therapists as part of the team. Some students may require even more specific expertise whenever technology is involved. States have established a system of technical assistance available to their school districts using assistive technology. These technology consultants may prove to be invaluable additions to the student-centered team.

No two students are alike; therefore, the process of selecting technologies should be based on student needs and strengths. Assessment of student needs includes information about student environment, including school, home, and community settings.

Conclusions

For many students, technology has given them a means of expressing themselves. For others, it increases their quality of life. Technology advances the academic performance of students with disabilities and helps them improve their behavior (Lewis, 1993). Technologies enable people with disabilities to accomplish goals never before thought possible (Lewis, 1993). Do not overlook the fact that technology can have the same outcomes for students without disabilities as they do for students with disabilities. Therefore, all of the preceding chapters in *Teaching Across the Curriculum* offer valuable information that can and should be applied to all students. As teachers become more aware of technology, we must all work to better support all of our students in reaching their full potential to become more successful in school and in life.

References

Assistive and Adaptive Computing Technology in Education. (n.d.). *Assistive & Adaptive Technology Terminology*. Retrieved August 10, 2001 from the World Wide Web: at_advocacy.phillynews.com/data/terminology.html.

Castellani, J., & Jeffs, T. (2001). Emerging Reading and Writing Strategies Using Technology. *Teaching Exceptional Children*, *33*, 5, 60–67.

EASI: Easy Access to Software and Information. (n.d.). *Assistive Technology and Special Education Terminology*. Retrieved August 15, 2001 from the World Wide Web: www.rit.edu/~easi/ak12/k12/k12glossary.html.

Family Center on Technology and Disabilities. (n.d.). Retrieved from the World Wide Web: fctd.ucp.org/fctd/techterms.htm.

Flippo, K. F., Inge, K. J., & Barcus, J. M. (1995). *Assistive Technology: A Resource for School, Work and Community*. Baltimore, MD: Paul H. Brookes Publishing Co.

Herlihy, D. (2001). Access to the Curriculum. *SETP: Special Education Technology Practice*, 3.3, pp. 39–41.

Higginbotham, D. J., Lawrence-Dederich, S., Sonnenmeier, R. M., & Kim, K. (1995). Assistive Communication Technologies for Persons with Expressive Communication and Cognitive Disabilities. In W.C. Mann & J. P. Lane, *Assistive Technology for Persons with Disabilities* (pp. 99–123). Bethesda, MD: The American Occupational Therapy Association, Inc.

Inge, K.J., & Shepherd, J. (1995). Assistive Technology Applications and Strategies for School System Personnel. In K. F. Flippo, K. J. Inge, & J. M. Barcus, *Assistive Technology: A Resource for School, Work and Community* (pp. 133–166). Baltimore, MD: Paul. H. Brookes Publishing Co.

Lewis, R. (1993). *Special Education Technology: Classroom Application*. Pacific Grove, CA: Brooks/Cole Publishing Company.

National Council on Disability. (1993, September). Study on financing assistive technology devices and services for individuals with disabilities: A report to the President and the Congress of the United States. Retrieved from the World Wide Web: www.ncd.gov/newsroom/publications/assistive.html.

New & Noteworthy. (2001). *SETP: Special Education Technology Practice*. 3.3, p. 6.

Ray, J. & Warden, M. K. (1994). *Technology, Computers and the Special Needs Learner*. Albany, NY: Delmar Publishers.

Sprigle, S., & Lane, J. P. (1995). Assistive Technology for Persons with Physical Disabilities. In W.C. Mann & J.P. Lane, *Assistive Technology for Persons with Disabilities* (pp. 33–73). Bethesda, MD: The American Occupational Therapy Association, Inc.

Tanchak, T. L., & Sawyer, C. (1995). Augmentative Communication. In K. F. Flippo, K. J. Inge, & J. M. Barcus, *Assistive Technology: A Resource for School, Work and Community* (pp. 57–79). Baltimore, MD: Paul. H. Brookes Publishing Co.

Technologies Provide Alternate Sensory Feedback. (1998). National Center to Improve Practice in Special Education Through Technology, Media and Materials. Retrieved from the World Wide Web: www2.edc.org/NCIP/library/vi/feedback.htm.

APPENDIX A

Useful Web Sites for Assistive Technology

Web Site	Description	Web Address
National Center to Improve Practice (NCIP)	Located at Education Development Center, Inc., NCIP is funded by the U.S. Department of Education, Office of Special Education Programs from 1992–1998 to promote the effective use of technology to enhance educational outcomes for students with sensory, cognitive, physical and social/emotional disabilities."	www2.edc.org/NCIP/
Center for Applied Special Technology (CAST)	Founded in 1984 as the Center for Applied Special Technology, CAST is an educational, not-for-profit organization that uses technology to expand opportunities for all people, including those with disabilities.	www.cast.org
National Council on Disability (NCD)	They provide freeware and shareware links for accessibility software.	www.ncd.gov/newsroom/ publications/assistive.html
Alliance for Technology Access (ATA)	This is a network of community-based resource centers, developers and vendors, affiliates, and associates dedicated to providing information and support services to children and adults with disabilities, and increasing their use of standard, assistive, and information technologies."	www.ataccess.org/
Equal Access to Software and Information	This resource to the education community provides information and guidance in the area of access-to-information technologies by individuals with disabilities. They offer information about developments and advancements within the adaptive computer technology field, and spread that information to colleges, universities, K–12 schools, libraries and into the workplace."	www.rit.edu/~easi/
Section 508: The Road to Accessibility	Section 508 requires that Federal agencies make electronic and information technology accessible to people with disabilities. The Center for Information Technology Accommodation (CITA), in the U.S. General Services Administration's Office of Government-wide Policy, has been charged with the task of educating Federal employees and building the infrastructure necessary to support Section 508 implementation. Using this Web site, Federal employees and the public can access resources for understanding and implementing the requirements of Section 508.	www.section508.gov/

APPENDIX B
Product Sources

Big Mack/Jelly Bean Button Single-Switch Latch and Timer AbleNet, Inc. 1081 Tenth Ave. S.E. Minneapolis, MN 55414 800-322-0956 www.ablenetinc.com	Board-Maker and Board-Builder Magic Touch and TouchWindow Writing with Symbols Mayer-Johnson P.O. Box 1579 Solana Beach, CA 92075
CoWriter/Discover Switch/Inspiration Kidspiration Write Outloud Don Johnston Inc. 800-999-4660 www.donjohnston.com/	Crespeaker Control Center Latch Switch Crestwood Communication Aids, Inc. 6625 N. Sidney Place Milwaukee, WI 53209-3253 414-461-9876
DECtalk Digital Equipment Corporation Continental Blvd. Merrimack, NH 03054 (800) 344-4825	Dynavox Sentient Systems Technology, Inc. 2100 Wharton St. Pittsburgh, PA 15203 800-344-1778
IntelliKeys IntelliTools 800-899-6687 www.intellitools.com	JAWS Synapse Adaptive Stop Speech Recognition & Adaptive Technology 3095 Kerner Blvd., Suite S San Rafael, CA 94901 Toll-free: 888-285-9988; Fax: 415-455-9801
Large-textured plate switch/vibrating plate switch/Gooseneck soft switch Flaghouse 601 FlagHouse Drive New Jersey 07604-3116 800-793-7900 FlagHouse.com	Liberator and Touch Talker/Light Talker Prenke Romich Company 1022 Heyl Road Wooster, OH 44691 800-262-1984
Magic Touch and TouchWindow Touch Screens Inc. 5761 Four Winds Dr. Lilburn, GA 30047 800-753-2441 www.touchwindow.com	PixWriter and Picture It Software Slater Software, Inc. 351 Badger Lane Guffey, CO 80820 Toll-free: 877-306-6968; Fax: 719-479-2254
Real Voice Adaptive Communications Systems, Inc. P.O. Box 12440 Pittsburgh, PA 15231 800-247-3433	Zoom Text Adapted Computer Technologies 16 Gingham St. Trabuco Canyon CA 92679 949-459-5241 sales@compuaccess.com
Soft Switch Tash Inc. 3512 Mayland Ct. Richmond VA 23233 800-463-5685 or (804) 747-5020 Fax: (804) 747-5224 tashinc@aol.com	

Integrating Technology Into The Curriculum

Linda C. Wojnar, EdD and Lawrence A. Tomei, EdD

11

Editor's Note: *The final chapter, "Integrating Technology Into the Curriculum," offers a look at how classroom teachers utilize the competencies, content ideas, and practical examples offered in the previous chapters to design, develop, and implement their own, teacher-made technology-based instructional materials.*

Whenever a teacher is introduced to the "latest and greatest," supposedly state-of-the-art tool for the classroom, they are often overwhelmed by the technical aspects of the technology, its cost in terms of time and money, and its lack of accessibility in their school. In other words, why learn a new technology if there is no one available to help me implement the tool in my curriculum, if my school cannot afford to purchase the package, or if we do not support that package or version in our computer lab? All are good questions.

In this chapter, the contributor offers three tools for creating technology-based instructional materials. Microsoft Word is the word processor of choice for creating text-based materials. Microsoft's Power Point is recommended for visual-based classroom presentations. And, Netscape Composer provides an environment for creating Web-based materials.

Chapter 11 offers a primer for creating technology-based instructional materials. Certainly, there is no attempt to provide a level of detail necessary to produce materials that would compete with commercial packages. Rather, consider the technology tools introduced in Chapter 2, combine them with the academic content offered in Chapters 3 through 9, take into account the implications of special needs students addressed in Chapter 10, and create individualized instructional materials using the skills offered.

If additional features are desired, readers are encouraged to locate a copy of Teaching Digitally: A Guide for Integrating Technology into the Classroom, by Lawrence A. Tomei, published by Christopher Gordon Publishers, Inc.

Text-Based Materials

Introduction

Teachers often find that concrete, hard-copy resources make effective learning tools for the classroom. Student handouts serve as assessment instruments, remedial content material, and enrichment activities. Study guides offer targeted instruction in the form of guiding questions for discovery learning and additional reading material for test preparation. No matter how many high-technology resources are available to the classroom instructor, sometimes, text-based material is still the best way to teach a lesson objective.

Microsoft *Office* includes a robust suite of office productivity tools including the word-processing package *Word*; the graphics presentation system *Power Point*; spreadsheet application *Excel*; database application *Access*; and, desktop publishing capability *Publisher*. Microsoft *Office* runs equally as well on both the Macintosh and Windows platforms with minimal differences reflecting primarily mouse functions. Microsoft *Word* employs many of the commands, options, and menus of a full-featured word processor and is the tool of choice for designing, developing, creating, and implementing text-based educational resources.

Handout and study guide materials are constructed with a common set of components. As a minimum, they should contain the following elements:

- **Title of the lesson.** In addition, a graphic or image appropriate for the content material contained in the resource could be added.

- **Student name.** Materials to be used by learning groups would offer room to identify all students participating in the experience.

- **Date of the lesson/section number.** Successful materials are used year after year. The date of the lesson identifies use in multiple sessions over the course of a semester or multiple academic years.

- **Teacher's name.** Self-explanatory.

- **Page numbers.** Sequential numbering of pages eliminates student confusion and enhances classroom discussion.

- **A variety of sensory aids to student learning.** This can include Clip Art, images, and text.

Perhaps the most straightforward method of preparing text-based instructional material is to first locate a document that already closely mirrors the final desired product. Just such a document is provided in Appendix A. The four-page handout, prepared using Microsoft *Word,* serves as a guide for developing handouts and study guides for the classroom. It contains all the required elements listed above. The required features of Microsoft *Word* necessary to "cut and paste" new content material are discussed below. Examine the handout first, and then follow the explanation of *Word* features to modify the example to fit your learning objectives. To demonstrate the explanation, specific instructions are provided following each feature; the instructions are displayed within a text box.

To speed the process of entering text into a document, the authors of this book have prepared an online Web site containing the examples depicted in Appendix A. The URL for this Web site is: www.duq.edu/~tomei/TAC (*Teaching Across the Curriculum*). Readers may visit the site, locate, view (only), or download the **STATES.doc** file and concentrate on applying the features introduced to create a new handout appropriate for your classroom.

Selecting (Highlighting) Text. Before editing, any text to be modified must first be highlighted or "selected." To select:

- A *word*. Position the cursor on the desired word and double-click the mouse.

- A *sentence* or *line*. Place the cursor anywhere in the middle of a sentence or line.

  - Windows machines, hold the Control key and click once.

  - Macintosh systems, hold the Command key and click once.

- A *paragraph*. Position the cursor within the paragraph and triple-click the mouse.

Practice selecting text using STATES.doc downloaded from www.duq.edu/~tomei/TAC. Note: a tilde (~) precedes the directory name

---

Moving Text. With a line of text highlighted, try the Cut, Copy, and Paste commands to move text to another location in the document.

- *Cut, copy, and paste*. Find the set of icons that look like a pair of scissors, two identical documents, and a clipboard. The scissors Cut, or delete the selected text. The twin documents Copy text or images. And, the clipboard Pastes the text into a new location.

- *Click the scissors* and watch how the Cut text disappears from the body of the document.

- The *Copy* command is identical to the Cut command except that the text is duplicated to an area of memory called the "clipboard."

- The text may be *Pasted* to another location elsewhere in the document.

> **Practice cut, copy, and paste to move text. Remember that the "copy" command duplicates the text to the clipboard; no on-screen activity is evident until you paste the text to its new location.**

The Undo Command. After any change such as deleting text or bolding an entire paragraph, a simple click of the Undo button on the Toolbar reverses the operation and returns the text to its former appearance.

- Click Undo to reverse the last action. To undo an action, click the left arrow icon. Undo is an important feature that saves time and recovers user mistakes.

> **Click the Undo icon to reverse any changes made to STATES.doc and return to the original document.**

Changing the Appearance of Text. Once text is selected, several editing commands are available to change the look of the line.

- *Bold, underline, and italics.* Clicking the icons for Bold, Italics, and Underline alters the appearance of the text. The buttons toggle appearance when clicked to indicate the feature is ON. A second click toggles the feature OFF.

- *Left, center, right, and justify.* To the right of the BIU icons are the alignment functions. Left alignment lines the text along the left margin. Centering is done with the second icon. Right alignment is appropriate for address lines and dates. Justify aligns text against both the left and right margins.

- *Changing fonts and font size.* To the left of the menu line are pop-down menus for changing Fonts and Font Size. The Font window offers various typesets, while Font Size sets the size of the type.

Highlight text within the handout and experiment with the appearance icons. Remember to reset the text to its original appearance by clicking the Undo icon.

Saving a Document. Whenever editing a document, a good rule of thumb is to save the file after each paragraph or after completing a series of extensive changes. The first unexpected power outage, mechanical failure, or computer virus will support this recommendation.

- *Save the document* by selecting File '! Save from the menu. If the file has never been saved, the Save As dialog box appears.

- *Identify the location* by clicking the Save In box until the correct folder appears. Enter a File Name for the document, and then click Save.

Save the changes to the file STATES.doc

Text Color. Students often search for visual clues in text-based materials. Of course, a color printer is required for effective learning. To change the color of text, highlight the target words with a mouse click and drag.

- Find the *Font Color* icon on the Drawing toolbar located at the bottom of the window and click the icon. To change to another color, click the down arrow and select from among 40 primary colors or click More Colors.

Try changing the title text to another color. Remember to highlight the text before attempting to change color.

Inserting Clip Art and Pictures. The Microsoft Clip Art Gallery offers images, sounds, and video clips for inclusion into a handout or study guide. Activity #3 of the STATES.doc handout incorporates two clip art graphics.

To Insert Clip Art into a document, follow these simple steps:

- *Position the cursor.* Before inserting clip art, the cursor must be at the point in the document where the image is to appear. Click the mouse button once to position the flashing cursor at the desired location.

- *View the Clip Art Gallery.* To load a gallery of available images, click the clip art found on the Drawing Menu at the bottom of the screen. Select the desired category, and click the Insert button to place the image into the document. Once there, the image may be resized or moved as desired.

- *To resize Clip Art.* Click the image to activate the "anchors;" little square boxes that appear on the perimeter of the image. Place the cursor on one of the four corner anchors to transform the cursor from a pointer to a diagonal arrow. Hold the mouse button and drag diagonally to resize the image proportionally.

To Insert a Picture into a document, follow these steps:

- *Position the cursor* as described above.
- *View the file.* Locate the file to be inserted by clicking Insert → Picture → From File.
- *Select the file.* Double-click the file name, then Insert. The image appears in the body of the document. Once inserted into a document, the picture may be resized, moved, copied, pasted, or deleted exactly as clip art.

> **Examine the clip art in Activity #3. Click on the mountain and try to resize the image. Then, click on the image, delete it, and replace it with another piece of Clip Art from the Gallery. Undo any unsatisfactory modifications.**

Inserting Tables. Tables are rows and columns of cells filled with text or graphics. There are at least four tables in the STATES.doc handout. To insert a Table:

- Click *Insert Table or use the Table icon* to choose the number of rows and columns to be appended to the table.

> **Examine the table in Activity #2. It contains four columns and 50 rows. Try adding your own table to the file, and then Undo the changes to return to the original handout.**

Inserting Hyperlinks. A "hyperlink" connects users to Web sites. The document must be online (i.e., connected to the Internet) to use this feature. To insert a hyperlink, select the text to serve as the link.

- Click the *Insert Hyperlink* icon or select Insert '‡Hyperlink from the pop-down menu.
- *Enter the Web page name* and click OK.

First, move the mouse on top of the first link (www.50states.com) **shown in Activity #1. Notice how a small window displays the hyperlink to be accessed when the reader double-clinks on the hypertext. Next, highlight the link and click Insert ? Hyperlink to view the URL for this link.**

Summary of Text-Based Materials

The four-page STATES.doc handout serves several purposes. First, it provides a structure for individualizing additional text-based materials. Second, it offers a forum for experimenting with the basic features of Microsoft *Word*. And, third, it demonstrates how text materials are effectively integrated into a Social Studies lesson. The text continues with visual-based instructional materials next.

Visual-Based Classroom Presentations

Introduction

While concrete learners often prefer text-based materials for reinforcement, abstract learners frequently identify visual classroom presentations as their preferred style of learning. Microsoft *Power Point* provides a collection of graphics design and presentation tools that create persuasive slide shows incorporating text; pictures, sounds, and video; hyperlinks to external and internal Web sites; charts and graphs; and a variety of hard-copy output. A well-designed classroom presentation consists of the following mandatory elements:

- **Slide 1** introduces the lesson.
- **Slide 2** displays the learning objectives of the lesson and any prior student knowledge of the content area expected before the lesson commences.
- **Slides 3 through 7** present the developmental activities for the lesson. Images are reinforced with textual material to support student learning.
- **Slide 8** offers vocabulary words and some form of assessment to ensure that student understanding has occurred.
- **Slide 9** provides an enrichment opportunity for students who complete the presentation early. Links to additional information are offered in the form of preselected Web sites, workbook material, and outside research to further explore the topic.

Similar to text-based material, the best way to prepare visual-based presentations is to locate a presentation that imitates the final desired product. The 15-slide **BEES.ppt** presentation, prepared using Microsoft *Power Point*, guides the development of a classroom presentation and contains all the required elements listed above. As with the text-based document, first examine the presentation, then follow the modifications to fit your learning objectives. Specific instructions are provided following each feature and are displayed within a text box.

To speed the process of creating a presentation, the authors of this book have prepared an online Web site containing the examples depicted in Appendix B. The URL for this Web site is: www.duq.edu/~tomei/TAC (*Teaching Across the Curriculum*). Readers may visit the site, locate, view (only), or download the **BEES.ppt** file and concentrate on applying the features introduced to create a new presentation appropriate for your classroom.

Viewing a *Power Point* Presentation. *Power Point* uses a series of five view modes that appear at the bottom of the screen. From left to right, the views include:

- *Normal View*, which provides the outline of the presentation in the left frame and the slide view on the right.

- *Outline View* for editing the content of presentation rather than its graphic elements.
- *Slide View*, which must be selected to insert Clip Art, images, and text as well as centering, background color, text size and color, and drawing.
- *Slide Sorter View*, which assists in building transitions effects and rearranging slides.
- *Slide Show View*, which displays the actual presentation on-screen.

For practice, click the *Slide Show View* and advance through the presentation.

- **Click the mouse, press the space bar, use the Up (Forward) and Down (Back) arrows, or press the Page Up (Forward) or Page Down (Back) keys to move through the slide presentation.**
- **After viewing the final slide in the show, Power Point ends the presentation and restores the screen to the previous view mode. A show may also be terminated at any time by pressing the escape key.**
- **At the conclusion of the Slide Show, select the <u>Outline View</u> before continuing with the exercise.**

Editing the Presentation. NOTE: You must be in the <u>Outline View</u> before continuing with this exercise. Before editing, text must be highlighted or "selected." To select a:

- *Slide,* position the cursor on the slide icon next to the slide number and click the mouse button to select all the text on that slide.
- *Bullet,* place the cursor anywhere in the middle of the bullet sentence and:

- Windows machines, hold the *Control* key and *click once.*
- Macintosh systems, hold the *Command* key and *click once.*
- *Word,* position the cursor on the desired word and *double-click* the mouse button.

Bold, Underline, Italics, and Shadow. Click the *Bold* icon, *Italics*, and *Underline* to see how they affect the look of the selected bullet. *Power Point* also provides a *Shadow* command. The buttons change appearance to indicate that the feature is ON; a second click toggles the feature OFF.

Alignment Left, Center, and Right. To the right of the BIU icons are the alignment functions. *Left* alignments line the text along the left margin. *Centering* is accomplished by clicking the middle icon, and the *Right* alignment moves text to the outside margin.

Changing Fonts and Font Size. Pop-down menus for changing Fonts and Font Size appear on the toolbar. Click the down arrow next to the *Font* window to view the available formats, and follow the same procedure to set a new *Font Size.*

Moving Text. Practice the cut, copy, and paste commands to move text to other locations in the presentation. The icons are in the same location as the word processor and, of course, have the same purpose. *Cut* deletes the selected text. *Copy* places text and images on the clipboard. *Paste* adds the text to a new location.

The Undo Command. After any editing changes, a click of the Undo button on the toolbar reverses the operation and returns the text to its former appearance.

Examine Slide 3, "What is a Honeybee?" in BEES.ppt. Remember, you should remain in the Outline View for this exercise. Practice the editing features explained above. Try the appearance commands (bold, italics, etc.), the alignment features, and the font controls. Finally, practice moving text, and then Undo the changes to return to the original slide.

Adding a New Bullet/Sub-Bullet. To add a new bullet, place the cursor on text immediately following the preceding bullet and hit the Enter key. *Power Point* assumes that another bullet is to be added at this location.

Promoting/Demoting Bullets. *Highlight the new bullet* and locate the icons that Promote/Demote text.

- Click on the right arrow to **Demote** the bullet, effectively creating a **sub-bullet** up to five levels deep.
- The left arrow **Promotes** each bullet until it reaches the status of the highest level of a new slide.

Examine Slide 2, "A Lesson About Honeybees." Again, remain in the Outline View for this exercise. Practice adding a new bullet to this slide and demonstrate what happens if the newly added bullet is promoted then demoted. Undo the changes to return to the original slide.

Saving a *Power Point* Presentation. Presentations should be saved after each slide is created or modified. Click the *Save* icon on the Toolbar or select the *File '! Save* pop-down menu. If the file has never been saved, the Save As dialog box appears. Set the location, and enter a new file name for the presentation. Click the *Save* button.

Inserting Clip Art and Pictures. In addition to clip art and pictures, the Microsoft Clip Art Gallery offers sound and video clips for presentations. To insert Clip Art into a presentation:

- Enter the *Slide View and Select the Slide*. Before inserting clip art, Power Point *must be in the Slide View mode*. Move to the slide where the image is to appear. Unlike documents, the flashing cursor may be placed anywhere on the selected slide.
- Insert the image. Select the clip art icon found on the Drawing Menu at the bottom of the screen or use *Insert → Picture → Clip Art*. Select a Category, then select the image. Click the *Insert* button to insert the image into the body of the presentation.

To Insert a Picture into a presentation, follow these steps:

- Enter the *Slide View and Select the Slide* as described above.

- *View the File*. Locate the file to be inserted by clicking Insert → Picture → From File.

- *Select the File*. Double-click the file name, then Insert. The image appears on the slide. Once inserted in the document, the picture may be resized, moved, copied, pasted, or deleted exactly as clip art.

> **Examine Slide 15, "Learn More About Bees." In the <u>Slide View</u>, practice adding Clip Art and an image from the file. Try to resize, move, and copy and paste the image. Undo the changes to return to the original slide.**

Inserting Sounds. To insert a digitized sound file into presentations, remain in the *Slide View*. Place the cursor anywhere on a selected slide.

- Click *Insert → Movies and Sounds → Sounds from Gallery* to view the gallery contents. Select the category and scroll through the available sounds to locate an appropriate file.

- Double-click the sound icon or click a sound icon once, then the *Insert* button. An image that looks like a speaker appears on the slide. Opt to have the sound play when the slide is first displayed or choose to have the viewer initiate the sound by clicking on an icon.

- Run the *Slide Show* to listen to the sounds.

- Sounds are inserted from the file by choosing *Insert → Movies and Sounds → From File* rather than the gallery; the remaining instructions for selecting files apply.

Inserting Movies. Inserting a video clip from the Gallery following the same procedure. Remain in the *Slide View* and place the cursor anywhere on a selected slide.

- Select *Insert → Movies and Sounds → Movies from Gallery* to insert movie clip from the gallery.
- Choose *Insert → Movies and Sounds → From File* Sounds to add movies from the file.

Slide 1 contains a short sound file taken from the Internet and inserted into the introductory slide (locate the speaker icon). In the Slide Show, you will hear the clip as soon as the presentation is launched and the show is initiated. (Note: presentation must be downloaded to hear sounds.)

Try adding your own sound file from the Gallery to another slide and run the Slide Show to listen.

Inserting Hyperlinks. Hyperlinks connect the presentation to an Internet site and may be tied to any object on a slide such as text, clip art, and images. To insert a hyperlink, remain in the *Slide View*, and move to the target slide.

- Select the text or image to serve as the hyperlink.
- Click *Insert → Hyperlink* and enter the target URL (Web address). Click *OK* to retain the link.
- Run the *Slide Show* and click on the link to launch the Web browser. Notice that a hyperlink is a different color (usually blue) from the rest of the text.

Advance to Slide #15 in the BEES.ppt presentation. Enter the Slide Show and move the mouse to one of the hyperlinks. Also, move the mouse to the bee (clip art). Notice that the URL appears in a text box. Click on the links and watch how the Internet browser launches to the desired site. You must, of course, be connected to the Internet to use this feature.

Selecting a New Design Template. *Power Point* comes with a wide variety of professionally designed templates. When a new template is applied, the background color, font size, and font color change. Before applying a new template to a presentation, *Save* the presentation first in case the results prove unsatisfactory. Change templates <u>early</u> in the design process before a considerable amount of text and images are inserted. To select a new template, follow these instructions.

- Enter the *Slide View* Mode. A new template may be applied in any mode; however, the Slide View displays the changes immediately.

- Click *Format* → *Apply Design Template* to preview a list of available templates. NOTE: Macintosh users may need to click *Find Files* → *Search Files* → *OK* to locate templates.

- Select the desired template and click *Apply*, then *File* → *Save* the presentation and *View* the Slide Show to view the results.

> In the Slide View mode, practice changing the Design Template. Examine how the new template results in changes to the background color, font size and color, and type. The Undo command is available to revert to a previous template format.

Printing the Presentation. A *Power Point* presentation may be printed using several options, all of which rely on the best use of technology for teaching and learning in the classroom. The choices available for printing also depend on the platform, so review the appropriate procedures. Click *File '‡Print* to open the Print Window. For Macintosh users, click the *General* print window of Microsoft *Power Point* to see a complete list of available options. Windows users will see these options immediately. The most common options when printing a presentation include: Print Range, Number of Copies, and Print What.

- Print Range. *All* prints every slide in the presentation; *Current Slide* prints only the single slide presently viewed; and *Slides* allows the user to enter a range of slides.

- Number of Copies. Enter the *Number of Copies* to be printed. Requesting the copies to be Collated prints them in order from first to last slide, then repeats the process again for additional copies.

- Print What. Another significant feature is the option to print Slides, Handouts, and Outlines. Click on *Slides* to print one slide on a page. Print multiple slides on a page by selecting *Handouts* 2, 3, 4, 6, or 9 slides to a page. The Handouts option is excellent for producing copies of slides for use in classroom situations.

> **Practice print the BEES.ppt presentation using first All, then Slides, then Handouts.**

Summary of Visual-Based Materials

The 15-slide BEES.ppt presentation follows the recommended format for classroom material. The opening slide introduces the lesson and attracts the attention of the learner with its sound clip. Slide 2 presents the learning objectives of the lesson, and slides 3 through 12 present the content for the lesson. Slides 13 and 14 offer vocabulary words by using a partner exercise, and the final slide provides links to additional information offered in the form of preselected Web sites.

Web-Based Lesson Home Page

Introduction

The Internet enhances teaching of all disciplines, student ages, and a variety of classroom delivery systems, including the traditional classroom, hybrid classrooms (combination of traditional classroom teaching and online teaching), or even cyber classrooms (all classes are taught in an online environment). Teachers who create their own Web sites tailor existing Web-based materials to meet the individual learning styles and the needs of the student.

A well-designed lesson home page consists of the following mandatory elements:

- **Banner Title and Image** to lead into the topic of the lesson and confirm the location of the page
- **Introduction**, complete with a brief explanation of the topic, key elements to be covered, and student instructions
- **Lesson Objectives.** Teachers should share the learning goals with their students; let them see the actual learning objectives that will be used to evaluate their understanding
- **Web Sites for Student Exploration**. Include links to other Web pages
- **Student Assessment Information**, including the criteria for grading the lesson
- **Address Block** that provides policies regarding use of Web-based materials including author citation (with name, affiliation, and email address); copyright and Fair Use statement; and created and revised on dates

Similar to text and visual-based material, the best way to prepare a lesson home page is to locate a site that contains as many of the required elements described above as possible. The **CIVILWAR.htm** page, prepared using Netscape *Composer,* will provide an example home page for Saint Jude Elementary School—Grade 5 Social Studies, created by Dr. Larry Tomei.

As before, to speed the process of creating a lesson home page, the authors of this book have prepared an online Web site containing the examples depicted in Appendix C. The URL for this Web site is: www.duq.edu/~tomei/ TAC (*Teaching Across the Curriculum*). Readers may visit the site, locate, view, or download the **CIVILWAR.htm** file and concentrate on applying the features introduced to create a new page appropriate for your classroom.

Planning the Web Site

Before accepting an example Web site for modification, consider its appearance and overall design. Does it include all the elements of a good home page shown above? Invest 90% of the time to plan a page and the remaining 10% to implement the Web site. It will save countless hours of revisions. When assembling a puzzle, regardless of the size, the border or outside framework is usually the area that is assembled first by most people. Once the framework is completed for Web sites, as for puzzles, then build the area within the structure. Replacing the example page progresses more smoothly if the new content, photos, and URLs are identified before beginning the technical exchange. Organize all documents, photos, URLs, and other content on one diskette (zip disks preferred). Keep all data in one location when designing Web sites. The example that follows uses Netscape *Navigator* and *Composer* and not Internet Explorer for designing the home page.

Lesson Home Pages

Launch Netscape Communicator and enter the edit mode by clicking *File → Edit Page* to change from Netscape *Navigator* (the preview mode) to Netscape *Composer* (the design mode). A new set of toolbars appears in *Composer* (see Figure 1).

Find CIVILWAR.htm on the *Teaching Across the Curriculum* Web site (www.duq.edu/~tomei/TAC). Click on the link to view the Course Page and scroll through the site to view its contents.

Enter Netscape *Composer* (*File → Edit Page*) and practice the skills described in the subsequent instructions.

Figure 1. The *Composer* Toolbar

Editing Text. *Composer* provides a similar suite of text editing features as Microsoft *Word* and *Power Point*. However, because *Composer* is a product of Netscape Inc. and not Microsoft, there are some differences in the icons provide by the toolbar. To change the course title, highlight the text, and enter the new name and grade and title of the lesson. At this time, you can also change the font type, color, and size using the tools on the second line of the toolbar.

Edit the <u>Course Title</u> to reflect a lesson or unit of instruction in your classroom. Practice changing the font type, color, and size. Notice that the bold, italics, and underline icons are different from the Microsoft products.

Edit the <u>Lesson Objectives</u> and <u>Introduction</u> text that appear next on the Course Page. Experiment with the bullets and numbering icons as well as the alignment window to center, right, and left justify text.

Inserting Images. Position the cursor at a desired location on the Web page. Click the Image icon on the toolbar or *Insert " Image* from the pop-down menu. Double-click Choose File to locate the image on disk, and click OK to insert that image onto the page. Images may be replaced by clicking on a current photo (such as the Civil War painting). Click *Insert " Image* to open the dialog box and choose another file.

Resizing an Image. Once the image is placed on the Web page, it may be resized by following one of these methods. First, select the image, and move the cursor to one of the four corners of the image until a double-ended arrow (1) appears. Click and drag the image diagonally to increase or decrease the size of the photo proportionately. Dragging from any other portion of the image will distort the image vertically or horizontally. Clicking the image and selecting the Image icon to display Image Properties may also resize images. The dimensions of the image (width and height) appear in pixels. Change the size of the image by varying either the height or width dimensions. Click *Apply* to view the results or click *Original Size* to return the image to its original dimensions.

> **Replace the Civil War painting image with another image more appropriate for your lesson. Practice resizing the image until it suits the lesson objective. Save the file and give it a file name other than CIVILWAR.htm.**

Inserting Hyperlinks onto a Web Page. Hyperlinks connect Web pages to other instructionally rich Internet sites, to email addresses, even to other documents. The use of hyperlinks avoids many of the problems associated with the World Wide Web, such as sending students to invalid sites; avoiding the "dark side" of the Internet; eliminating unproductive searching and surfing; and overcoming obstacles to the discovery process (e.g., typing skills). To insert a Hyperlink:

- Create and Select the link. Hyperlinks may be linked to <u>any</u> text or images displayed on the page. Select the text or image by highlighting the item.

- Insert the Link. Click the *Link* icon from the Menu bar or the *Insert → Link* pop-down menu. In the dialog box, locate Link to a page location or local file, and enter the URL beginning with *http://* for an external link residing on the Internet. Omit http:// to access internal links or files located on your computer. To insert an email address, substitute *mailto:* as the prefix to the link.

- *Save* the Web page, and *Preview* the link in *Navigator* to test the connectivity to the selected site or email address.

> **Double-click on the Instructor's Name and examine the link. Notice that the example provides an external link (beginning with http://) to an existing Internet address. Next, double-click the instructor's Email Address to view the syntax for linking to email. Substitute your email address as the instructor.**
>
> **Scroll down to Web Sites for Student Exploration. Double-click each Civil War link, replace the text, and click *Insert ?   Link* to change the Web address, sending the student to your selected sites. Save the file.**

Page Properties address the visual composition of a Web page and provide general properties, colors, and background images. Click *Format* → *Page Colors and Properties*. The *General* tab edits the *Title* of the Web page. Ignore the Author information, because it is included only in the page source code for security purposes. The *Colors and Background* tab controls the predefined colors for text, links, and background. To place an image on the background, click the *Use Image* option box, and enter the file name or click the *Choose File* button to locate the file on disk. *Save* the Web page to retain the changes.

> **Examine the Page Properties of the Civil War site and make the following modifications to suit your lesson:**
>
> **1. Revise the Title of the page in the *General* tab.**
>
> **2. In the *Colors and Background* tab, locate the background image (brown.jpg) and change the image or de-select the *Use Image* box and select an appropriate *Background* color. In addition, experiment with the text and hyperlink colors to suit the new background.**
>
> **3. Save the changes made to your lesson.**

Summary of Web-Based Materials

For credibility, add the original Created date for the Web site, the Name of the page designer, and Revision dates, when applicable. Save your work often, and place all images, sound files, video clips, and Web pages on the same diskette or hard drive folder. Consider using a 100 or 250 megabyte zip disk, because 3.5 inch floppy diskettes reach capacity very quickly when graphics are involved.

Conclusion

When the design phase is complete, view the new site using other Internet Web browsers. If the page was created in Netscape *Composer*, open the site using Internet Explorer. Try using America Online (AOL). Students view Web sites using a variety of browsers from home, school, and the library. This step eliminates problems with page distortions, missing links, unsupported elements, and the like. Finally, when incorporating Web addresses and links into a classroom lesson, remember that Web sites have a tendency to move almost as often as people. Conduct a dry run of the Web page before each class, and be sure to retain the original files for the inevitable revisions necessary, if the site is truly integrated into your curriculum.

Appendix A

50 States Worksheet

The URL for this Web site is www.duq.edu/~tomei/TAC (*Teaching Across the Curriculum*). Readers may view or download the **STATES.doc** file to use when practicing the skills demonstrated in this chapter.

Student's Name _____   Date_____

Mrs. Brown's Third Period Social Studies

Activity #1. Visit the World Wide Web site www.50states.com. Select your favorite state, and provide the following information found on the respective state site.

State: _____

Capital City: _____

Bordering States: _____

                          _____

                          _____

                          _____

State Flower: _____

State Bird: _____

State Flag: (Draw your state flag in the box below using the correct colors.)

State Nickname and Motto: _____

State Tree: _____

Provide two other interesting facts found at the Web site.

1) _____

2) _____

Student's Name _____   Date_____

Mrs. Brown's Third Period Social Studies

Activity #2. After visiting the Web site www.statecapitals.org, complete the missing information on the chart with the appropriate State, the Year it became a state, and its Capital.

	State	Year of Statehood	Capital City
1	Pennsylvania		
2			Atlanta
3			Tallahassee
4			Columbia
5	California		
6	New York		
7			Columbus
8			Raleigh
9	Maine		
10	Wyoming		
11	Alaska		
12			Springfield
13			Honolulu
14	Missouri		
15			Richmond
16			Madison
17	Minnesota		
18	Oregon		
19			Boise
20			Frankfurt
21	Washington		
22			Phoenix
23			Santa Fe
24	Texas		
25			Lincoln
26			Montgomery
27	Mississippi		
28	Oklahoma		
29	South Dakota		
30	North Dakota		
31			Nashville
32			Des Moines
33	Louisiana		
34	Arkansas		
35			Concord
36	Vermont		
37			Raleigh
38			Providence
39	Massachusetts		
40	Connecticut		
41	Delaware		
42			Carson City
43			Baltimore
44	Montana		
45	Colorado		
46			Indianapolis
47	Minnesota		
48	West Virginia		
49	New Mexico		
50			Salt Lake City

Student's Name _____   Date_____

Mrs. Brown's Third Period Social Studies

Activity #3. Using the library's Almanac, provide the following facts about the United States of America.

United States Fact Sheet

Highest Point (Name, State, etc.):

Lowest Point (Name, State, etc.):

Provide four additional interesting facts about the United States that you found in the Almanac.

1) _____

2) _____

3) _____

4) _____

Appendix B

Honeybees Visual Presentation

The URL for this Web site is www.duq.edu/~tomei/TAC (*Teaching Across the Curriculum*). Readers may view or download the **BEES.ppt** file to use when practicing the skills demonstrated in this chapter.

Honeybees

What's All the Buzz About?

Learn all about bees and how they
make our lives better

Appendix C
Civil War Lesson Home Page

The URL for this Web site is www.duq.edu/~tomei/TAC (*Teaching Across the Curriculum*). Readers may view or download the **CIVILWAR.htm** file to use when practicing the skills demonstrated in this chapter.

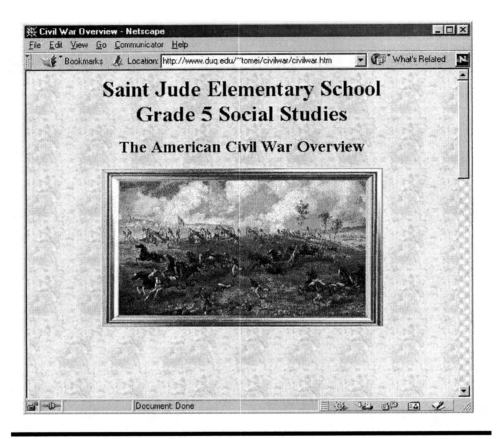

Index

L

language arts Web sites 178
Launch Netscape Communicator 309
learning challenged students 208
learning objectives 13
lesson home pages 309
lesson plan ideas for database 48
lesson plan ideas for graphics and paint & draw utilities 54
lesson plan ideas for hypermedia/multimedia 62
lesson plan ideas for spreadsheet 41
lesson plan ideas for word-processing 34
lesson plan ideas for World Wide Web 68
literature resources 15
Lotus 1-2-3 246

M

MacWrite 29
manipulatives 121
McCluhan, Marshall 136
Microsoft Windows 246
Microsoft Word 29
mineral bonding 108
model for designing technology-based lessons 9
moving text 294
multimedia and hypermedia application 58
multimedia computer 248
multiple intelligences 94

N

National Council for Accreditation of Teacher Education 249
National Council of Teachers of English 161
National Council of Teachers of Mathematics 114, 117
National Council on Disability 273
National Educational Technology Standards 249
National Educational Technology Standards for Students 26

National Science Education Standards 93
National Standards for Arts Education 217
National Standards for Technology in Teacher Preparation 161
NCSS 141
Netscape Communicator 66

O

ocean currents 108
open education 7
operation and maintenance costs 202
organization 148

P

page properties 312
paint and draw 2
Pennsylvania Department of Education 93
performance and exhibition 222
planning the Web site 308
PowerPoint 57
Principles and Standards for School Mathematics 118
printing the presentation 306
prior knowledge 6
problem solving 122
problem-solving programs 252
procedures 167
productivity software 252
promoting/demoting bullets 303
Public Law 19-142 273

R

reference/research sites 257
reinforcement 94, 184, 192
resizing an image 310

S

satellite dishes 201
satellite receiver 201
satellite-link transmission 201
saving a document 296
saving a PowerPoint presentation 303
schemata 7

About The Editor

Lawrence A. Tomei was born in Akron, Ohio, on July 22, 1950. He earned a Bachelor of Science in Business Administration (BSBA) from the University of Akron in 1972, a Masters of Public Administration (1975) and a Masters of Education (1978) at the University of Oklahoma, Norman OK, and a Doctorate in Education (1983) from the University of Southern California.

He authored numerous journal articles and three books on educational technology, including: *Professional Portfolios for Teachers* (1999); *Teaching Digitally: Integrating Technology into the Classroom* (2001), both published by Christopher-Gordon Inc.; and *The Technology Facade* (2002), published by Allyn & Bacon.

Dr. Tomei is a Certified Computing Professional - Management Endorsement (1978), Certified Data Processor (1980), Certified Data Processing Auditor (1979), and Certified Information Systems Auditor (1979). In addition, he holds a Vocational Education Certificate from the State of Colorado (1989) and the Pennsylvania Instructional Technology Specialist Certification (2001).

About The Authors

A native of Medford, Massachusetts, **V. Robert Agostino** has been at Duquesne since 1968. His interests center on History and Social Studies Education. Dr. Agostino taught the first courses on Instructional Computing at Duquesne, with the certainty that technology and computers would have a major impact on teaching and learning. This book demonstrates his foresight.

Claudia A. Balach is a middle school Science Teacher for Quaker Valley School District in Sewickley, Pennsylvania. She is a National Board Certified Teacher and a doctoral candidate at Duquesne University. Her research interests include Professional Development Schools, Learning Communities, School Reform, and the Professionalization of Teaching. She has presented at the national level on teaching with technology and on middle school science education.

Robin J. Ittigson is a Residential Resource Mathematics Teacher in an elementary school in Pittsburgh, Pennsylvania. In addition to teaching fourth grade mathematics, she trains district colleagues "Thinking Math," a mathematics professional development course authored by the American Federation of Teachers. She received her doctorate in Educational Leadership from Duquesne University. Her research focused on patterns of questions asked by middle and high school mathematics teachers to develop problem-solving thinking.

Linda M. Lengyel has been working in the field of Special Education for 20 years and is committed to supporting persons with disabilities in inclusive environments. Dr. Lengyel has used technology to support many persons with disabilities. Currently, Dr. Lengyel is an Assistant Professor at Duquesne University, where she has taught graduate level courses on the use of Assistive Technology.

Barbara M. Manner is an Associate Professor in the Bayer School of Natural and Environmental Sciences (BSNES) and the School of Education at Duquesne University. In BSNES, Dr. Manner teaches Earth Science classes as well as an Environmental Hydrogeology course in the Environmental Sciences and Management (ESM) graduate program. In the School of Education, she teaches elementary and secondary science methods classes. Dr. Manner has done extensive science education and environmental geology research and has published articles related to her research in both areas.

Marilyn J. Narey is currently a Visual Art Teacher and Department Chair in Canon-McMillan School District. She has been the recipient of numerous awards and grants for her innovative projects and partnerships, including *KDKA Thanks to Teachers, Pennsylvania Department of Education Best Practices, PAEA Middle Level Educator of the Year Award*, and a *$24,100 JCPenney Community Education Grant*. Her teacher workshops and presentations have been conducted at local, state, and national levels and include topics such as *Understanding Children's Art, Technology: A Tool for Learning, and Re-Thinking the Secondary Art Curriculum*. Ms. Narey also serves as PAEA Middle Level Division Director, Chairperson of the Southwestern Pennsylvania Teachers of Distinction, and editor of *Dialogue: A Journal of the Teachers Excellence Foundation*. She recently served as Head Writer of the visual art segment of the Pennsylvania Department of Education publication, *Crosswalks: A Guide to Implementing the PA Arts and Humanities Standards*. Ms. Narey is the mother of two sons, Daniel and Nathan, who assisted and supported her early ventures into the exciting world of technology.

William J. Switala has spent 37 years in the field of education. He earned his BA degree in philosophy from St. Vincent College, an MA in Latin from Duquesne University, and a PhD in classical languages from the University of Pittsburgh. Dr. Switala spent 31 years in basic education before joining the faculty at Duquesne University. Fifteen of those years were devoted to teaching languages and history in Grades 6–12 in schools near Pittsburgh. The next 16 years were spent as an Administrator supervising curriculum in a suburban Pittsburgh school district. For the past 6 years, he has served as an Assistant Professor on the faculty of the School of Education at Duquesne University. He has also taught in an adjunct faculty capacity for the University of Pittsburgh, The Pennsylvania State University, and California University of Pennsylvania. In addition to teaching, he has had 95 articles, books, reviews, and translations published. These deal with topics in education, languages, and history. Dr. Switala has also delivered papers at local, state, and national conferences, served on numerous educational committees and advisory boards, and has been a consultant on curriculum matters in a number of school districts. In addition to his training in classical languages, Dr. Switala also reads 6 modern languages.

Derek Whordley began his career teaching in British primary schools and went on to become the Headmaster of the British Embassy School in Ankara, Turkey. As a Department Chair and subsequently a Dean, he introduced study abroad programs in the United Kingdom. His work has included visits to schools in Canada, Russia, Jordan, and Haiti. Dr. Whordley is active in the accrediting commissions of the International Baccalaureate Association and the Association for the Accreditation of Career Schools and Colleges of Technology. He has traveled throughout the United States. He is interested in work associated with literacy and pedagogy for young children. His published work includes two practical texts for nursery and Head-Start teachers and one piece on global education.

Linda C. Wojnar is an Assistant Professor at Duquesne University in the Instructional Technology Program and teaches the Certificate and Master's Degree Programs-Distance Learning Strand. Her dissertation August 2000 was the *Design and Implementation of a Best Practice Model of Online Teaching and Learning*. Her teaching background has included teaching in higher education, the military, and community colleges. She has conducted accreditation visits as an Education Specialist. She is a Project Consultant with the School Performance Network and has done postsecondary consulting in curriculum and instruction. Dr. Wojnar is published in the field of Distance and Online Learning and has presented in conferences locally, nationally, and internationally. Dr. Wojnar holds a Pennsylvania Instructional Technology Specialist Certification and is currently teaching a cohort of distance learning participants from Northern Ireland.

John (Jack) G. Zewe received his BA in Business Administration from Walsh College and a Master of Science in Education from Duquesne University. He is currently an Elementary Teacher for the Pittsburgh School District.

International Journal of Distance Education Technologies (JDET)

The International Source for Technological Advances in Distance Education

ISSN: 1539-3100
eISSN: 1539-3119

Subscription: Annual fee per volume (4 issues):
Individual US $85
Institutional US $185

Editors: Shi Kuo Chang
University of Pittsburgh, USA

Timothy K. Shih
Tamkang University, Taiwan

Mission

The *International Journal of Distance Education Technologies* (**JDET**) publishes original research articles of distance education four issues per year. **JDET** is a primary forum for researchers and practitioners to disseminate practical solutions to the automation of open and distance learning. The journal is targeted to academic researchers and engineers who work with distance learning programs and software systems, as well as general participants of distance education.

Coverage

Discussions of computational methods, algorithms, implemented prototype systems, and applications of open and distance learning are the focuses of this publication. Practical experiences and surveys of using distance learning systems are also welcome. Distance education technologies published in **JDET** will be divided into three categories, **Communication Technologies, Intelligent Technologies, and Educational Technologies**: new network infrastructures, real-time protocols, broadband and wireless communication tools, quality-of-services issues, multimedia streaming technology, distributed systems, mobile systems, multimedia synchronization controls, intelligent tutoring, individualized distance learning, neural network or statistical approaches to behavior analysis, automatic FAQ reply methods, copyright protection and authentification mechanisms, practical and new learning models, automatic assessment methods, effective and efficient authoring systems, and other issues of distance education.

For subscription information, contact:	For paper submission information:
Idea Group Publishing **701 E Chocolate Ave., Suite 200** **Hershey PA 17033-1240, USA** cust@idea-group.com **URL: www.idea-group.com**	**Dr. Timothy Shih** **Tamkang University, Taiwan** tshih@cs.tku.edu.tw